The Enchanted Candle

The Enchanted Candle

CRAFTING AND CASTING MAGICKAL LIGHT

Lady Rhea

WITH EVE LEFEY

CITADEL PRESS
Kensington Publishing Corp.
www.kensingtonbooks.com

CITADEL PRESS BOOKS are published by

Kensington Publishing Corp.
850 Third Avenue
New York, NY 10022

All Kensington titles, imprints, and distributed lines are available at
special quantity discounts for bulk purchases for sales promotions,
premiums, fund-raising, educational, or institutional use. Special book
excerpts or customized printings can also be created to fit specific needs.
For details, write or phone the office of the Kensington special sales
manager: Kensington Publishing Corp., 850 Third Avenue, New York, NY
10022, attn: Special Sales Department; phone 1-800-221-2647.

CITADEL PRESS and the Citadel logo are Reg. U.S. Pat. & TM Off.

Art by Lord Apollo

First printing: August 2004

10 9 8 7 6 5 4 3 2 1

Printed in the United States of America

Library of Congress Control Number: 2004100516

ISBN 0-8065-2578-9

To the two most important people in my life:
my beautiful, loving, and compassionate daughter, Tara,
and my loving wife, Sandra,
who from the very first has stayed by my side.
Both of you have contributed to this book every step of the way.

—LADY RHEA

Contents

Foreword

It was in the summer of 1980 that I first met Lady Rhea. I stumbled into the Magickal Childe in New York City on my way to a rehearsal. It was a bit of a spooky place—an old-fashioned occult shop with cobwebs, books, and supplies on both the dark and the light side of magickal workings. Yet, as I made my way to the oil office in the back, I was met with the alluring smile and wise eyes of who I thought must be the Goddess herself. There was Lady Rhea, tinkering around with the potions, and at once she made me feel at ease. I was very moved by her compassion, humor, and the light in her heart. A week later I came back for a tarot reading, which ended with a prescription for a candle spell for success. I still have this spell, handwritten by her, taped into my witch's grimoire. I continue to use it through the years and it always works.

After several months, Rhea invited me to join a women's study group on Wicca. This was a big deal for me because I was a confirmed solitary in my practice. If not for Rhea, I would never have experienced the wonder and power of working with a coven. I remember the day in late September of 1982 when I showed up for a witches meet. Rhea had a mischievous grin on her face and ushered us all out of the Childe into a beautiful garden in the East Village. She had spoken about getting her own shop with her partner and now it seemed she had achieved this in the blink of an eye. I thought to myself, "This is a woman who gets things done, makes things happen!" I was present at that first circle in the Enchanted Garden, and have since been to many other rituals led by Lady Rhea. A year later, I was initiated under her hand and became a priestess of Wicca.

Rhea has always represented the embodiment of the Mother Goddess for me. And I was there for the birth of her daughter Tara, which fulfilled this role on an earthly plane. To my amazement, her acceptance of the role as a mother did not take away the Mother energy that flowed through her constantly, and if anything, it made her give more to those who sought out her help.

In the two decades that have passed since then, I have had the opportunity to study many magickal paths, and I always return to the work of Lady Rhea. It was she who correctly combined the powerful energies of talismanic magic with the burning of candles. The joining of these magickal forces creates the most powerful form of magick I have witnessed. She adds a third powerful element in *The Enchanted Candle* with rituals or spells to accompany each candle seal.

The thing I admire most about Rhea is her willingness to give and educate. With this great work she instills the confidence in each individual to follow the heart's desire and manifest the will. There are no strings attached, for like the Goddess, Rhea demands nothing in return. Like the best kind of mother, she teaches her children to walk—to fly—to soar. No matter what you seek, you will find an Enchanted Candle spell here to achieve your aim. Follow the instruction Lady Rhea provides, and I have no doubt you will be empowered on your path.

—Lexa Roséan
a.k.a. Lady Venus
New York City

PART I

The Elements of
Enchanted Candle Craft

Enchanted candles are powerful tools to bring into your life whatever it is that you most want to manifest. Is it love you seek? Money? Luck? Good health? Whatever it is you want to bring into your life, an Enchanted Candle can be crafted and burned to invoke those energies and bring them directly to you. In the course of this book, you are going to learn how to create something truly magickal and life-changing.

I could give you a quick fix and tell you how to carve the physical candle, what colors to use, and where to buy glitter, and send you on your merry way, but that would be cheating you out of something truly precious. So bear with me as I explain why enchanted candles work. Each element of creating an Enchanted Candle—choosing the colors, the oils, the seals, the deities invoked, the planetary alignment, the phase of the moon—all of these need to be taken into careful consideration, and I will share with you not just the *what* but the *why* as well. When you truly understand the magick of the enchanted candle, you will be amazed at how well your candles will work for you.

In this part, I will be explaining the elements of the enchanted candle. In part two, you will learn how to actually make one. I suggest that you read the book all the way through before crafting your first candle.

You may be thinking, "But I need to do this spell now!"

Magick should never be rushed. If it is worth doing, then it is worth the time and patience to do it well. That being said, in this book I am going to teach you to use ingenuity—to know how to use items that you have on hand. You will see various candle types and suggestions for substitute ingredients. There's no need to get hung up on one or two ingredients if you don't have them available. For example, let's say you do not have a pullout candle (a pillar candle which slides in and out of its glass encasement) on hand. You need to do the spell now. Look around you and see what you do have available to you at the moment. Do you have a candle that is thick enough to inscribe on? Don't have an exacto blade? How about a sharp ballpoint pen, a knitting needle, or other pointed implement? Do your candle spell with what you have available. Most important, say the incantation provided and let it go out into the Universe. This art takes time to build up, but it so worth it as you will see!

Within this book, you will find ingredients such as iron filings, Dragon's Blood, perfumed waters, and items with names you might not even be able to pronounce. You will likely think to yourself, "this witch must be a few straws short of a full broom. Where am I ever going to find these things?" Not to worry. I have personally worked in the occult store business for the last thirty years. Appendix C contains a list of stores that carry all of the items listed in this book. You can contact them via e-mail, by writing for a catalog, or phoning the number given. If you cannot find a store near you, just go on to one of the Web sites listed—you will find excellent store directories listed by state.

Supermarkets and bodegas often carry plain seven-day glass candles, herbs, and sometimes even some oils.

To keep a well-stocked apothecary for your enchanted candle work, I have listed a few general items that you may find helpful to keep on hand. Essential colors are white, red, and green. White will cover for any color, red is always good for love and fast action, and green is always good for money. All of these colors are used in healing. Iron filings, honey, sugar, cascarilla (powdered eggshell), and camphor are staples. Keep dry herbs on hand for specialized spells you may often repeat. Any time you get flowers, dry the petals and keep them in a container. Even when a spell calls for fresh red rose petals, dry ones will revive once they hit the liquid. For incense and oils I suggest you keep the sacred seven oils in stock: sandalwood, rose, lily, frankincense, lavender, musk, and mint. For incense, sandalwood, frankincense, or a frank-and-myrrh combo, musk, rose, and sage are always a good bet. This general listing can cover just about anything you need to do. Build up your apothecary and enjoy the magick.

1.

Enchanted Candle Craft

Throughout the ages, the art of making talismans (a charm inscribed with magickal writing or symbols that brings luck to the person carrying it) has entailed the use of various materials. For example, certain precious metals were used for planetary seals (a magickal talisman made during certain planetary hours). The ancients ascribed a metal to each planet, such as lead for Saturn, tin for Jupiter, copper for Venus, and so on. Insignia rings were carved from stone by the Greeks, Romans, Egyptians, Sumerians and many other cultures. Magickal rings were also created by casting a ring, and etching a magickal seal on the place where the stone was to be set. Once the stone was in place, the symbol would no longer be visible, but the stone's energy would forever empower the seal beneath it.

Talismans can also be made from clay, wood, cloth, parchment paper, or whatever else the imagination can conjure. One of the most powerful mediums for a magickal talisman is wax. The reason I prefer the wax talisman is because it can be in the form of a candle, and when the candle is burned, it slowly releases the magick of the talisman into the Universe. All the mediums for making talismans are good, but how many talismans does a person want to carry around? Each time I want to do a specific spell, I simply carve the talisman into the wax candle and release it. Once the candle is lit it starts to release the spell and the magick is on its way.

ENCHANTED CANDLES

When burning a talisman etched in wax, the seal is released into the astral realm. Before I go any further, let me define for you exactly what the astral realm is. It is believed by many practitioners of the Craft that the astral realm is one of the three planes of existence. The physical plane is where our bodies live and operate; the mental plane is where our thoughts process what happens to us on the physical plane. The astral plane is in between the two. On the astral plane, there is a body of existence just like there is on the physical plane— a twin self, or a mirror world of the physical plane. But on the astral plane, everything exists on a different energy vibration. It is based on the belief that we are made up of energy. On the physical plane, this energy takes the form of matter. On the astral plane, that energy consists of the essence or spirit of that which is on the physical plane. In the astral realm, the world and all the living creatures in it (including us) are not hampered by the limitations of the physical world. It is the world of spirit existence where magick happens and time is irrelevant. This is where thoughts can take hold and become real and then they can manifest back on the physical plane.

When an enchanted candle is burned, the talisman doesn't disappear—rather, it is transformed through the energy of fire and manifests on the astral plane. All spiritual and physical matter coexist. Just because you cannot see something on a regular basis does not mean that it does not exist. There is a world of microscopic life that we cannot see without the help of high-powered microscopes. There is the astral world that we cannot see without the assistance of training the physical self to let go of its need to "see to believe." Many believe that the astral plane is the main domain of existence because this is where our physical world gets its form. It is where things are conceived and created in order to make things happen here in our physical world. Therefore, before we do anything physical, it must first take place on an astral level. For example, when an artist creates a sculpture, that piece of art is first conceptualized on an astral level. Form is only the baby or infantile state of a concept that started on the astral plane. The concept that originated on the astral plane begins to manifest by forming on the physical plane. When a person gets a new job offer, she first sees herself in that job—doing the tasks, getting the higher paycheck, traveling in her business suit, receiving her paycheck—before she accepts the position. Essentially, she is creating her new reality on an astral level before creating it physically. It doesn't matter whether you are a "good visualizer" or not. Even if it's as simple as seeing yourself getting the paycheck at the end of the week, there's a reason you want that job. After all, if you look ahead at the job being offered and see nothing, what's the motivating force to make you accept? I believe everyone visualizes to some extent, and that's what drives people to create new circumstances for themselves. We often refer to this as "daydreaming" or "fantasizing." What will it be like to actually land that job and get started? What outfit will you wear the first day on the job, what will the people be like?

You may be wondering how to focus intention and direct will into the candle work. Visualization cannot be forced. I have seen people concentrate so hard that the expression on their face is one of constipation. When you do that kind of concentration that is exactly what is happening to your magick—it becomes constipated. Backed up in your astral body, it cannot release itself. The astral body is a duplicate of you that carries out your life in the magickal realm. It is where all things happen before they manifest on the earthly plain or our physical world as we know it. To slip into this world, communicate our desires, and mold our life, we must be one with this world.

In order to do this, you must relax. Being anxious and hurried will not allow you to be in the proper frame of mind. Direct the mental image of the life you desire as if directing a movie in your mind. Set the stage, the players, and let it roll. This is what I call the daydream method. Allow the scene to run over and over in your mind for a period of time while sitting in front of your candle, and then let it go. Do not obsess about it.

Allow your spell the time to ripen and appear in your life as it should. I cannot count how many times people have lit a candle for a lover to return and then called the next day to complain that it wasn't working. Talk about putting the kibosh on your spell before it even had a chance to start working! If it took time for the relationship to break up it stands to reason that it's going to take time for it to return. Real magick is not Hollywood—a wave of the fairy godmother's wand and all is well. Let your magickal thoughts flow from you into your work, and do not fret over it every minute. This is why I suggest including a petition to the deity with whom you are working in the candle spells. When you sit down and write your thoughts out on paper, you become focused on what you want and it flows from you. Be positive and sure of your intentions.

When crafting an enchanted candle, many factors that affect the astral plane need to be taken into consideration, such as colors, shapes, astrology, oils, incenses, altars, and tools. This chapter will discuss them and their relevance to enchanted candle making.

CONCERNING MAGICK

The magick candle allows an individual to express herself. No two candles are exactly alike. Candle crafting allows your personal expression to come through. You may choose to do a love healing candle in pink with green, silver, and pink glitter, while someone else may choose to make a love healing candle in white using dark pink, turquoise-blue, and gold glitter. Using magick is to create a lifeline connection between that which you desire and attainment of that objective. It can also be used to help loved ones. You can make a candle for someone who is in need of healing, or for someone who needs help in any area of life. In short, its potential for opening doors to all facets of life is limitless. Any kind of talisman can be used in any fashion or in any tradition of magick you choose to work with. Even the alphabet is a form of magick, so long as it communicates your thoughts. An enchanted candle can be carved with Anglo-Saxon runes, Tantric syllables, hieroglyphics, Goddess/God images—even stick figures. As long as the pictures are clear and precise to you, they will act as functioning talismans.

Caution should be taken whenever practicing magick: *Be clear about what you want.*

If you are prone to indecision and/or being fickle, the magick will reflect the same. Always remember: be careful what you invoke, because you may receive it! Here's one of my favorite little stories that illustrates that theme:

A man and his wife living in a coal-mining town lost their only son in a coal mining accident. One day, an old man came to the door asking for money. The husband gave him some pennies, and the old man grinned toothlessly and said, "For this I shall reward you. Here is a magic charm. It will grant you three wishes. But only three!" With that he slipped a severed monkey's paw into the man's hand, and when the man looked up, there was only a fog outside the door.

When the man's wife came home, an argument about the charm ensued. For her, a severed monkey's paw was ghastly, and who believed in such nonsense anyway? The man soon became weary of arguing with his wife, and without thinking said, "I don't want to fight anymore. I wish I could just have a bowl of soup and go to bed!"

To their astonishment, the bowl of soup appeared. Now both were angry that a wish was wasted. They considered the art of patience and thought of a plan. They soon agreed to wish for their son back, never considering that the son was embalmed and at peace in his grave. When the son appeared at the door, he was screaming in torment and pain.

So with only one wish left, they wished him back to his grave.

(paraphrased from "The Monkey's Paw" by W. W. Jacobs)

Be very clear regarding an intention! Think about the consequences of actions. Think things through. Magick is like a chess game: it takes more than one move to win. It requires strategy. This means you should watch out for moves that produce a failure to win. Sometimes we must sacrifice for the greater good of winning our objective. This means sometimes you may have to do something you are not happy about, but in the end you will get what you are going after.

Magickal will is the power that directs the seal on the candle into the astral plane. Magickal will is basically your desire, being put forth by way of magick. You are consciously creating a talisman to achieve something that has not been possible by ordinary means. What you believe is what will manifest. This basic principle has been taught since the early ages. All personal motivators will tell you that you need to be positive to get the right results. If you only half believe in what you are doing or make self-defeating statements like "This will never work," "Nobody will ever love me," or "I will never be wealthy," when getting ready to do a candle spell, you defeat your magickal work immediately.

You must program your magickal work through the subconscious mind to obtain what you desire. The subconscious mind will not buy a lie. For example, if you run around saying "I have money in the bank," you are making a positive statement. But if you *don't* in fact have money in the bank, your subconscious mind knows this, and the money won't manifest. However, if you say, "I am going to put money in the bank, and I am willing to do my best to get it there," the subconscious mind will understand and help you achieve your goal.

One more thing about magick: any of the spells in this book can be done by and for both men and women of any race, culture, background, and sexual preference. There is no discrimination in magick. Only in people.

CONCERNING SEALS

The authenticity of seals are often called into question. Many people claim that only an ancient symbol found in an old cave somewhere can be "real." Some people believe that if it hasn't been handed down from some ancient text of magick or was created by someone from this day and age, it has no power behind it. This is not true. Take a stop sign, for example. It is certainly not of ancient origin, but it wields a lot of power—it causes people to stop their cars, and look both ways before moving forward again. A question I have been asked often is "Can I use other seals with an enchanted candle?" Yes, you can. There are of course some very powerful, well-known ancient seals. Particularly the Seals of Solomon, and spirit seals. If you are good at carving these seals into the wax, then by all means use them. I have used a pentacle of Venus with a Love seal on the same candle. In other words, I can use one of my seals and empower it with another seal designed by someone else. As long as the seals are working toward the same goal, any combination of them is fine. I like to carve a Love Healing seal on the front of the candle and a seal of the spirit Barbatos to heal emotional hurts on the other side. I might also add a Tara seal to ferry one across from sorrows, or a Banishing seal to neutralize past trauma. The candle seals in this book have been created for help with everyday problems. Thousands of fellow practitioners have been using my candle seals with the greatest of results. So can you.

SIGNIFICANCE OF COLOR

The astral world is composed of highly concentrated color. Everyone from the ancients to present-day psychics who have traveled the astral plane know and see these colors. I have had my own great experiences with astral travel both through meditation and consciously practicing the art of astral projection. Astral projection was part of my training as a High Priestess in the Craft. When practicing astral projection, I actually see colors like neon lights behind my closed eyelids—it's like when your closed eyes have been exposed to a sudden, bright light.

Everything that exists on the astral plane has a color. Each plane of correspondence vibrates to a particular color energy. The principle behind the plane of correspondence is that like attracts like. For example, the color of anger on the astral plane is red, and the color a person's face turns on the physical plane when they're angry is also red. Blue has been scientifically proven to invoke feelings of peace and calm in people. On the astral plane, blue is also the color of peace and calm. Therefore, it is important to be careful in choosing the correct color to use when selecting a candle for a talisman. When working on a special spell that requires more than one candle, try to choose colors that are complementary and suitable to your main purpose. This will be discussed further as we go along.

The following color guide will make choosing the colors for an enchanted candle a little easier, as it explains the magickal meaning of each color. When in doubt, however, you can always use white, gold, or silver, which will be accepted by all spirits, gods, or energies you are trying to reach. Both gold and silver have long been recognized as the colors we relate to moon and sun, male and female, and white has always been recognized as a color of neutrality.

Red

Pure energy, sexual prowess, and "focused manifestation" are its properties. Red can be used for love magick and/or healing magick. Love, passion, and marriage fall under red. Venus rules love, but Mars rules marriage. We attribute red as a color related to love, but also to lust, and both Mars and Venus have primary aspects that have to do with lust and love. Red is a good color to use for attraction magick, especially that of physical attraction, the rekindling of a current relationship, and seduction. Red is also perfect for an ongoing relationship where marriage is desired and a push in the right direction is required.

When red is used for healing, Mars will energize the physical body into action. There is a great driving force to create life and motivate life in this color. Use red for weight loss, and for renewed energy. Red also covers muscle injuries, some sexual dysfunction (such as men not having enough physical drive to want to make love), and blood disorders. Do not use red for burns, abrasions, rashes, fevers, or any disorder that involves a volatile Mars nature. This is because red inflames these disorders rather than healing them. You would want to use cooling, soothing colors for that kind of healing.

Pink

Pink brings us Venusian love. This color is good for attraction, devotion, and healing. Pink works on a more subtle level than red, but don't let it fool you. It is the combined action of Mars (red) and the Moon (white). Together, the two colors bring the drive of Mars and the receptivity of the moon. This color is also good for flirtations, passions, and the renewal of emotions. Devotional love and soul-mating can be invoked through this color. Most of the love seals work with pink unless otherwise indicated. Erzulie is a Haitian goddess of love, one of my favorite goddesses for working with pink. She works equally well with red, yellow, or white. Other deities that correspond well with this color are Venus, Aphrodite, Freya, Dwynewen, and all love Goddesses.

Blue

This color is associated most with peace: a bright blue sky, tranquil blue Caribbean waters, the royal gleam of a sapphire, lapis lazuli revealing wisdom in the eyes of ancient Egyptian statuary. Blue is considered a strong and protective color. Yet the coolness of the color is peaceful and brings serenity. Blue is a color that fortifies the aura. One way to see this for yourself is by doing a simple color test. Take two sheets of paper—one pink, and one a deep blue. Hold up the pink sheet of paper and stare at it for one minute. Now hold out your arm. Tell a friend to push down on your arm. They should find very little resistance. Now repeat the process with the blue paper. When your friend pushes down on your extended arm this time, he or she will likely find much greater resistance in your arm. Blue is the invisible color of the sun—just picture the color blue in a gas jet flame. We see the sun as a yellow orb in the sky, but the blue flame color is not visible to us. When doing work for peace in your life, family, and home remember that blue is the color that will build a strong force field of protective energy around you.

Green

Green is the color of cash, plain and simple. Many people think that this is because the American dollar is green. This is a common misconception. Green is the color of cash because Venus rules the money flow in our lives. Green corresponds to planetary Venus in Taurus, which governs earth matters and rules over money. In the material world all art, treasures, antiques, and worldly possessions are her domain. Venus also works well with Mercury—one can use an orange candle in conjunction with green to open doors quickly and remove obstacles so that a desire will manifest more easily.

Green is a calming color used to heal female problems, diseases of the heart, and to help with most cancers. For heart problems, I use a Love Healing seal on a green candle with pink glitter. The calming effect of this combination promotes mental reassurance and confidence—since most diseases are associated with emotional pain, this is often the mandatory first step of healing the physical body.

Green is also associated with divine providence, material abundance and well-being, as taught to us by the ancient astrologers and magicians of centuries past, and is the devotional color for Mother Earth.

Orange

Communication is the key word here. Mercury, divine messenger of the Gods, rules this color. Going through a lot of red tape lately? This candle can be the scissor that cuts through it. Orange is best suited for success spells and favorable decisions. If you're having trouble getting your thoughts collected, are distracted, or are finding it difficult to express your desires, use this color. Orange is an excellent color to use in job-hunting spells.

Purple

This is a color that denotes majesty and pride. Purple is Jupiter's color, for his notorious bestowment of honors, recognition, knowledge, and his wisdom through psychic vision. Jupiter is a royal planet that bestows honors onto people, as does the god Jupiter in ancient mythology. Use a purple candle for spells dealing with legal issues and to overcome difficult problems, and Jupiter will bring a favorable judgment. (However, this does not mean that if you commit a crime and light a purple candle, you will get away with it!) It can help bring mercy from the courts: a lighter sentence, probation, or some good fortune may come from your time spent in jail. For instance, many people have made great changes while in prison and have helped many others.

Purple signifies abundance, and Jupiter is a planet well known for its qualities of generosity and abundance. This is why it has been the color of the royals for centuries. Whatever your desire or goal, there is an abundance of wealth that comes along with its accomplishment. Power and strength are also attributes of purple. This comes from the blend of the color red for power, and blue for strength. Use the color purple wisely and the power and strength that comes with it will bring you happiness, balance, and opportunities rich in beauty, art, and personal fulfillment.

Gold

There are many shades of gold, but in a seven-day pullout candle, gold is actually a dark yellow or a golden light brown. This color brings successful results in magickal use by its sympathetic vibration to the earth tones. After all, where does gold come from?

The metallic gold only comes in taper candles, but works wonderfully for devotional offerings. A devotional offering in Wicca entails making an offering purely for the sake of giving, and thanking the gods for their many blessings. Most of the deities and saints understand when gold is used instead of another color. However, a word of caution: metallic candles are not quick to burn, and sometimes have a tendency to go out. However, they are accepted as devotional offerings just the same. Gold-colored candles can also be used in money spells, success spells, and as an alternative to yellow or orange candles.

Yellow

This is the color of Apollo, golden Sun God of the fiery chariot, riding across the sky. It is used for building up the ego, so that one can walk in a state of balance. Yellow will clear away all auric debris that weighs down the soul's natural development. Auric debris culminates over time and is made apparent in the personality. Are you low on self-esteem? Do you feel like your life is worthless? Then you need some sunshine in your life to clear away that auric debris. Use this color for any work requiring mental clarity as well as for its ability to attract what you desire.

Sunny, warm and inviting, yellow's exuberant, joyful disposition is contagious. This is why I often use it for spells dealing with love—its optimistic vibration helps invoke a better frame of mind. Be flirtatious! Wear a golden, gleaming aura. Be a Love Goddess and shine with a mantle of glowing love for beauty, receptive warmth, and responsiveness to all.

White

The serenity of white produces a clearing effect. Whether we are using it on a person or to sweep away obstacles, it is the best purging color in the spectrum.

It is advisable to do an uncrossing spell before the undertaking of most spells, as this will open doors and set a clear path before you. If there are any negative blocks that have been stopping you from attaining your successes in life this candle will be good for clearing them away before you proceed with other spells. This can also be done while you are doing your other spells. For instance, if you have decided to do a love spell and you do not necessarily feel that there are any particular blocks in your way but want to play it safe, this candle will help clear away any obstacles that you may not be aware of. You can burn any white candle spell with any other candle spell together at the same time. White will cleanse, purify, and absorb like no other. It will also absorb any other color. For example, if I had a spell that called for a green candle, yet none were available, I could substitute a white one for it. If the user envisions a green light passing through the white candle, then the candle "becomes" green. White corresponds to the moon because of its receptive qualities.

I recommend that white candles be kept in stock for various Enchanted Candle uses. All deities respond to white, therefore a white devotional will help call your master guides to help in all emergencies by bringing about divine solutions in troubling situations.

Gray

The realm between black and white, gray is neutral in its vibration and is used mostly to quell or stop negative energy. This color works well to put an end to gossip or arguments, and to void another's harmful projections. However, many people do not enjoy the vibrations of this color in a working atmosphere, for it tends to act like a sedative to everyone in the vicinity. This is great if relaxation is the desired result, but if you are doing a hot love spell or money magick, use white to uncross, unless there is someone specific stopping you from attaining your goals. In that case, use gray. You can also use gray with other colors to banish or neutralize another person's harmful thoughts to you. Gray or silver is another color associated with the moon. Metallic silver candles are often used as devotional candles to the moon goddess. Silver metallic and gold metallic are used as moon and sun candles. They are also both used in money spells.

Brown

Brown is the color of work. Brown has always been a serious color. That is why we use it when there is a job or project that needs strict attention and focus. Being a color close to black, many people mistake brown for the "safe" black. This means people who feel that they need a justice spell can safely use brown, because being a color of the earth it will cause no harm. Many times I have read spells that refer to using a brown candle for justified retribution. As if intentions carry no karma! The truth is, brown is born from fire—the interaction of red and green. Fire is the element of the will. Being an earth color, brown embodies the forces of action at work. Let's look at society for a moment shall we? Men wearing brown suits usually imply a sense of business. Commonsense style is what brown is really about. If you feel people in your life are lacking common sense when dealing with you, then brown would make a good color choice for a Justice candle.

Black

This color is representative of Saturn. Traditionally the God is associated with the negative and malefic. To this day, some misinformed people consider our Horned God to be the devil. Black candles were once considered to be used for the devil's work and magick was thought to cause harm. Hence, modern black candle magick has received the same reputation. For the most part this is true, but only because there are those people who are misdirected and would use this energy for ill will. Often in my years of being in the occult business, people purchase black candles to get back at someone who has harmed them. They are sold commercially for this purpose. They can be used for this purpose if you so desire—but I do not recommend it. Let's examine our culture for a moment. Black here is considered a color of mourning. In China black is a color associated with water and money. White in China is considered a color of mourning. Does this make black good and white bad? Certainly not. Some banishing spells require a black candle, as do some Kabalistic workings—black isn't always bad. But it is recommended that you are very certain that your intentions are not harmful before going forward. For example, some people associate black with sexuality (like sexy black lingerie), so for them a black candle may be appropriate to use in a love-calling spell. Even when I do recommend retribution, it should be only under severe circumstances of violence, such as murder, rape, or mugging. For these I recommend the Justice seal accompanied by a calling for a balance of karma. Along with this call for justice, I recommend a white candle with a Banishing seal to help break the connection to the act that was committed. A person feels violated when an act of violence has been committed against them. A black candle gives the victim a sense of returned power, and gets them in touch with their anger and the darkness that was called up within them by the act of violence, thereby allowing them to release it as the candle burns. They might want to follow this with a yellow Solar Blast to help realign and rejuvenate the afflicted party. Once the anger has been released into the black candle spell a yellow candle will rejuvenate the spirit.

Seven Colors

Some occult stores and Botanicas carry seven-color pullout candles. They are difficult to work with because they are seven candle rounds strung together like a set of buttons. Each color relates to a chakra, a planet, a god or goddess, or a saint. They begin with the base or root chakra. Next comes the spleen, then the solar plexus, the heart, the throat, the brow, and finally the crown. Often used for uncrossing spells, they can be very effective in unblocking the seven chakras. This candle will open all of these energy centers and put them in alignment. Any spiritual blocks present will be alleviated. For example, say you are attempting to study for an important exam in school but everything around you is falling apart while you are trying to focus. The phone keeps ringing. Your dog makes a mess in the living room. Everyone in the house keeps shouting. These are all minor examples of the blocked energy that surrounds you. By doing an uncrossing spell to release those blocks, you are now free to study for your exam. This is a candle that has a lot of work to do, so when burning these be patient—they often take a long time to burn, despite their name. They can burn anywhere from seven to ten days.

SIGNIFICANCE OF CANDLE TYPES

My first impression of the candle section in an occult store when I was first studying Wicca was a delightful mixture of confusion and awe. A myriad of colors was the first thing my eyes took in; next were the varying sizes and shapes. Mixed into this display of color and shape were candles in glass jars with images printed on the glass. Thirty years later, I'm still intrigued by it all!

He who understands the principle of vibration
has grasped the scepter of power.

—THE KYBALION-3 INITIATES

When we look at the picture of a saint, our immediate reaction is to recall information. This is a person who has lived and accomplished great feats of physical and emotional strength. They have conquered evil, resisted temptation, suffered torture, and shown high endurance or the ability to rise above pain. Some showed the ability to communicate with other life forms such as the animal kingdom or the spiritual realms. Others produced different kinds of miracles, such as St. Theresa, who produced flowers directly from her body. With such grand achievements, it's no wonder we gain courage from these superhuman images.

Many Wiccans use saint candles because they understand that many saints were once pagan gods. This fact is also essential in understanding candle burning. As a saint candle burns, it carries the memory of the picture that surrounds it along with whatever association we have with that saint in our minds. If we see that saint as a god or goddess, that is the energy which is carried out by the burning candle. For example the Caridad Del Cobre (which is a Virgin Mary) is associated with the African Goddess Oshun who corresponds with Venus. St. Barbara is associated with Chango, who is an African God associated with the Sun God of other cultures. Burning a saint candle vibrates the energies of these saints/gods and their associations into the astral plane, which in turn will then vibrate back to the material plane.

I'd like to add that even though I am a Wiccan high priestess, I deal with many different aspects of magick. My personal religion does not stop me from tapping into different realms of magickal or supernatural worlds. Whether those worlds are peopled by saints, goddesses, gods, angels, spirits, faery folk, or other spiritual beings from varying traditions, my references will tap into a world that encompasses all. Candle magick is not about dogma or staying within the confines of a specific religion. It's about tapping into the vast world of magick and using any aspect of that world that will help you. The Gods work through many hands and answer all who come with a sincere request. So yes, you can be Wiccan and ask a Catholic saint for help. Or you can have no Latin background and still ask a Santerian orisha for guidance. You get the picture.

Any candle can be carved—it depends on your dexterity. Practice and patience are the keys. The preferred candle size for the Enchanted Candle is a seven-day pullout—a seven-day, glass-encased candle that slides easily out of its glass container. This allows us to carve, oil, glitter, and feed our Enchanted Candle. It is the most elaborate of the spell candles. There are times when smaller versions are needed. For example, sometimes you just can't burn a big candle for seven days without being too conspicuous. Or sometimes the spell you are trying to cast is time-sensitive and you need something in a hurry. For cases such as these, I recommend a votive candle in a glass holder. Its broadness makes it easy to carve and the glass holder allows it to burn fifteen hours.

A few words about the timing of spells. The mere act of putting your intentions out there will certainly bring you some results. But it's the burning of the actual candle that releases the spell into the astral plane and sets the magick to work. Sometimes it may take several tries. For example, say you do a spell to get a job. You burn your candle, and the next day you get an interview, but in the end the job is given to someone else. Do you quit? Of course not. You still need a job! This is when you have to have trust in the Universe and do your spell again—that obviously wasn't the right job for you! Actions bring results. Never assume that all you need to do is wave a magick wand (or light a magick candle) and all good things appear. Magick takes work and concentration and lots of practice.

Next, we have the jumbo size candle. It is 1½ inches in diameter, and it is approximately thirteen inches tall. This is also broad enough for carving, but since it has no glass holder, its burning time is fairly short, and you'll want to put something underneath it to catch the dripping wax. The same goes for the coach candle. A coach candle is about six inches long and about one inch around. The coach candle got its name from the time when coaches were still in fashion and they were used to light the candle lamps on the side of the coach. They are wider than a taper candle and last a little longer. These candles, as well as tapers, can burn anywhere from three to eight hours, depending on the heat and breeze factors in the area where they are burning. Tapers are taller and thinner than the other candles. Some tapers are what we call "dinner candles" and are very long and thin. Now, of course, use common sense in choosing the right size seal according to the candle size. For example, Come to Me will only fit on a seven-day candle. For the smaller candles, good seals to use are the Seals of Solomon and spirit seals. Now, there are exceptions to the rule. I have carefully carved a Come to Me seal on a votive, but it wasn't easy. You have to have patience and accept a facsimile of the seal if every nuance cannot fit, knowing that the intention remains the same.

Next we have figure candles—those that represent images: humans, witches, skulls, cats, and devils, just to name a few. There are quite a few on the market. I have also seen some impressive dolphins, seashells, butterflies, unicorns and others. These candles are terrific for developing visualization. They represent a specific person or concept, which makes focusing easier. However, they are extremely difficult to carve and decorate unless you have a lot of patience and practice. I can carve very ornate seals in small replica on these candles, but a beginner may get very frustrated. When used in combination with a seven-day candle, however, they can be very powerful. Here are some uses for the most common ones:

Skull Figure

Use this for a thick skull! When you have to get inside someone's head, this is the ticket. Ellegua, remover of all obstacles, is a good deity to invoke here. Use Uncrossing oil and Special No. 20 powder on the candle (more on oils and powders in chapter 3). This, of course, is just one suggestion on how you might use a skull candle. There are green skull candles to get it inside of the subject's head to attract money, and so on.

Male Figure

This is used to attract a man. Use this with a female figure (or another male figure if the subject is gay), and a spell to bring the lovers together. I recommend burning these in front of a Come to Me candle or Hypnotique. With Midnight or Mystere oil on the figure candles, you have a very potent combination to attract the man you want. Burn Passionate Lover's incense while using this candle combination. Occult oils are stocked in all shops that carry magickal implements.

Female Figure

This works the same as the male figure candle, but here's an interesting variation for women who are shy, or just in a rut. Take your figure candle and anoint it with either passion oil or voodoo nights oil. Burn this in front of a flirtation candle, such as Mystere or Come to Me, and you'll not only find yourself meeting men, you'll be receiving a lot more attention from them to boot. Having problems keeping a man once you've met? Burn a white female figure candle dressed with Femme Blanche oil in front of a Femme Blanche candle.

Cat Figure

Luck is the key here. Many cultures such as the Japanese, the Egyptians, and Haitians just to name a few use cats for luck when gambling. Anoint a black or red cat candle with Gambler's Luck oil and burn in front of a Lucky Seven Candle. Black cats are either considered bad luck or good luck depending on the culture and your belief system. I personally consider all cats good fortune. Your lucky numbers can be inscribed on both your Lucky Seven candle (see seal on page 156) and your cat candles for extra power. Need a change of luck in general? Burn a red cat candle dressed with Lucky Lodestone oil in front of a Solar Blast candle that's been dressed with Nine Fruits oil or Ode to Joy oil.

Witch Figure

Care to bewitch someone special? Then use a red witch candle anointed with Bewitching oil and burn this in front of a Midnight candle. Both names should be included on the witch candle. Use Black Opium incense or Voluptuous Venus incense while the party in question is present. The effects are dazzling!

Devil Figure

Famous for their lucky attributes, these candles are very popular in voodoo. Are you familiar with the phrase "lucky devil"? Take a red devil candle and anoint it with Flying Devil oil. Burn it in front of an Uncrossing candle. I've seen people with the worst run of luck have everything turn around after this spell was performed.

Cross Candles

Did you ever hear the expression "he has too heavy a cross to bear"? This is a great candle to use when you want to lessen someone's burden, including your own. Burn a cross candle in conjunction with an Uncrossing candle anointed with hyssop oil or Uncrossing oil, while burning High John the Conqueror incense.

Devotional Figure Candles

These include dolphins, seashells, unicorns, and other figures. In this case, choose what best suits the spell. For example, lunar Goddesses or Ocean Mothers will love dolphin candles or something that represents the sea as much as Apollo (a sun God) will love a sun candle or a sunflower candle. If you're doing a love spell or a devotional altar to Venus or Aphrodite, you may want to use a heart-shaped candle. I have found that if the Goddess or God wants an offering they will guide you to it. For example, Erzulie is an ocean dweller, so seashells are appropriate. Lighting a seashell candle in her honor will most certainly get her attention and appreciation.

Seven-Day Saint

These candles with a picture of a saint on them normally include a prayer on the candle, which explains what the candle is for. If you're unsure who the image on the candle represents or what they stand for and you are buying your stock in a reputable store, the staff will be able to help answer some questions for you. I strongly advise you to buy your Magickal supplies in a store with good vibes, as these vibes will reflect in your Magick. Remember, inanimate objects will absorb negativity, which will lessen the strength and power of your spell. Some deities will not even come when summoned if the supplies the spell is conjured with are unclean with negative energy.

When no pullout candles are available and you still want to use a seven-day candle, there is still another possibility. Enchanted candles are carved into the wax, but you can still use a seven-day candle that does not come out of the glass. Instead of carving the candle itself, just draw the picture of the seal you desire on a piece of paper, and choose the appropriate candle color you want to use. Tape or glue the picture seal to the candle and then proceed with the spell as you would an enchanted candle spell. Place the feeding you would normally use in the bottom of the glass into a bowl instead (more about spell bowls on page 68), along with the rest of the spell ingredients. Be creative—use colored markers or glitter pens to draw your seal. The deity will lay his or her hand where his or her signature lies. For example, we all know what a peace symbol is. If you carve a peace symbol in a candle then you are contacting deities that represent peace. The symbol is a signature belonging to them—even though we created it, they inspired it. Whether the symbol is carved in the wax or drawn on paper surrounding the candle, the deities will still come. Say you are moving into a new apartment, and you want to do a house blessing candle and the only way you can get pullout candles is by mail order. Does this stop you? No, of course not! Just run to the supermarket or local store where they carry plain seven-day candles and purchase a blue one. And just start drawing! Of course it's preferable to carve the candles, but this is a good backup.

SIGNIFICANCE OF ASTROLOGY

Why is astrology so important when creating an enchanted candle? It is the timing of the universe that allows us to grow. The divine order in which we grow is made known to us over time, as astrologically we are given life lessons to live through. Some people just plod along allowing life to take them where it will. Others have an innate understanding of how to get what they want, and they go after it. Then there are those who have an interest in magick and decide to alter their lives by using the universal laws that are at their disposal. Having an astrological chart done for you will tell you a lot about yourself. It will even show you what sector of your chart shows your interest in the occult arts and sciences. How wide that sector is or how narrow may determine your amount of interest in magick. However, since you are reading this book, you are obviously interested!

Let us examine the timing of the universe and how it allows us to grow. Saturn is considered "the teacher" in astrology, and its placement in your chart shows what circumstances have come to you in order for you to grow. Two people can have the same placement of Saturn and have totally different experiences, but they will both still grow from these experiences. It is similar to the creation of a pearl. A grain of sand finds its way into an oyster. It agitates the oyster, which begins to secrete a milky film over the grain of sand. It continues this process over time, and a pearl is formed. Just as agitation gives us the pearl, so agitation or friction makes us grow. And no two pearls are exactly alike.

Magick is part of the universal plan of life. People use its principles every day whether they know it or not. Others often have chaotic lives because they have not grasped its principles to their fullest extent. People who believe in themselves and go for what they want usually get it. This is one of the basic principles of magick. We, of course, have free will, and are not at the complete mercy of planetary alignment. But the planets do affect our lives. A sun sign horoscope is a very general prediction of what is going to happen. I wouldn't suggest hiding away at home when your chart tells you a bad astrological aspect is coming up next week, but when I know I have a bad astrological aspect coming up, I start my candle magick early to start warding off the negative effects coming my way.

Take the moon, for example. The moon controls the tides of the oceans. That's a pretty big job. We as human beings are physically composed of a large percent of water. If the pull of the moon can control the tides, what can it do to us? We are but an individual speck in the universe. Are we really so arrogant that we think a large heavenly body has influence over the vastness of the oceans, and no effect on us?

It has been said that "a wise man rules by the stars but is not ruled by them." Basically, that means we should work with the planets to achieve the best of what they have to offer, but not let them control our lives. We have many choices and one of the basic ones is to gain control over our emotions. We still need to cry in order to appreciate our laughter, but we do not need to go overboard into an ocean of tears either.

Does this mean that you have to take astrology into account when crafting a candle or performing a spell? Well, let's look at what is happening astrologically to you that requires candle magick to begin with. For example, all of a sudden you might be getting many great job offers, and there's one you especially like. You may want to do a success spell to help ensure that you will get it. The influence of Mercury could open doors to communication, and solar power will make you stand out and shine, so you should take that into consideration when preparing to do your spell. Solar power is the soul and how it influences itself through its solar chart. For example, I am a Leo, and how I make my will known is different than how a Virgo would. Leo is loud and obvious, while Virgo is shy and retiring. But we can both get our points across.

On the other hand, if feeling uninspired and in a rut, you could do a solar spell to empower you with new inspiration.

Performing ritual magick during the right astrological aspects—meaning that everything is in fine cosmic order—is recommended. There are many examples of correct cosmic order for spell casting, which is why I am giving you both solar and lunar references. If the sun is in Gemini, ruled by the planet Mercury, which is all about communication, then this is a good time to do all kinds of communication spells. The sun stays in power for a month. So while the sun is in Gemini and the moon is in Taurus, it is a good time for you to do spells about communicating finances. While the sun is still in Gemini and the moon moves into Libra, you may want to do spells that deal with communicating about relationships. Read the meanings of the planets, sun, and moon, and you will see how they spell out for you your most powerful opportunities. Does this mean that you can only perform a certain spell when the planets are in a specific placement? Of course not. It simply means the planets are correctly aligned during that time. It does not mean that alignment is absolutely necessary in order for the spell to work. Go with the flow, see what aspect is at its optimum timing, and do spell work to keep your life moving.

Unfortunately, usually what has you running for a candle is anything *but* cosmic order: you may be thinking "my life is hell and I need to fix it now. I cannot wait for Venus to finish retrograding, and Mars to come into a more favorable sign." My advice: when you need to do magick, just do it. However, remember one rule of caution: try not to perform your spell during a void-of-course moon (they only last a few hours, so it's worth the wait.). Technically, the void-of-course moon is one making a transition from one astrological sign to another. There are astrological calendars that list this information for every day of the year, and they list how the moon is changing.

One question that people often ask me is: If I carve a love candle on Friday and do not have time to perform the spell, do I have to wait a whole week before I can start my magick? Well the good news is that you carved it on Friday, so it already has the Venus influence. You can begin the spell and light the candle whenever you are ready. Being ready is more important. Being relaxed, focused, and uninterrupted will effect your magick in a greater way than having every planetary position in perfect harmony. Remember: if every planet were in perfect harmony you would be out doing what you want instead of doing candle magick.

The zodiac really is a giant clock in the heavens keeping time to the vibration of the Universe and all it has planned. How those plans work out is up to each individual. The stars just set the stage upon which we are the players writing our own scripts. Knowing the special correspondence each planet has with the cosmos and all things in it is like having a special key to unlock the doors to the Universe. A "spiritual key" in this instance is a listing of all of their special attributes and when to apply them in your magickal operations. Each planet has deities that are connected to it. This will help you to decide your course of action. If, for instance, you have decided to do a love spell to meet someone new, naturally you turn to Venus. With our spiritual keys we can fine-tune the spell even more. Let's say that you desire someone who is vibrant, magnanimous, and fun loving. You can add a solar candle to your spell, such as Solar Blast or Love and Happiness. This will help you to attract a mate that is more vibrant and full of life. Or say you want someone who is nurturing and caring. Then adding some lunar properties to the spell will be the enhancement you're looking for.

Our first look at astrology is at the beginning of Cro-Magnon culture. Markings on reindeer bones are believed to record lunar cycles. From here history leads us to 4000 B.C. in Mesopotamia. Sumerians built ziggurats, the first astrological observatories. Astrology is recorded in cuneiform on clay tablets. So we know from early on that each planet was named after a deity because they share those attributes. Here is a partial list to give you an idea of some of the deities who are attributed to those planets.

Sun: Apollo, Sol, Ra, Helios, Krishna, Odin
Moon: Diana, Yemeya, Luna, Selene, Isis
Jupiter: Jove, Bacchus, Zeus, Mabon
Mercury: Ganesha, Mercury, Thoth, Hermes

Venus: Aphrodite, Erzulie, Oshun, Lakshmi
Mars: Aries, Oggun, Mars
Saturn: Cronus, Saturn
Uranus: Uranus, Ouranus
Neptune: Poseidon, Oceanus
Pluto: Pluto, Hades

THE PLANETS AND THEIR SPIRITUAL KEYS

Sun: *He who constructs*

The life giver. The sun will burn away all impurities. It is the great leveler. The Sun brings humility to one's enemies, clears away depression, and aids in building up self-confidence. The Sun's energy will help bring you recognition and put you in the spotlight.

SPIRITUAL KEY: Harmony.

Moon: *She who mothers*

Protectress from psychic and physical harm. Ruler of all hidden mysteries. The moon carries precedence over the tides of the oceans. She rules the house and keeps it together. Use for opening psychic doorways as well as protection.

SPIRITUAL KEY: Nurturing.

Jupiter: *He who expands*

This planet is for all work dealing with increase, rewards, abundance, tolerance, justice, joviality, extravagance, luck, gambling, idealism, wisdom, the ability to grow mentally.

SPIRITUAL KEY: Mercy.

Mercury: *He who communicates*

Mercury is the creator of language, tarot, and magick. He analyzes and opens new doors. He is a deity of mobility, perception, success, and is the messenger of the Gods. He is a clever trickster, so be very certain of what you require from him. I have a story I never tire of telling about Mercury's mischievous nature. First let me explain that he tricks you for your own good. There is always a lesson to learn from one of his tricks. Once you have learned that lesson, you are better for it, and when you get what you want it is a real treat. I once needed a new car, so using sympathetic magick I went out and bought a small toy car. I used it in a spell telling Elegua (the Santerian name for Mercury) that I needed a car. My daughter's father was working in the toy wholesale district of Manhattan at the time and often he would buy toys wholesale and then sell them to the truckers he would meet while working a freight elevator. That night he came home with two boxes of toy cars and said, "Look at the great deal I got today, I sold two boxes in the last hour at work, and I will sell these two off tomorrow morning." I paid five bucks for my little car to do my spell, and what did Elegua do? He sent me two boxes of the same car. I ran over to Elegua's altar and said, "Okay, very funny." I then told Elegua I would put the toy car in the crossroads when I got my car. A week later we had the money to get a used car and Elegua was happy playing in the crossroads with his new toy. What I learned was the importance of shopping for the best deal rather than diving into buying a car just because it seemed to be the best I could find in my price range.

SPIRITUAL KEY: Intellect.

Venus: *She who allures*

She is the ruler of cash flow, and of beauty and art. Her expressions are pleasure, art, music, beauty, and affection. She is mellow, peaceful, and sociable.

SPIRITUAL KEY: Love.

Mars: *He who gives energy*

Mars is the awakener and provides the drive for desire, initiative, adventure, war, and all projects that lack these qualities. Physical energy for healing is expressed through Mars.

SPIRITUAL KEY: Dynamism.

Saturn: *He who endures*

Saturn is the teacher, the dealer of unrelenting discipline and karmic balance. He oversees introspection, perseverance, and the working out of karma during the process of spiritual evolution. He also rules business and its foundation. Business requires a strong foundation and rigid rules, or standard procedures in order to flourish and grow. Saturn gives us that. It is the skeleton upon which all of life is built.

SPIRITUAL KEY: Wisdom.

Uranus: *He who perceives*

The perfect spiritual consciousness. The seat of intuition and altruism. Extremes and sudden change. Uranus destroys the constricting influence and crystallizations of Saturn. It displaces and overthrows established attitudes which have outlived their usefulness. Revolutionary, original, erratic, eccentric. It is related to intuitive knowledge.

SPIRITUAL KEY: Awakening.

Neptune: *He who is the absolute consciousness*

A higher vibration of Venus. Venus is beauty and all acts of love; Neptune is the spiritual love of mankind. All things that are creative can come from Neptune, as it rules the astral plane. Neptune is receptive, passive, and nebulous. He brings spiritual strength and opens psychic doors. He represents astral entities, artistry, and creativity from the astral realm.

SPIRITUAL KEY: Faith.

Pluto: *He who clears the way*

The higher vibration of Mars. Mars rules over generations. It stays in one orbit for approximately fourteen years, which means everyone born in that time frame is of one generation. Pluto's orbit covers the masses and has been a symbol of cleansing, healing catharsis through destruction, disintegration, and elimination.

SPIRITUAL KEY: Regeneration.

THE MOON

The moon has a very special relation to candle magick. She is the intuitive side of magick. As the Sun takes an average of thirty days to travel through one house, the moon only requires two to two and a half days. This means that there are more available changes of the phases of the moon going through the solar houses of the zodiac to work with. For example, if you want to utilize Aries energy, you do not have to wait for spring to come around—just perform your magick when the moon is in Aries.

But there are also different phases of the moon that make some work more auspicious than others. When the moon is waxing, it is growing from the new moon stage to the full moon stage. This is the best time for all spells that require growth, like love spells, money drawing, success, and so forth. When the moon is waning it is the best phase for spells for cleansing, releasing, and uncrossing. For less auspicious times, just be clear about your intention, and use the waning moon energy in a positive way. For example, if you're dying to bring new love into your life *now* and you don't want to wait for the moon to finish waning, then do a spell that will release any obstacles that are keeping you from meeting your mate. This method can be used for the casting of all spells during a waning moon. Overall, be sure of your intentions, stay diligent in your work, and you will achieve results.

Moon in Aries

Initiating new projects and speeding up old ones. Good for passionate relationships and situations where courage, energy, and initiative are needed. A witch I know named Pixie works in the environmental and ecological field. For months she had been agonizing about whether or not to return to school and study environmental law. She had the desire to do it, but she lacked the courage and the finances to actually see it through. We crafted a Road Opener candle in the new moon phase of Aries, and it opened up many new possibilities for her. The next day she inquired at work through the human resources department about their education program, and the doors flew open. Her company paid for her schooling and she is now getting a degree.

Moon in Taurus

For stabilization, solidity, and endurance. This moon is good for completing projects that have been left unfinished. The Taurus moon will enable you to become more focused at the task at hand. Taurus will move mountains slowly and methodically, even if it is one bucket of dirt at a time, but it will not quit until the job is accomplished. A waxing moon in Taurus is the time to begin money magick or stabilize a shaky relationship. The moon in Taurus grants boons for abundance. Raven always had a problem staying at a job. She was a hairdresser and very good in her field, but nothing lasted more than a couple of months to a year. She came to me for a reading and we charted out a plan. She was young and had a lot of savvy. The small neighborhood shops she kept trying to settle down in would never allow her to grow. She needed to work in New York City at a large salon where she could flourish and grow. So we began her job spell while the moon was in Aries. When she landed the job, she was so excited! She called me and gave me her start date. I told her no it wasn't an auspicious date. She said, "Are you crazy?"

I told her to call her new boss and tell him her present employer wishes her well but just booked a wedding party and really needed her for this one last job, and to see if she could start a week later if it wasn't too inconvenient.

She did as I told her. Her new boss admired her loyalty and allowed her to start a week later, when the moon was in Taurus. She has been with the company thirteen years, is a salon manager, and has refused offers to even go into her own business. She loves her job. The moon in Taurus is not the only reason she is still there, but it certainly helped stabilize her.

Moon in Gemini

Mercury is the ruling planet for Gemini, so when the moon is in this sign, a spell done under its influence has a lot of speed. The moon in Gemini rules all communication projects and will bring friends when asked for. This is a good moon for communication spells, for learning, and for giving courage to shy people. Tina decided to go to school to become a massage therapist. She had a lovely job working in a hospital running a department. Now going to school and keeping a full-time job was going to put a lot on her plate. She needed help to get through this. So we started a regular regime of Ganesha rituals to help her retain the information she was learning and to keep her job. We started the rituals with the new moon in Gemini. The Gemini twins also helped her to keep two major tasks going at once. She kept her job for the stable income and benefits, and the massage business gives her a nice extra income. Now she doesn't have to kill herself working two jobs all the time to keep up her lifestyle and independence.

Moon in Cancer

This is an excellent moon phase for the antique collector as it rules over the home and antiquities. It's an excellent time to go hunting for odd treasures. All matters dealing with the home are best for the waxing moon when passing through Cancer. A house blessing is especially potent at this time, as is invoking a new apartment, or stabilizing a difficult home-life situation. The moon in Cancer is a very emotional time, but you never know what good may come from something bad. If people bother to listen to someone's emotional outbursts they might actually learn something about that person, as well as about themselves. The nurturing moon in Cancer can help you do that. Bless the home and all its inhabitants during this moon phase. It will bring mothering love to the home.

Lady Zoradia helped another witch named Connie during a difficult phase in her life. Connie needed money to get an apartment right away. Lady Zoradia did a Lakshmi candle for her under the Moon in Cancer and told her to strongly visualize what she needed. Connie did and she attended an open ritual for Lakshmi that we held at the store where we worked. A week later someone she had once loaned money to came to her and gave her several thousand dollars to thank her for the time that she helped him out. She needed nurturing help and that is just what she received.

Moon in Leo

This moon phase expresses royalty and ceremony. It promotes all acts of loyalty through friendship. What an ideal time to throw a party! If you cannot throw a party during this time, then initiate the magick when the moon is in Leo. Appropriate spells are the Solar Blast, Uncrossings, and House Blessings. This is also a great time for magickal work regarding attraction, recognition, creative flair, and for self-expression. I am a Leo, and I love this moon. If you're down in the dumps, this is a good moon phase to bolster up some self-esteem. Theresa suffered a long bout with depression. I advised her to light Solar Blast candles each time the moon entered Leo. Amazing things started to happen. For one thing, her doctors finally found the right medication to help combat her depression. Theresa actually started getting up earlier in the morning and singing with the birds! Her friends started gravitating to her more because she was having fewer mood swings. Her whole life improved. This, of course, is not the only time to do a Solar Blast spell, but the influence of the Leo moon certainly did wonders for Theresa!

Moon in Virgo

Initiate magick on finding solutions to problems that you haven't been able to solve and need some help analyzing. This is a good moon phase for tests and school projects. It's also an excellent time for magick pertaining to employment matters. Communications are under focus at this time. Healing magick and all sixth house health matters—related to diet and health in general—should be dealt with at this time. A good example is candles for weight loss. This moon phase can help you put into perspective the concept of "eating to live, not living to eat."

Speaking of diets, I prefer to start diet magick during a new moon, either in Aries for new beginnings or in a fixed sign for staying power. Fixed signs are Taurus, Leo, Scorpio, and Aquarius. If the diet is health-related, for reasons such as high blood pressure, diabetes, or any other diet-related disease, then the new or waxing moon in Virgo is perfect.

Merlin, a high priest in the craft, has his sun in Virgo, and always likes to start new projects under that moon sign. He feels it empowers him with intuitive insight. There is an alliance between his sun and the moon at this time, and he has had many successful ventures when he aligned the moon and the sun. The truth is, even if you do not have your sun in Virgo, this moon phase will still help you to analyze problems. Many of my clients have burned an Uncrossing Candle during this moon phase and have found the key to ending their troubles as a result.

Moon in Libra

This is a harmonious time for initiating love magick to find a soul mate, or simply a friend. This is a great time for socializing and meeting people. It's also a good time to redecorate the house or change your appearance—beauty knows no bounds during this lunar shine. If there are squabbles and disputes to be settled, then it's a good time for situations where compromise, diplomacy and a sense of fairplay can be invoked. When the moon is in Libra, something is in the air—people come to me in swarms, looking for help in finding that special someone to be in their lives.

Michelle was in love with a man who was always in and out of her life. His indecision was driving her crazy! I did a reading for her and saw another man in her immediate future. She found this very hard to believe. I promised her she would soon forget all about the man she was currently so crazy about (even though he was making her miserable) if she just gave herself a chance and went out that weekend.

I convinced her to let me make a Spellbound candle for her. The moon was in Libra, and I wanted to take full advantage! A week later, she said it was as if I plucked this guy out of the sky and he fell into her lap. They have been dating ever since, and I hear wedding bells in the future. When Libra moon is on the rise, romance, partnerships, and love are more possible than ever.

Moon in Scorpio

This is the moon that rules over secrets and magick. It's a great time to do some soul-searching to seek out spiritual avenues that can lead you to answers. The key here is strategy. If you are looking for intimacy then this is a great moon phase as well. Scorpio feels things deeply and forever. Need a little detective work done? Put the old gumshoes on this moon to work and you will have your answer. The effects of this moon phase are very strong, being that this is a fixed moon and the sign of secrets—both those that can be kept hidden and, if you so desire, those that can be exposed. Most occultists use this moon phase to discover the keys to unlock magickal information. This is a regenerative sign. It can bring relationships back from the dead. This is a great moon phase to start spells to return a loved one to you.

This is my favorite moon phase to perform spells with Martha Dominadora or "The Sorceress." If there are any obstacles between two people reuniting, I turn to her, especially when the moon is in Scorpio.

Morgana and her lover were always under stress from his family. They didn't like her, and would deliberately cause friction between them. Eventually, it got so bad that they split up. At first, Morgana did not want to do love magick on her man because she felt it was too controlling. I told her that there is no amount of magick that can make someone love you. A love spell is simply to help you both have a clear shot at being together. Once you two are together, if it is not what you both freely desire, it will end. So she did a Sorceress candle along with a Scarlette's Seduction candle while the moon was in Scorpio. They not only got back together but he now asks her to create candles all the time because he loves the effect they have on their bedroom! This is just one example of what the moon can do in Scorpio. Experiment and see what you come up with.

Moon in Sagittarius

Positive energy abounds during this phase. If you have been hoping for a miracle, now is the time to ask for it. This is a good moon phase for success in legal matters because Jupiter (who rules Sagittarius) rules over courts and mercy in judgment. People who work for tips, such as waiters, bartenders, street musicians, dancers, hair dressers, taxi drivers, maids, and so on, would benefit from this moon by doing money magick during this time. In fact, people who make a large part of their pay through tips should always have a Jupiter candle burning during this phase. If you have a penchant for philosophy, light a wisdom candle such as a Purple Wisdom, or any candle to help expand knowledge in the direction you are headed, and travel the spheres of the magickal planes. These planes or spheres are where all ancient mysteries live and this phase of the moon helps you tap into these secret places.

Ancient knowledge is prevalent during this lunar phase. I always advise my clients to perform spells for school, classes, and general guidance that will attract powerful ancient masters or guides from the astral plane that will bring them to a better place in life. For example, a new supervisor may come to your job who is positive and working to benefit all. This way opportunities open up for you to grow in your job potential. If you are flying high on the market in your job skills then this can open wide the windows of opportunity.

Many use this auspicious phase of the moon for magick having to do with luck and games of chance. Natalie always does spells during this phase of the moon to increase her chances with luck and gambling. She wins often but I do not know whether to attribute her luck to gambling magick or just to wonder if she is just on the lucky side of Lady Fortune!

Moon in Capricorn

When you have a project that requires no-nonsense answers and a lot of hard work, tedious labor, and difficult business situations, this is the time to engage. This is the best time for all situations that call for self-discipline and ambitious effort. My daughter, Tara, is a very serious student. She likes to do candle spells under this moon phase to help her get through a tough project in school. Her favorite candle is Road Opener. It helps to clear her path to knowledge and the Saturnian moon phase helps her stay focused. This is a great moon phase for helping you get focused for any difficult situation or any problem in life that keeps alluding you.

Moon in Aquarius

This moon phase is a great time for performing any magick of a progressive nature. Progressive magick means that you have accomplished a degree of what you are after and you wish to continue. It's a time of inspiration and sudden brilliant insight. Creative blocks are removed, the doors of communication are opened, and new possibilities emerge.

I love this moon because it has a cool head. Its emotional ideal is to be aloof and removed from the trappings of drama. This is why progressive magick happens here. There is logical thinking that only allows the necessary concerns of what you are after to come through. The last of the fixed signs, it also brings stability to your work.

Aquarius is called the sign of the humanitarian. I love to do rituals for humanitarian acts under this moon phase, such as lighting a White Tara candle for world peace.

My friend John had been doing a spell to get himself transferred to another state with his federal job. John was getting really flustered and angry that the spell did not seem to be working. He was closing on a house in the state where he desired to move. He had to sell his current apartment and move out right away. He just couldn't seem to get it together. To make matters worse, his new bride was having second thoughts about moving. What a mess! Finally I suggested he try a White Tara Candle under this moon phase. He did as I told him, and soon he was transferred to an office just three blocks from his new home.

Moon in Pisces

This extremely psychic phase of the moon brings guidance through internal wisdom and intuition. This is a good time for developing all phases of psychic development—write in a dream journal, learn the tarot, or simply meditate. It is also a great time to practice divination. I have the moon in Pisces in my birth chart. It is one of the aspects in my chart that helps me to commune with the spirits. Astral entities come under the sign of Neptune, which is the ruler of Pisces. Many empaths, psychics, and healers have the sign of Pisces either as a sun sign or moon sign. It is not the only sign for psychic ability, but certainly wherever it lies there is some form of psychic ability present. Under this moon phase I often recommend a High Priestess Initiation candle for people who wish to commune with astral entities, guardian angels, master guides, animal totems, departed loved ones, and to develop their own psychic powers. This moon phase can often be an emotional time for those who are inclined to empathy. I often recommend a Love Healing candle in this phase of the moon as its powers are great for healing. One of the members of my coven, Lord Tammuz, lights a Love Healing candle in the Moon in Pisces every month for his lover who has passed into the Summerlands. It helps him to communicate his loss and helps him to feel brighter and better about life.

* * *

We have come a long way since our early ancestors recognized the importance of calculating the phases of the moon. Now you can get a horoscope reading online. There is an obvious need for us to recognize what the stars have in store for us and how we can best apply this information. A wise astrologer named Michael Cunningham taught me the basics of astrology in my twenties. I will always be grateful for what I learned from this man. He taught me to embrace the bad aspects as well as the good. It was hard to accept his wisdom at the time. I would become infuriated with him and often cry. But with the years I learned more from what he taught me. It was basically this: if everything was all good all the time, then there would be no need for good. Good would be totally impotent without the bad. There would be no basis for comparison. Do not be afraid or very disappointed when the stars are not pointing in a favorable direction, for it is then that you are being challenged to work through something and make a change. Michelangelo was challenged by the Pope for every brush stroke he made, but he still painted the Sistine Chapel. Look at your life as blank canvas: There will be obstacles, but there is a masterpiece waiting to be painted.

2.

Altars and Tools

ALTERNATIVES TO GLITTER

Some people don't like glitter. They find it difficult to work with, messy, or they don't like the idea of using something synthetic in their spell. There are alternatives, however, that can be used in creating enchanted candles. Herbs, for example, give quite a bit of power to a spell. They are a gift from Mother Earth herself and contain both healing and magickal powers. Each herb carries its own magickal portent. For example, mint carries the element of fire, and is used magickally to bring luck, and medicinally for stomach ailments. Tracing a candle with glitter in different colors is the same as shamanic or Buddhist sand painting. Using herbs for the same purpose not only employs the magickal properties of those herbs but also gives the enchanted candle an appealing natural look. Dry mint powders easily, or it can be crushed for a more leafy look. Some herbs are large and hard and therefore need to be powdered, such as allspice berries, cinnamon, frankincense, and dragon's blood, to name a few. I suggest using an electric coffee grinder for this. A mortar and pestle can also be used, but it's difficult to get thoroughly powdered herbs with them. Experiment with the different herbs listed for the spell work to see what you like best.

Let's say you are making a success candle and don't want to use glitter. Take some ground allspice berries and mix them with some ground cinnamon. This will be brown in color, and when you rub it into the carved and oiled candle, it will define your carving so that you will see it clearly, and have the benefit of the magickal properties of that herb added to your candle spell. Carve your candle, dress it with the oil, and simply sprinkle the powdered herbs all over it, or you can spread the herbs on a sheet of waxed paper and roll your oiled candle through them. The oil will darken your powder and the outline of your carving will come through.

Some herbs are soft and do not necessarily need grinding. Lavender flowers and life-everlasting are good examples—you can sprinkle them on whole, and they will give your candle a very magickal and earthy look. Some herbs, such as peppermint, are very dry and can be crushed with your fingers.

Another alternative to glitter is powdered incense. Incense will also outline your carving and add great power to your spell—as the candle burns the incense will burn as an extra offering to your spell. To choose an appropriate powdered incense keep your intention in mind. For a Come to Me candle, you can use Come to Me incense, or Venus incense, or Egyptian Musk incense.

Yet another substance that can be utilized in candle dressing along with glitter or alone is magickal powder. Magickal powders are colored talcs to which a few drops of a magickal oil has been added. As you probably know already, a magickal oil is a blended oil such as Come to Me oil or an essential oil that you have chosen for a spell, such as rose for the purpose of a love candle. A magickal oil contains certain properties that will help enhance your spell. Magickal powder works much like powdered herbs—you can sprinkle it on the candle or roll the candle in the powder—and some find it smoother and easier to work with.

CONSECRATING TOOLS

To consecrate means to bless and make an object serviceable for magick. Once made sacred for ritual purposes, a tool can only be used in those acts of magick; it no longer will serve a mundane purpose.

To consecrate your carving instrument, meditate and focus on the magickal energy within you. Envision a tiny white light pulsing in your heart, growing with every heartbeat until it fills your entire body. Gather that white light into the hand that holds the tool. Point your index and middle fingers together on the handle, and as you envision the white light enveloping it, say these words:

> Oh implement of earthen metal, thou shalt serve me in the scripture of the Gods. As I use thee, thou shalt become a writing instrument, so that I may call upon the sacred presence of the Mighty Ones to lay their signatures upon my work. With this intent, I do conjure thee with power for so long as I use thee for the good of mankind and myself. So mote it be.

ALTARS

The altar is a sacred table space that is sanctified by being used only for magickal purposes. Some altars are dedicated to certain deities and their offerings are brought here. If you are a worshiper of Diana, for example, you may go to her for all of your needs whether they be financial, love, protection, or whatever you may have need of.

In city living, we find that sometimes other arrangements need to be made. If you can provide the space, then great. But if you cannot, don't worry; that is one of the many blessings of the enchanted candle. This living talisman is an altar unto itself, because within its own container offerings have already been made to the spirit world. The glass provides a safe, contained space for the candle to perform its work.

On the other hand, some people like to keep altars dedicated to their Gods or Goddesses where they leave offerings, keep spells, and worship. A few examples follow of what can be done in a more elaborate altar setup. This is by no means the only way—every person identifies with the Divine in his or her own personal manner. But if you find a more "magickal atmosphere" helps you focus, then here are some suggestions

Basic Magickal Altar

There are many people who do not wish to erect an altar to a specific deity, even though they are performing a love spell, or a money-drawing spell, or have some other specific intention. In answer to this, I'm including a universal altar or basic altar. This represents the four elements, which correspond with the four quadrants of the Universe: North, South, East and West.

DEITIES: You can invoke any deity at this altar (but one at a time, please!).

COLORS: Whatever colors you choose. Can correspond with what you most want to bring into your life. When in doubt, use white, silver, and blue.

ADORNMENTS: Crescent moon, clear water, salt, incense, hounds, deer (you can use pictures or statues of these animals). Statues of Yemaya, Diana, or any Goddess or God image that invokes the feeling in you of magick, peace, love, and your higher ideals of life. Camphor, mirrors, any lunar symbols, crystal or glass for candle holders, bowls etc. Small statues of nymphs or fairies, anything that comes along that you feel relates to your deity of choice.

GEMSTONES: Moonstones, clear quartz, black stones, blue stones.

FLOWERS: White roses, blue roses, all blue or white flowers, orchids, gardenias, gladiolas, moon flowers.

Uncrossing Altar

Sometimes obstacles need to be removed in order to bring something good into one's life, like releasing the fears left over from an old relationship before seeking a new one. All over the world, in every culture, a system of uncrossing can be found—prayers with the power to remove that which opposes. To give you a few ideas of how different people perform uncrossings, let's look at a few examples. First, in my own culture—Italian—we are famous for our belief in *malochia*, the "evil eye." If you are the victim of the evil eye, you will experience bad fortune until someone removes this hex for you. There are even ways of preventing the evil eye, according to some. One way that I heard from neighbors when I was a child, was to pull in your ring and index fingers and thumb, leaving the pinky and pointer fingers out, forming a horn. This you did under the table when you knew some one was throwing the *malochia* on you.

Some British people call the evil eye "putting the Reagans on you." In the Latino culture it is called *malo de ojo*. They have several common phrases for ridding oneself of the evil eye or negative forces: *quita maldicion, kita mal, contra envida, sal pafueda,* and *desenvolvimento* (which is the common term to mean *uncrossing*), to name a few. The Greeks wear evil eye jewelry all of the time as a preventative measure. Catholics and Christians wear a cross to protect them from harm as much as they wear a cross to announce that they are Christian. Wiccans wear their pentagrams as a protective amulet, as well as to show that they are Wiccans. All of these symbols are related to uncrossings. They protect and remove negative thoughts thrown at them—deliberately or accidentally—from others.

DEITIES: In Ceremonial Magick, an appeal for an uncrossing is often made to the Lord of Obstacles. Let me explain who or what the Lord of Obstacles is. We have many obstacles placed in our life. For instance I know a witch who wants to go to school for gemology. The course is very expensive, but he can receive financial aid from the government because of the time that he served in the Navy. However, he must first put down a couple of thousand dollars out of his own pocket before the government will fund the rest. This is his obstacle. He needs a job that will fulfill this expense, and he is having trouble getting that job. So whom does he turn to? The Lord of Obstacles, because he is the remover of obstacles that stand in one's way. In Wicca, one of the popular Lords of Obstacles is Mercury. The Hindus pray to Ganesha, keeper of the threshold of life, the door that allows good or bad to flow in at will. In Santeria, the appeal is made to Elegua, and in Haitian Voudoun, the appeal is made to Legba or Simbi.

COLORS: White, orange, or violet (or a red and black combination for Ellegua). These are the colors that work best with uncrossing. Orange and violet, according to many ancient texts that refer colors to planetary schemes, are the colors of Mercury.

ADORNMENTS: Certain items can be placed on the altar to add power to the spell that you are doing. Following are a few suggestions that may add some atmosphere to your magickal space, thereby helping you focus on your intent. Use your intuition to decide what will work best for you.

In a bowl filled with water, you can float a small vial which contains a few drops of Mercury Oil. Seal it tight with wax so water does not get in. Crosses can also be placed on this altar. The pagan definition of a cross is related to a crossroads where all elemental planes—North, South, East and West, ruled by Earth, Fire, Air and Water—all converge at one point. Therefore, a cross is a good symbol to use, despite the Christian connotation it may initially engender, as it indicates the removal of all obstacles no matter what direction they are coming from or what elemental plane may be causing the obstruction.

Skeleton keys crossed together can be used on the altar, and then as a talisman afterwards. The skeleton key, or any key for that matter, is a symbol of an unlocked door. You can carry keys as a talisman to prevent or remove obstacles. Always return your key to your altar to be recharged when you are done.

All pictures and statues representing Mercury, Thoth, Ganesha, Ellegua, Legba, Saint Anthony, and Guardian Angel can also be used to adorn this altar.

GEMSTONES: Smoky quartz, black tourmaline, clear quartz, or fluorite octahedrons in white opposite dark purple or blue octahedrons (double pyramid). Use four stones: two dark and two clear, placed opposite each other. These are unblocking gemstones and their energies are best for uncrossing purposes.

FLOWERS: Carnations (red and white), lilies, freesia, anemones, red and white roses, and blue and white irises are some suggestions for flowers that are good for an uncrossing altar. Their properties are for clearance. White flowers with a dark contrasting color are especially good.

Protection Altar

When the need to cleanse or protect arises, it is best to call on the nurturing, protective qualities of the moon. The moon rules over all dwellings, and is also associated with the sea and the element of water. Since the human body is mostly made up of water (also governed by the moon), water is also the element that houses the soul. The moon has the power to soothe, illuminate, and inspire. Protective deities such as Hecate, Kali Ma, Durga Anubis, and Saturn, are associated with the dark side of the moon. They are not negative, but they are very powerful.

DEITIES: Yemaya, Artemis, Athena, Luna, Isis, Triduana, Mahesvari, Kwan Yin, Tara, Kali Ma, Hecate, Sekhmet, and other lunar goddesses; Epona, Bast, and Diana for protection of animals.

COLORS: Blue, silver, white, green, black, and black and white.

ADORNMENTS: Seashells, fish; zodiac signs of pisces, cancer, or scorpio; coral, seaweed, dried starfish and seahorses; combs, handmirrors, and ornate fans. Place a pretty bowl of water mixed with sea salt on your altar, or if you live by the ocean, fill it with ocean water. Pictures of the ocean, mermaids, the moon, and sea creatures can also decorate this altar.

GEMSTONES: Quartz, pearls, coral, moonstone, obsidian, smoky quartz, onyx, black kyanite, lapis lazuli, turquoise, bloodstone.

FLOWERS: Gardenias, white or blue carnations, gladiolas, white pompoms, white chrysanthemums, moonflowers, any blue or white flower.

Healing Altar

All altars are really a personal affair. No two are alike. Altars are like living things because they grow and change with time. A healing altar can be set up for a specific spell, and when your work is done can be taken down. If you are dedicated to the healing arts then you may wish to establish a permanent one.

If you're making an Aesclepius Healing candle you may want to use an image of St. Lazarus or Babaluaye to be the deity on your altar. These are commonly found in botanicas and occult shops. There is no set rule except the intention of the healing magick that you are performing, and which deity or spirit you personally feel a link to. You may want to place a picture of the person you are trying to heal on the altar. If a picture is not available, you may want to use a small doll to represent that person. Bless the doll by giving it the name of the person to be healed, and pass it through incense, salt, and water.

DEITIES: Aesclepius, Babaluaye, Obatala, Mars, Huchi, and Gaia are a few of the many deities associated with healing.

COLORS: White and green.

ADORNMENTS: A picture of or personal symbol associated with the person to be healed is beneficial for this altar, but it is not mandatory. The recommended practice for healing is meditation and sending energy to the person to be healed, which can be done with a sincere heart and clear intent. Some people feel you need to get permission from the subject to perform a healing spell. To me it is a matter of your personal ethics. If you feel that permission is needed, then take the time to ask for it. However, I personally feel that doing a healing spell puts good energy out into the world, and therefore permission is not necessary.

The photo or symbol can act as link between you and the person to be healed—something to focus on to help you channel your energy. Your healing altar can also contain a clear bowl of water, healing stones, and pictures or statues of the deity or deities being summoned.

GEMSTONES: Clear quartz, rose quartz, and amethyst.

FLOWERS: Lilies, carnations, mums, or other white flowers

Love Altar

An altar created with elegance, taste, and style achieves greater recognition than one strewn with disregarded valentines from unwanted paramours. Keep your love altar up to date and clean of debris and excess trinkets and offerings. Even if everything that adorns your love altar is a token of devotion from the one you love, it can begin to reflect negatively on your personal love life. Treat all love requests with respect, for how you invoke them will reflect back to you. Sometimes folks can be fickle when it comes to love. They may want several lovers at any one given time. You may want a past lover back, but then when that person does not return fast enough, you meet someone new. So you pursue the new lover and then the old one returns and now you want both. I've found that if you invoke more than you can handle it will manifest quite a mess in your life.

DEITIES: Venus, Erzuli, Aphrodite, Oshun, Aine, Kamuhata Hime, Ishtar, Freya, Iseult, Lugh, Cernunnos, Pan, and Lakshmi.

COLORS: Red, pink, green, lilac, peach, copper, gold, and yellow.

ADORNMENTS: Rich fabrics, crystal perfume bottles, small hand mirrors, fancy hair combs, fans, small heart-shaped boxes filled with potpourri, luxuriant items, luscious sweets, jewelry, champagne, elegant lingerie. A decorated bowl of water and a beautiful statuette of a love goddess will make your love altar complete.

GEMSTONES: Clear quartz, rose quartz, amethyst, malachite, green tourmaline, watermelon tourmaline, kunzite, bloodstone, and sodalite.

FLOWERS: Roses, tulips, lilacs, gardenias, baby's breath, Queen Anne's lace, and wildflowers.

Money Altar

According to astrology, Venus rules cash, Saturn rules business, and Jupiter rules abundance and expansions. When the need for money is apparent, we appeal to the universal law of abundance—that everything we need is out there and that all we need do is reach for it. It is important to remember to ask the Universe to provide us with what we *need*, and not to ask for excess. There are many deities that exist in the realms of abundance. The one you feel a special connection to is the one you tap into for that magick.

DEITIES: Habonde, Lugh, Danu, Cerridwen, Damara, Erzulie, Apollo, Venus, Lakshmi, Ganesha, Thoth, Ellegua, Oshun, Kwan Yin.

COLORS: Green, yellow, gold, and copper.

ADORNMENTS: A bowl filled with water and pennies, a dish of change, Chinese Buddhas, acorns, dry rice or grains in a bowl, birdseed, sea salt, fruit, a dish of candy, mirrors placed behind the offerings to double your abundance, small tabletop water fountains, and articles that you feel represent money.

GEMSTONES: Goldstones, carnelian, copper, citrine, iron pyrite, aventurine, jade, or jadeite.

FLOWERS: Yellow or gold chrysanthemums, marigolds, orchids, carnations, and gardenias.

Psychic Divination Altar

"How will I know?" This is the question that plagues the mind of anyone who is faced with a decision in life. The plain truth of the matter is that only time will tell! But you can take steps to strengthen your intuition and psychic awareness so that you at least know you are not deceiving yourself in the choices you make. For example, sometimes you can paint a picture of what you want in your mind. Be sure your information is accurate by keeping track of your predictions and seeing what comes true and what does not. Always remember that like attracts like, and as above, so below. This applies to psychic awareness in that a sort of mental "wire service" connects all minds, so that when we reduce the pictures in our minds to one focused image, we connect with that image on the astral plane. Having an altar devoted to psychic divination can help us to focus on the matter at hand, and clear away any clutter for our minds that blocks our vision.

Sometimes people have several desires that are connected to one another. For instance, someone may want money, psychic power, and success in the workplace. Well, this is the intricate part of planning out your magick. You can use psychic power to attract success in the workplace, and success in the workplace can lead to wealth. So this person might want to set up an altar and do a spell for psychic power first, then do his success and money-drawing spells on that same altar. Keep a log of all your magick and the results of what it has brought you if you need to think of more than one thing at a time.

DEITIES: Psyche, Mercury, Aradia, Diana, Yemaya, and Apollo.

COLORS: Purple, white, blue, and black and white.

ADORNMENTS: Divination tools such as runes, tarot cards, pendulums, crystal balls, and magick mirrors can be placed on this altar. However, these should be removed from the altar when you are ready to divine. Incense should be burned to cleanse and invoke spiritual aid, and a bowl of clean fresh water should be laid out. One of the gemstones used for psychic divination may also be placed in the water to absorb all the leftover electric activity psychic bodies emit.

GEMSTONES: Clear quartz, phantom quartz, amethyst, fluorite, obsidian, jet, onyx, moonstone, smoky quartz, and black opals.

FLOWERS: Lilies, gladiola, chrysanthemums, roses, orchids, gardenia, and irises.

3.

Apothecary

Pulling a spell together becomes much easier once you understand the basic principles behind the use of certain things. For example:

- Incense is used to create the atmosphere and to make the spell more productive. For thousands of years we have used incense to please the Gods. Much is written about incense in ancient texts from all of the great schools of magick from early history throughout time. There are Biblical references to the use of incense, as well as in old Egyptian, Greek, Celtic, and Asian texts.

- Oils are used to anoint the candles as well as the body to prepare the way to the world where your magick will happen.

- Baths are a ritual to cleanse your body and aura so that both your physical and psychic worlds are purified and you are prepared to commit to your work.

- Floor washes are used to cleanse your space and attract the appropriate deities and spirits to accomplish your work. By the way, if you have carpet on your floors and therefore can't use a floor wash, then you can do the following: take about a cup or two of baking soda, put it in a mixing bowl and add a few drops of the oil that you are using in your spell. Stir it well clockwise, and sprinkle it on your carpet. Wait five minutes, then vacuum it up. The baking soda is a natural cleansing product used in spiritual work and when you add the oil you empower your cleansing.

◦§ Powders are similar to, but slightly different from, powdered incense. They usually come in colored sachets and they are used just like we use talcum powder after a bath. They are sprinkled over candle spells, as well as on the body.

INCENSE

Smoky fingers spiral through the air ready to alert the Mighty Ones of your call. Incense creates atmosphere, and this serves a double purpose: the gods are attracted to certain scents, and incense can be a powerful tool to invoke the aspect of the deity best suited to your cause. Secondly, and more important, it helps to activate those aspects within *you*. For example, the scent of incense inspires psychic awareness the moment it is lit. It also acts as a purifier. Unclean spirits and energy can hide in corners—the right incense purifies and keeps a well-balanced home. It also represents the element of air interacting with the element of fire, or thought process (air) transformed through the will (fire). Like a mist, the smoke of incense colors the air making it visible. Incense arouses our senses and helps us to commune with the realms beyond ordinary sensation—it helps bring us "between the worlds."

There are four basic types of incenses available today. Stick and cone incenses are made of a compressed wood base dipped in fragrant oils and dried, then dipped again. They usually consist of a single fragrance, like jasmine, honeysuckle, rose, sandalwood, patchouli, or almond. Stick and cone incenses are good when a single fragrance is desired, but they can be used in a combination of two or more if you have more than one candle requiring different scents. If you are doing a money-drawing spell, for instance, you may want to use sandalwood or frankincense. If you happen to be doing a love ritual at the same time, you don't want the woodsy scents to overpower the love call. So when close work is required, sticks work well, because they have a lighter smoke in your space than an herbal or powder incense.

Herbal and powdered incense always requires a charcoal in order to burn, and they require sturdy heatproof incense burners. Powdered incense has become very popular for several reasons. One of the best is that it comes in colors. These colors relate to the same astral vibrations that are listed in the color guide, pages 11–18. The colors often correspond to the candle color magick you are doing. For instance, love magick incense is often made up out of a red or pink wood base. Wood base powdered incense is usually sold in occult shops or botanicas. If you want to buy unscented wood base so that you may add oils to make your own fragrance, check the shopping guide in Appendix C.

Herbal incense is still considered by many magick practitioners to be the best. It is a mixture of herbs and essential oils blended together. The combination is very potent. As a warning though, herbal incense can be especially smoky—make sure you keep a window open when burning it, or it may activate your smoke alarm!

Oils

The purpose of oils is to direct the candle to the proper plane of existence. For instance, a yellow Solar Blast candle needs oils that inspire joy and a positive outlook, such as Sun oil, Frankincense oil, Orange oil, or Heliotrope oil. Just as colors and incense correspond to certain aspects, so do oils.

To dress a candle, put some of the oil in your palm or on your finger and rub from the center all the way up to the top of the candle. Then take some more oil and begin the same process working your way down. All the while, you should be envisioning what you desire. The reason for this is first you are sending your prayer upward, then downward—"as above, so below." As the candle dissolves into the atmosphere it will bring your will with it in all directions.

If your hands are sensitive to the oils you should use gloves. I like rubber hospital gloves; they are sold by the box in surgical supply stores and large pharmacies.

The following pages are listings of some of the most popular oils available. The first listing is essential oils—that is, basic oils of one plant with certain magickal properties that can be used for many purposes. Some oils or fragrances can be used for more than just one purpose. The second listing is of magickal blended oils— several different oils combined for one magickal purpose. These oils can be found in many occult shops (see the shopping guide in Appendix C).

Essential Oils

Acacia: Meditation, psychic development, friendship.

Allspice: Determination, energy. success, luck, money.

Almond: Prosperity, money, abundance, hope.

Amber: Protection, healing, joy, prosperity.

Ambergris: Love, seduction, psychic, astral travel.

Anise: Divination, psychic development, love. Sacred to Oshun.

Apple blossom: Love, joyfulness, success.

Apple: Fresh start, friendship, health, money.

Balm of Gilead: Love, protection, healing.

Basil: Romantic love, harmony, cleansing, money, protection.

Bay: Victory, success, money, uncrossing sacred to Apollo. Solar magick.

Bayberry: Financial blessings, success, overcoming obstacles.

Benzoin: Purification, peace of mind, financial luck. Sacred essence of the Gods.

Bergamot: Protection, prosperity, joy, success.

Camelia: Love, luxury, abundance, allure.

Camphor: Cleansing, uncrossing, purification, one of the more pleasing essences of the Gods. Good for moon magick, sacred to Diana, and Yemaya. Also sacred to Obatala and Ochanla.

Cardamom seed: Spicy love, money, luck.

Carnation: Energy, restoration, healing, love healing, love.

Cedarwood Purification, wealth, protection.

Chamomile: Healing, soothing, sweet dreams, calming.

Cherry: Stimulating friendships, parties, happy times.

Cinnamon: Personal protection, female sexual stimulation, meditation, illumination, money-drawing, success, attraction. Sacred to Oshun.

Citronella: Clearing, expelling, hex breaking.

Civet: Sexual stimulant, attraction, lusty (use very little).

Clove: Attraction, aphrodisiac, memory enhancer, stimulant, inspiration, money-drawing, domination.

Coconut: Luck, money, fortune, sacred to many gods such as Ganesha, Elegua, Obatala, Lakshmi, and Erzulie, just to name a few.

Coriander Seed: Love, attraction.

Cucumber: Cleansing, healing, calming, house blessing, moon magick.

Cyclamen: Love, marriage, easy birth.

Cypress: Protection, blessing, consecration, psychic awareness.

Damiana: Sexual stimulant, mood setter, good times.

Dragon's blood: Protection, uncrossing, banishing.

Eucalyptus: Healing, purification, strength, power.

Frangipani: Love, enchantment, seduction.

Frankincense: Purification, exorcism, blessing, money, solar energy, one of the highest essences to offer the Gods. Good for solar magick.

Galangal root: Hex breaking, winning court cases, overcoming enemies.

Gardenia: Love, attraction, protection, wealth, spellbinding to captivate one you desire.

Garlic: Uncrossing, jinx removing, protection.

Heather: Young love, first blush of youth, makes you feel and look younger.

Heliotrope: Clairvoyance, sun energy, protection, happiness.

Honeysuckle: Clear thinking, memory, prosperity, business, love. Sacred to Oshun and Venus.

Hyacinth: Peace of mind, relaxation, gay love, new love.

Hyssop: Prosperity, abundance, purification, uncrossing, banishing.

Jalup root: Overcoming obstacles or enemies, high magickal workings, court cases.

Jasmine: Love, attraction, moon magick, relaxation, psychic awareness. Alluring and highly seductive. Sacred to Oshun, Venus, and Erzulie.

Juniper berry: Purification, luck, protection, banishing.

Labdanum: Dark seduction, dark moon magick (magick that is done during the dark phase of the moon).

Lavender: Love, healing, purification, attraction, banishing, uncrossing, money drawing. Good for moon magick.

Lemon: Cleansing, uncrossing, banishing.

Lilac: Memory, past lives, clairvoyance, love, spiritual love, romance.

Lily of the Valley: Marriage, love, healing, purity, sacred essence to the Gods.

Lime: Uncrossing, sometimes used in money and luck formulas.

Lotus: Spirituality, wealth, prosperity, healing, pacifying, soothing. Sacred essence of the gods. Especially sacred to Tara, Lakshmi, and all Buddhas.

Magnolia: Meditation, psychic development, peace, harmony, seduction, charm, love.

Mastic: Door-opener, purification, sacred essence to the gods.

Mimosa: Healing, prophetic dreams, attraction, romantic love, allure.

Muguet: Marriage, love, healing, purity, sacred essence to the gods.

Musk: Sexual attraction, stimulating, enticing, sensual love.

Myrrh: Purification, protection, uncrossing, banishing, healing, sacred to Saturn.

Myrtle: Love (note: the fragrance does not stimulate olfactory senses for attraction. Its scent is not so pleasant to wear as a perfume).

Narcissus, black: Peace, harmony, relaxation, hypnotic seduction, self esteem, love attraction.

Neroli: Attraction, peace, marriage, love, success.

Nutmeg: Meditation, relaxation, protection, success, gambling luck, money-drawing.

Orange: wealth, luck, happiness, health, success.

Orange Blossom: Attraction, love, marriage.

Orris root: Romantic attraction, love, pure intentions.

Patchouli: Attraction (to attract women), peace of mind, protection, sensuality, luck, money-drawing.

Peach/peach blossom: Sensuality, luck, money.

Pennyroyal: Luck, purification, peace.

Peppermint: Change, relaxation, cleansing, luck, money-drawing.

Pine: Financial blessings, male lust, protection.

Pineapple: Joy, friendship, money, luck.

Pear/pear blossom: Romantic love, peace, harmony, sacred to Obatala.

Rose: Sacred to Venus and all love deities, peace, harmony, purification.

Rose geranium: Protection, cleansing, luck.

Rosemary: Healing, promotes prudence, common sense, and

self-assurance. Protection, aids mental powers and memory, remembrance.

Rue: Personal protection, uncrossing, money, change of luck.

Sage: Cleansing, purification, wisdom, opening the mind to knowledge.

Sandalwood: Protection, healing, past lives, good fortune, abundance, psychic work. Pleasing to the Gods.

Strawberry: Friends, parties, hot attraction. Sacred to Erzulie.

Styrax: Purification. Opens doors to astral realms.

Thyme: Love, psychic cleanser, protection, healing.

Tonka: Wealth, luck, gambling

Vanilla: Energy, aphrodisiac, love, joy, good times, healing and soothing to the soul.

Verbena: Love, purification, change of luck.

Vervain: Creativity, success in the arts, obtaining material objects, love-drawing, purification, psychic inducer.

Vetivert: Love domination, power, money.

Violet: Love, sexuality, attraction, fairy magick, healing, removes shyness.

Watermelon: Money, house-blessing, joy. Sacred to Yemaya.

Wintergreen: Uncrossing, healing, money-drawing.

Wisteria: Divination, clairvoyance, psychic development, meditation, love.

Wormwood: Seduction through otherworldly means, protection, power, enchantment.

Ylang Ylang: Sexual attraction, job-seeking, healing.

Magickal Blended Oils

Here are some of the more popular blended oils, which can be found in occult shops and botanicas. Keep in mind that formulas may vary, so you may want to ask the salesperson what ingredients are in each particular oil blend to make sure it contains the elements you want. Some shops buy preblended oils or are not willing to discuss their formulas with you as they are private information and well-kept secrets. In that case, if the oil smells pleasing to you and you like it, go with it. You will see in the spells in part two that I list essential oils as alternatives to the blended oils, just in case you can't find the blended oil listed.

This is a listing of oils that were created by me for achieving a specific desire or for devotion to a specific deity. I have been formulating blends of oils for over thirty years dating back to when I first worked for the Warlock Shop, one of the first occult stores ever opened in the United States. Some of the names are my rendition for that formula. There are many formulas for Come to Me oil, for example. If you purchase it from our shop then you will be getting my formula for Come to Me oil. This doesn't say that someone else's is not as good as mine—as long as the essential oils used in the blend contain the aspects that relate to the desired result, and the blended oil is infused with intent, it will be a potent magickal tool. You need to shop and find someone who makes an oil that works for you.

Adam and Eve oil: For couples.

All Night Long oil: Relieves sexual problems.

Ambrosia oil: Delights the Gods. Good to use for special requests such as abundance, happiness, and joy.

Amethyst oil: Wisdom, clairvoyance, and for breaking habits.

Ancient Wisdom oil: Helps concentration, clarifies muddled thinking.

Aphrodite oil: Makes a woman irresistible and charming.

Arabian Nights oil: Attracts new friends and many lovers.

Astarte oil: Increases sexual awareness; use for a love formula.

Astral Travel oil: Enhances meditation and journeying.

Attraction oil: Love formula. Incites passions; also attracts good luck and money.

Banishing oil: Rids one of negative forces and hexes.

Bast oil: Sacred formula for the Egyptian Cat Goddess.

Bat's Blood oil: For hexing others.

Bewitching oil: Power formula that adds greater potency to your spell. Good to use in conjunction with commanding and compelling spells.

Blessing oil: For blessing all work when you need an extra blessing from the deity to which you are appealing. Benefits all spells.

Black Star oil: Opens psychic channels and communications with Gods and spirits.

Call Me oil: Opens communications on all levels.

Cast Away oil: To rid one of evil spells and black magick.

Cernunnos oil: Classic Horned God oil; for honoring the God; also for fertility.

Cleopatra oil: For lovers. Entices a desired stranger.

Come to Me oil: Attraction recipe specifically for sexual purposes.

Commanding oil: To get others to do your bidding.

Commanding Love oil: To command your will, stay at home with me.

Concentration oil: Clears the mind; inspires insight into problems.

Crossing oil: For hexing.

Crown of Success oil: Stops those who would intend to block your success.

Crystal Healing oil: Enhances energy, clears away all troubles. Same properties as a quartz crystal.

Delight oil: Removes lovers' inhibitions; increases pleasures.

Dove's Blood oil: For solving problems of the heart; brings peace of mind and joy.

Dragon's Blood oil: For uncrossing a friend; protection.

Earth oil: Invokes all elementals (spiritual beings) of the Earth plane; good for spells dealing with grounding, stability, nurturing, hearth, and home.

Egyptian Musk oil: For love and allure.

Elegua oil: Uncrossing, brings luck, opens doors, devotion to the God of Santeria

Enchantment oil: An aid to magickal spells. Not to be used for negative spells.

Erzulie oil: Haitian goddess of love, devotions, and spells.

Faith, Hope, and Charity oil: Represents the three graces, for help in all problems having to do with finances, love, and faith.

Fast Luck oil: Classic luck attractant. Works quickly.

Fire oil: Invokes all elementals of Fire; good for spells dealing with passion, transformation, and creativity.

Fire of Love oil: Draws lovers, increases sexuality.

Gambler's oil: Favorite luck charm for gambling.

Ganesha oil: Hindu God of success, remover of obstacles.

Gold and Silver oil: Money drawing and luck.

Healing oil: Promotes rapid healing and bliss.

Helping Hand oil: Brings harmony and aids in finances.

High John the Conqueror oil: Brings great fortune, overcomes obstacles.

High Priestess oil: Use for lunar rituals, psychic initiations, and high priestess initiations.

Horn of Plenty oil: Overcomes poverty, and brings wealth and prestige.

House Blessing oil: To cleanse and purify a home. Protects from all evil.

Inspiring oil: Boosts one's morale, confidence and optimism

Joy oil: Attracts friends, and brings joy when depressed.

Jupiter oil: To invoke Jupiter for his beneficial aspects.

Justice oil: To bring justice to one's life.

Kindly Spirit oil: Brings sympathy and overcomes loneliness

Lady Luck oil: For supreme luck when gambling.

Lakshmi oil: Hindu Goddess of multiple blessings.

Leather and Lace oil: Commanding, compelling love. For those who want it now.

Lodestone oil: Brings good luck and breaks hexes.

Lady Silk oil: Love attraction and for keeping an ongoing love.

La Flamme oil: Causes a loved one to think of you.

Love oil: The classic formula for love.

Love Healing oil: Heals emotional hurts, opens communications, restores love.

Love and Protection oil: Protects lovers from those who wish to separate them.

Lucky Lottery oil: Helps you connect with those six little numbers that stand between you and happiness. This is good for any kind of lottery both legal and illegal wherever you live.

Lucky Seven oil: Protects from hexes and aids in gambling luck.

Lucky Thirteen oil: Changes the superstitious bad-luck number to a lucky one.

Mars oil: Formula for action, energy, and war.

Meditation oil: Enhances meditation and spirit work that deals with communicating with helpful spiritual forces that surround us every day.

Mercury oil: Planetary blend for communication, knowledge, and wisdom.

Metropolis oil: Success in apartment hunting and purchasing a new home or space.

Milagrosa oil: Miraculous Mother, Holy Mother Diana, Virgin Mary.

Money-Drawing oil: Protects against financial losses. Draws money.

Money House Blessing oil: To bless the home with money, and chase away poverty.

Moon oil: Planetary blend for the moon. Good for devotion, spell work involving the moon such as blessing a home, getting a new home or for any spell work involving the moon or the Goddesses of the moon.

Moon Goddess oil: Sacred blend for the Moon Goddess.

Mystere oil: Mystique, glamour. Works on love in a mysterious way. For example, it can cause two strangers who have passed each other every day and never noticed one another before to finally meet. It brings out the unknown and a sense of magick. It smells a little bit different on each person who wears it.

Nine Indian Fruits oil: Famous money house-blessing formula—blesses the house and helps bring in extra finances and gives joy and happiness in the home.

Obatala oil: Virgin Mercedes, clearance, peace, clarity, and mercy.

Ocean Mother oil: Psychic inducer, for devotional purposes use with all water deities.

Oshun oil: Love, flirtations, charity, and marriage.

Osiris oil: Sacred formula for the Egyptian God of Justice. Can be used on Justice Candles and for personal protection.

Pan oil: Sacred blend to the great God of Fertility, earth, nature spirits, and for good sex.

Peace oil: Gives peaceful conditions in your life, home, and all environments.

Peace and Protection oil: Rids bad vibes and gives strong protection.

Prosperity oil: Draws success and money.

Protection oil: Protects one from magickal attacks.

Purple Wisdom oil: Psychic wisdom, higher learning, invites spirit guides to come to you in your sleep.

Rainbow oil: Joy, healing, and resurrection of our sense of being alive and being happy about it. It makes you feel good about a brand new day.

Rhea's Love Haunt oil: The memory of you will linger for days after they see you.

Road Opener oil: Removes all obstacles, gives you a clear path.

Rose Quartz oil: Good for the physical and psychic heart, emotional trauma, and healing love.

Scarlette's Seduction oil: Love, lust, attraction of lovers.

Saint Lazarus oil: For healing, cleansing, and a giver of great wealth and success.

Saint Martha oil: Resolves all problems in love, power, and strength. Saint Martha is a saint who I have called "the Sorceress" for her powerful allure to bring back lovers.

San Cipriano oil: This formula specializes in returning a lover, wife, or husband. Also helps give a favorable outcome in court cases.

Sappho oil: Lesbian love attraction and love spell blend.

Saturn oil: Planetary blend for respecting rules and restrictions.

Serenity oil: Blissful peace, tranquility, and calm.

Showers of Gold oil: Wealth and prosperity.

Sirens oil: To make you bold and alluring.

Special Favors oil: Grants wishes that seem impossible.

Spellbound oil: Captivate them with your charm and hold them spellbound.

Spiritual Cleansing oil: Clears away all malignant spells and leaves a calm clear effect.

Success oil: Good fortune and success in all endeavors.

Sun oil: Solar power, burns away all impurities, success.

Tara oil (Green): Remover of all sorrows, financial blessings.

Tara oil (White): Mother of Peace and protection, who sees in all directions. She has seven eyes, which in Buddhist belief means that she sees all who call upon her.

Tramp oil: Total seduction, flirtations, and downright sexiness.

Uncrossing oil: Removes any hex or spell.

Venus oil: Draws love toward you. Makes you irresistible.

Voluptuous Venus oil: Love formula designed for luring a lover.

Voodoo Nights oil: Blend that calls up the spirits of lust and
    passion.
Weight Loss oil: Helps to inspire you to shed those pounds.
Witch Love oil: The magick of love. This is a love formula that
    was created in the Warlock Shop in 1971.
Wolf's Heart oil: To overcome fear and gain courage.

Those of you who have bought earlier editions of this book know
that I have many more formulas. The reason I have not listed them all
is that it simply becomes too large a list for the practitioner of candle
magick to choose from. I do intend to publish my formulas for all of
my oil blends in the future so that you can make them for yourself or
your local shop can blend them for you. This is why under all of the
oils suggested I have listed some single fragrances so as to make it
easier for the candle practitioner to be able to make a candle without
hunting down a formula blend that was created by me. Experiment for
yourself and see what you can come up with. Always write the formula down and label your bottles so you remember what is in them.
Do not trust your nose to decipher what is in a bottle. For example,
patchouli has a distinct smell so you know when it's straight patchouli.
But it's more difficult with a blended oil. A good apothecarist always
labels all bottles and keeps a file with dates of all formulas.

Sometimes I change or make a new formula for the same name.
For example, I might have three different formulas for Love Oil. All
of them are dated and numbered. Sometimes I even include the location where I was inspired to make the blend. I will even include my
source of inspiration. A new and wonderful world of alchemy awaits
you in creating candles, spells, and formulas for magick. Keep a journal of your work by writing down everything you create and what
the results were.

4.

About Candle Spells

Enchanted candles are spells unto themselves. Carving a candle with a specific design that represents a deity, or a magickal seal that represents a concept, is the same as creating a document or petition. The important document must reach the right party. You cannot send it Federal Express, so in order to deliver the message you will light this candle. The seal carving, the oil, the glitter, and the "feedings", or offerings, are all a part of the package you are sending to your deity.

However, you may desire to enhance your candle spell work with a specific ritual, so I have suggested a spell and ways to prepare each candle. The preparations I have suggested include a specific cleansing for each candle, so that you can cleanse it of any previous energies and make it clean and new just for your purpose. You can also use just the preparation for the candle and not the spell if you choose. Or you may have your own ritual or spell you want to use your enchanted candle for. There is no "right way" in this work—you do not have to follow my spells for your candle to be effective.

PREPARATION OF CANDLES

In the pages that follow, each spell includes its own separate recipe of oils and incenses to use for cleansing your candle. Here I am offering basic, generic cleansing instructions that would work well with any candle. You can fill in the oils and incenses depending on which spell you are preparing for. Or, you can use this cleansing ritual to cleanse the outside of seven-day candle glasses, such as commercially made saint or spell candles. These, too, need to be wiped down and cleansed of the energies they pick up while sitting on the shelf. This way, your candle is being neutralized, leaving a clean slate on which to work your magick.

Make sure that you gather the necessary items that are listed under your spell before you start carving your candle. All four of the elements will be used to cleanse your candle in preparation for your spell.

Now pass your candle through the incense.

Step 1: Cleansing Your Candle

Remove your candle from the glass. To represent the elements of water and earth, use water and salt. A quarter of a cup of water should be more than enough. Add three drops of oil and three pinches of salt and stir clockwise three times. The type of oil you use depends on your spell's specifications. There is an intensive list of oils and their magickal uses in the apothecary section in chapter 3, but here is a short list for quick reference:

Love oils: Rose, lavender, musk, jasmine, honeysuckle, and ylang ylang.
Money oils: Bayberry, sandalwood, orange, cinnamon, and bay.
Uncrossing oils: Lavender, basil, carnation, frankincense, and lemon.
Protection: frankincense, vervain, mint, sage, and amber.

Dip a cotton ball in the water/oil/salt mixture and cleanse the top of the candle three times in a clockwise motion. Then start going down the candle to the bottom in downward strokes, saying the following words:

> With water and earth I do conspire to blend together as I desire, to banish all that's been before, so I may conjure this candle pure evermore.

Once this is done, you are ready to purify your candle with fire and air.

Burn the desired incense and grasp the candle by the top and the bottom leaving most of it exposed. If you are using a candle that has a glass holder but does not come out of the glass, then proceed as you would with a regular candle. Slowly start to pass the candle through the smoke, envisioning all impurities being swept away and dissipating into the air. Speak these words:

> Fire and air burn bright, and put all that was before to flight. Cleanse my candle with magick might so I may cast my spell and put all to right.

Now it's time to cleanse the glass holder of the candle if you are using a pullout candle. Place it in the sink and run hot tap water into the glass. Add about three capfuls of ammonia, and three pinches of salt and let it sit for a few minutes. This will not only clean the glass of wax smudges and dirt, it will remove previous energies from the glass. This is a practice I always do because I like a clean glass to insert my beautiful candle into. You can either dry it by hand or turn it upside down and allow it to air dry. When the glass is dry you are ready to feed your glass holder.

Step 2: Carving Your Candle

After choosing the seal(s) you want on your candle, hold your candle in one hand and carve the seal with your utility knife or hobby blade. If you do not have either of these, any sharp knife or even an old ballpoint pen will work. As you carve, you should be envisioning the desired result of what you are trying to manifest.

Visualize what you feel comfortable with. Magick needs flow and rhythm. If you are doing a money spell, don't stop and say, "Oh, I saw an image of myself greeting the person who is going to hire me for the job, and the book expressed seeing myself in the job." That disturbs the harmony of the magick. Let it flow in your own natural rhythm for the best results and always trust in the Gods to provide for you and all will be fine.

Step 3: Feeding ~~Your Candle~~ The glass holder & candle

Unless a spell indicates otherwise, the traditional feeding is done with a pinch of iron filings and a drop of honey. I recommend you always taste the honey you are offering. There is a story that some-

one tried to poison the Goddess Oshun's honey, which is her favorite
offering. Ever since then she would not accept honey without the
offerer tasting it first. It's good practice to do this with all offerings to
all Gods because we commune with them when we share in their
gifts. In the Craft, when we make a libation of wine we offer some to
the Gods, like a toast. Then we take a sip. This is based on the same
principle. We are certainly not going to taste iron filings, which are
used for attraction or as magnetic sand to draw to you what you
want. But where applicable, taste an offering before giving it to the
Gods.

Each enchanted candle spell lists a suggested feeding. Some, such
as Femme Blanche, are restricted to certain kinds of offerings. Others
leave a lot of room to be creative. The following are some offerings
that you can use: herbs, incense, pennies, cascarilla, sugar, melao,
palm oil, bluing powder, cocoa butter, a few drops of oil, perfume, dirt
from corresponding areas (like a bank for a money spell), hair, nail
clippings . . . the list goes on. Use your imagination. Be creative and
see if you find something small that can be used in conjunction with
your spell.

Step 4: Oiling Your Candle

Pour a small amount of your chosen oil into the palm of your hand.
Starting at the center, rub the oil up the candle first, then down.
Make sure you cover the entire candle with the oil. It can be a little
messy, so you may use rubber gloves if you wish. It's also a good idea
to have newspaper spread on your workspace to catch spilled oil and
glitter.

Step 5: Glittering Your Candle

Take a clean spice jar and make a small hole in one side of the cap.
This makes a perfect container from which to pour your glitter. Outline your seal with the glitter by tilting the jar over the seal and
lightly tapping it with your finger so a small amount of glitter comes
out. When you become proficient in this tapping technique, you will
begin to see that the glitter jar works almost like a pen or paintbrush
because you are controlling the flow of the glitter. As you tap, move
the bottle along the outline of the seal.

Allow the deity you are working with to guide you in your choice of colors. No two enchanted candles are exactly the same—they are individuals just like us. All the spells listed in this book are different for everyone, for each person has a different story and purpose behind doing their individual candle work.

After you finish glittering the seal, very slowly slide the candle back into the glass sleeve. You may want to carve and glitter a hexagram, pentacle, or a solar cross (a cross with four equal arms that represent the crossroads, four elements or the four watchtowers of a circle) on the top of the candle. I call this the "hat" of the candle. It is the sendoff as you light it. The hexagram on top represents "as above so below," and "as below so above"—what we vibrate up to the astral plane will mirror its effects down to the earthly plane. A pentacle represents the four elements and spirit. The solar cross in glitter on top is so that what you are trying to manifest should come from all directions.

Now your candle is ready to light as it is or you can elaborate on your magick with a spell.

SACRED SPELL BOWLS

When it was first suggested to me to add separate spells to this book, I said, "well that's something to think about." Enchanted candles are spells already, as by having been infused with a talisman they contain an intent, so at first I felt it was a great challenge to think about how to enhance them. I am a psychic and the candles were communicated to me through guides, so I figured that my guides would communicate to me once more on what to do. Thank the Goddess they did! I wanted a format that would be consistent just as the enchanted candles are uniformly prepared in the above sequence. Then it occurred to me that I was always giving offerings to the deities when I was lighting the candles. So I would teach people how to use herbs, flowers, fruits, and other ingredients in conjunction with their enchanted candles! They will make offerings to the gods that they are invoking with their candles.

One of the reasons people love my candle system is that everything is done on one candle and it doesn't require a lot of altar space. Now folks could be putting out a separate glass for the wine and a plate for any kind of fruit, honey, sugar, or other food offering. Plus there might be a separate vase for flowers and probably a charm bag to hold all the herbs for each candle that requires an herb offering. That sure seems like a lot for one candle spell, and can be very unruly and cluttered. Sometimes people need multiple spells, like one for love and maybe an uncrossing or money drawing. That could take up three different altars alone! Then I realized sacred objects— the offerings you will be giving to the very Gods themselves—are what is being sought after here. A circle is a sacred symbol to a witch and necessary in the art of magick. I would put the candles in a circle with a spell and an incantation. Now, whenever I think about a witch in her circle I always see a cauldron in the picture. For a witch, a cauldron is a natural part of their tools. It suddenly became clear to me what was needed: sacred bowls! They are a sacred circle and a cauldron all in one. This would eliminate the need to cast a circle before doing the spell, since everything is already within a sacred circle. Furthermore, all the ingredients and offerings can be put together in one space without taking up a lot of room. Finally, I had a formula and I was eager to start trying it out. After much experimenting I came up with spells that really work.

You should purchase special bowls for spell work. I like large cut-crystal bowls or glass with a cut-crystal look. This allows for the candlelight to come through, and you can see all of your offerings through the clear glass. This is just one suggestion—use your imagination when shopping and experiment with different styles. Perhaps you are in kindred spirit with the Goddesses Tara or Lakshmi (the Hindu Goddess of supreme compassion and financial blessings) and want to get a green glass bowl just to burn sacred candle offerings to them. Get a yellow one for Oshun (the Yoruban Venus who gives love, money, and multiple blessings), or maybe colorful ceramics are more to your taste. You might have a beautiful bowl just waiting in your cupboard for this very purpose—perhaps an heirloom from Grandma. Now you have a great way to use it besides as an occasional odd bowl for green beans. Put Grandma's love for you to work. Now you can turn that love into a magick tool.

Another added bonus in using bowls is the candle burning safety feature. After being in this line of work for the last thirty years, I cannot count how many times candle magick has gone wrong and started fires. If you are using a pullout candle to make your enchanted candle, the offerings, such as iron filings, honey, sugar, or herbs and flower petals are being fed into the bottom of the glass. When the candle melts down to the bottom of the glass, the offerings can catch fire, or the glass can overheat, causing it to break or explode. If your candle was on a wooden surface, that could then catch fire. In bowls filled with liquid this is less likely to happen.

For those of you who will be using pillar style candles without glass casings, having a bowl gives you an instant candle holder and can still include liquid offerings. However, I never suggest you leave a candle burning unattended, even when it is in a bowl. If you feel it is important to leave a candle burning nonstop for seven days, then take the whole spell and move it into your bathtub for an extra safety measure.

LETTERS OF INTENTION

It is of greatest importance to me that you clearly understand why we use letters of intention. We are petitioning the Gods to intervene with our life's problems. Written words carry as much power as pictures. They are vehicles of communication.

When you write something out it makes you become extra clear about what it is you want. When you desire something your mind can run wild with random thoughts. Writing down all of these needs and desires allows you to realize exactly what you want and helps you focus. Have you ever gone shopping at the supermarket without a list? Have you ever then forgotten to buy what you went there for? You wouldn't be alone! I watch customers on a daily basis come in with a book of spells and a shopping list. If your spell is important to you, then writing a letter of intention should be easy. Be specific about what you want. Remember the story of the monkey's paw? Take heart if all of your letter cannot be answered the way you want; the Gods you are petitioning will find ways to inspire happiness for you.

I personally always end a petition with alternatives. My ultimate happiness is what I am after in the end. For instance, say I want to win the lotto in New York. But I win it in Conneticut. Will I say, "Oh no that's not good enough, I said New York"? No way! As long as I am happy in the end it is good enough for me. I like to leave an open door when petitioning the Gods.

Here are some examples of what your letter of intention might look like:

Dear (name of deity you are working with):

My name is _____. I have been dating _____ for two years now. We have a good relationship, but I do not see it growing in the direction that I desire. I do not want to waste my years being a companion and lover to this man, only for him to leave me for someone else. If we are meant to be together then bring this man closer to me, seeking marriage. Let none stand in the way of our union in this life nor turn him aside because of their petty jealousies of our happiness together. Let all obstacles to marriage be removed from our path. So Mote It Be.

The end lines "Let all obstacles be removed form our path. So mote it be" are the open door. You just covered areas you may not even know about yet.

Dear (name of deity):

My name is _____. I have desired to be with _____. We see each other on occasion, have great sex, and then he does not call me for weeks. I always must be the one to try to put myself in his path so that we can see one another. I always feel as though I am chasing him until he sees me. Then he wants me and we are happy together. I know he desires me and enjoys my company, but our relationship seems to be going nowhere. Please inspire his heart to seek me out so that our efforts to be together are mutual. If this is impossible, if we are not meant to be, then please send me someone who is meant to be happy and in love with me. Help me so that I may pursue my life's happiness and continue on in my path with someone at my side who loves me and desires to be my partner, with no reservations. So Mote It Be.

Again, the end line—"with no reservations. So Mote It Be."—allows you to open a door with a specific instruction.

Special note: In love spells, if you have any doubts about the object of your affection at all, I always recommend that you keep the door open for someone else to come into your life. I know that when you want one particular person this is hard to hear, but you will be amazed at the results you can achieve with this if you keep an open mind and do not obsess over a person who may not be the right one for you.

A Word About Wine, "The Nectar of the Gods"

When I first started rereading all of the spells in this book to be used in conjunction with alcohol, I said to myself, "My Goddess, I sound like a candidate for an AA meeting." Then it occurred to me that the spells in this book would be difficult for someone who is in recovery for drug or alcohol addictions. Then I thought about the age issue with regard to wine and hard liquor. Many practitioners are minors and I do want to consider their circumstances. So, below is a list of exchanges for the wine and alcohol offerings. Clear water can be used as a general substitute for all the liquid offerings.

RED WINE: substitutes are dark grape juice, red grape juice, cranberry juice, and nonalcoholic red wines.

WHITE WINE: White grape juice, apple juice, pear nectar diluted with water, and nonalcoholic white wine.

ROSE WINE: Seltzer or sparkling water, or with a light rose-colored fruit juice mixed in. Red grape and cranberry also work.

CHAMPAGNE: Sparkling apple cider, or any nonalcoholic sparkling beverage.

STREGA AND OTHER LIQUEURS: Nectars are excellent for this purpose, although I suggest you use water to dilute them, as they are thick and sticky. Peach, pear, papaya, even orange juice is great for success spells. Strawberry nectar works for love spells. Any fruit nectar or juice is fine—just choose something that you are guided to by instinct. For example, if you see cranberry juice on the shelf, and you think "Ah, that deep red looks like it would be perfect for my love spell" then go for it. Allow some of your natural magick to flow with the choices of your spell. Your natural magick is the instinct that guides you and that is influenced by your spirit guides. Each person's ability to flow with his or her guides varies. For some, it comes naturally; others have to concentrate a little harder. But it's always there.

While wine is the best offering, it will not make the Gods happy if your magick is causing you a struggle for choices and temptations that are not good for you. If you are in recovery for alcohol do not use the wine, since it may tempt you to start drinking again. Magick needs flow, not struggle and strife. However, if you do not have an issue with alcohol than toasting the Gods is fine.

Spell Offerings

Just how messy are they? Well if you work in a neat and organized fashion, then this shouldn't be a problem. You should gather all of your ingredients and prepare your spell just like you see food prepared on a cooking show. If you stop to answer the phone or take care of another errand and you do not have everything in front of you, your magick will be like the old adage "a chicken running with its head cut off." Prepare everything first, then set out to do your spell.

A warning, however: candles burning in bowls of wine, or water with honey and other offerings, can attract unwanted visitors—bugs, rodents, house pets. Once you've done your spell and lit your candle, you can either leave the bowl with the offerings in it until the candle is finished burning, or you can dispose of the offerings the next day and finish burning your candle without them. Once you have made your offerings to the deity and the candle is lit, the offerings have already been accepted by the gods. How long you intend to keep the offerings on your altar is up to you. If you are concerned about attracting pests, then feel free to dispose of the offerings right away.

Disposal of Spells

When you flip through these spells, you may think to yourself, "Wow, these spells are great, but what a mess when they're done!" I've looked down at a bowl with seven days of wine, flowers, and herbs sitting in it, and the red wine left rings and the flowers were all mushy. The question is, what do you do with all the leftover stuff when a spell is finished? Many magickal practitioners will answer, "If it is for a deity you have to bring it to the river," or "Leave it under a tree," or "That deity takes her offerings in the ocean." Yeah, well, what if you are living in Arizona? Are you supposed to just hop on a plane with your spell in a neat and tidy Tupperware container and take a short flight to the nearest ocean? Ridiculous isn't it? What I have learned in all these years is that not every spell requires that the offering be brought to the location where a deity rules. The deities will come down to the spell work and consume spiritually what you have offered them. Once they are done, and the spell has been completed, it matters little what happens to the physical material left behind.

So what am I telling you to do with it afterward? It's simple—you dispose of it in the garbage and wash the rest away. I'm very practical about this. The deities have already taken what they wanted from the spell. The rest is really insignificant to them. Your Letter of Intention has already been recognized, and can be discarded as seeing it done. Don't worry about insulting the Gods. They love the offerings and enjoy the praise.

In the previous chapters, I have given you all the information you need to understand the elements of the enchanted candle and why they work. You have learned how to carve and empower your candles with oils, incenses, powders, colors, glitter, altars, and, of course, intent. Now you are ready to put those candles to use. One way to use your candles, as I've said, is to simply burn them. Another way is to use them in a spell. In the next several chapters you will find spells for all sorts of purposes: spells for love, spells for money, spells for power, spells for protection, spells for healing. You will find unusual spells, commonly needed spells, universal spells, and spells for specific minority groups. You will find spells for people and spells for animals. You will find spells for couples and spells for individuals. Some spells will apply to you and some won't. The idea is to use the spells that would most benefit you or your loved ones.

Each spell contains an illustration of the seal to carve into the candle, the candle color, the purpose of the spell, the oils and incenses to use, the magickal cleaning agents and feedings, the deity to invoke, ingredients for the spell, and the rite. So enjoy these spells, and let the magick begin!

PART II

Seals and Spells

5.

Enchanted Love Candles

Let us part the veil and enter into the mysterious world of love. Here is where some of life's greatest mysteries live. That is why romance is the hardest thing to figure out. "I love him but he doesn't want me." "Now he wants me and I don't want him." "All we do is fight then make up." "Do you think he'll ever ask me to marry him?" These are some of the common gripes I hear every day about love. Sounds terrible, doesn't it? What is it about love that makes us go through such great lengths to have it? Because when love is right, there is nothing in heaven or earth that can compare to it. The following spells are to bring, enhance, and celebrate love, and have been devised over the years in direct response to the most common love requests. These love spells are for situations that are universal. Each seal can cover more than one situation and I offer more than one suggestion of what each seal can be used for. Whatever your specific needs are, there is a spell here for you. May love find its way to you swiftly!

MYSTERE

Become a sizzling-hot Sex Goddess!

PURPOSE: The seal for Mystere was designed to bring an air of mystery to the subject. Mystery serves as a magnet to most people. Curiosity is a part of human nature, and when someone mysterious enters a room, people are drawn to her or him. Once you have a person hooked, there is a whole lifetime of things to learn about each other and still your personality keeps growing, and then that makes for new things to be discovered. But sometimes it is that initial intrigue that we lack—the glamour that makes someone notice you. Mystere surrounds you with a glamour that makes you different and intriguing to others. It is essentially an attraction spell to draw a lover.

CANDLE COLOR: Pink, red.

DEITY: The goddess Erzulie. There are many aspects to Erzulie, but the one to focus on for the purpose of this spell is her sense of mystery and intrigue.

CLEANSING: Rose water, narcissus oil, lilac oil.

OIL: Mystere, Venus, Attraction, narcissus, strawberry, rose, lilac, apple blossom.

INCENSE: Mystere, Rhea's Love Haunt, rose.

Mystere

FEEDING: Iron filings, honey, cinnamon powder.

Mystere Spell

ITEMS NEEDED

A letter of intention to
  Erzulie telling her your
  goals and desires
A small plate
Seven strawberries
Honey
Seven pennies
Powdered sugar

Champagne
A glass bowl
Pink rose petals
A hand mirror
Lilac, musk, and narcissus
  oils for blending
An empty bottle for perfume
  oil

CASTING THE SPELL: The love incense should be lit just before carving the candle to call forth Erzulie, and during the incantation below. First compose the letter telling Erzulie how you wish to change and become more alluring. When this is done fold the letter in half and place it in the center of a medium sized bowl. Place your candle on top of the letter.

Now place the bowl with the letter and candle on top of a large plate. Place the seven strawberries around the plate telling Erzulie this is an offering to her. Now drizzle the honey over the strawberries asking Erzulie to make you sweet and alluring. Put a penny next to each strawberry and sprinkle powered sugar over the tops. Next, pour the champagne into the bowl. Float the rose petals in the champagne. Prop the mirror in front of the bowl. Reserve the three oils for mixing in the empty perfume bottle—you will be creating a special perfume to wear when you go out.

INCANTATION: Light the candle and say these words:

> I surround myself with the exotic perfume of mystery. My inner
> self blossoms like night-blooming jasmine captivating the one I
> desire. Like the hummingbird you are seduced by my nectar, sweet
> with attraction, desire and passion yet to unfold. With this allure
> I do summon you forth to come and explore the mysteries of me.

When you are finished saying the incantation, fill the bottle with the three oils, one-third of each, and add a few drops of the champagne and a pinch of sugar. Put the cap on and shake well. Place the perfume in front of your candle and leave until your candle is finished burning. The incantation should be said three times in a row once a day. When you say it is not important as long as the timing is right for you and you say it with intent and feeling. Each time you say the incantation, look in the mirror and see how you are improving, and speak to Erzulie, the Goddess of Beauty, of your desires. When the candle is finished burning, wear your magick perfume when you go out for a night of adventure. Know that you now carry an aura of mystery. Be confident that Erzulie walks with you and enjoy yourself!

SAN CIPRIANO

To get back a lover and have great sex!

PURPOSE: I have used this intoxicating spell for rejuvenating a romance and for adding spice and newness to a marriage. San Cipriano was a native of Carthage who lived in about 249 A.D. He resided in Antioch, and received his formal training at Mount Olympus start-

ing at age seven. In life San Cipriano continued his studies in Argos, Egypt, Memphis, Sparta, and Chaldea. He is a saint who reunites estranged lovers. Speculation has it that he learned black magic before converting to Christianity. I believe now he was a local witch, shaman, and even a magician. Resistance to conversion at this time was equal to public humiliation, torture, and death, so people's choices were narrow. This also gave the magistrates the right to pick and choose those of the occult world that would benefit them. Many of the Christian prayers have occult meaning woven in their fabric. For example, there are prayers to St. Michael that include lines revoking evil magick that others have sent to individuals. St. Martha has prayers to bring domination over obstacles. A prayer to the Caridad del Cobre (Our Lady of Charity) starts out with the words "Oh unique spirit, without begin-

San Cipriano

ning or end, ever present, ever powerful, in whose ocean of life I am but a drop, let me feel the presence of your power." St. Francis of Assisi wrote the "canticle to the sun." This means "circle of the sun" and it includes incantations to Mother Earth. Proverbs eight and nine are where Lady Wisdom speaks to us in the Bible. These and other prayers are designed to have occult power.

San Cipriano was united with another pagan soul named Justina who also later became a saint. It is their great love for each other that has compelled many to turn to them for help when separated. In one story it was Cipriano the magician who helped another young man try to achieve the love of Justina. According to the tale, when he tried to unite them however, all of his magick failed and he fell in love with Justina and converted to Christianity himself.

CANDLE COLOR: Red, pink.

CLEANING: Water, red wine, Florida water.

DEITY: San Cipriano. Invoke the aid of this powerful saint along with Saint Justina to accomplish your task.

OIL: San Cipriano, Come to Me, Astarte, musk, cinnamon, or jasmine.

INCENSE: San Cipriano, Come to Me, Fire of Love, La Flamme, jasmine, musk, and rose.

FEEDING: Iron filings, honey, jasmine flowers.

San Cipriano Spell

ITEMS NEEDED

A letter written to San Cipriano stating your desires
A bowl
The petals of one dark red rose
3 tablespoons of brown sugar
2 teaspoons of basil
4 pinches of iron filings
Honey
A glass of red wine

CASTING THE SPELL: Incense should be lit during this ritual. Fold your letter to San Cipriano in half and place it in the bowl. Place the candle on top of the letter. Scatter the rose petals around the bowl. Next, sprinkle the brown sugar and the basil on top of the rose petals. Now place a pinch of iron filings north, south, east, and west inside the perimeter of the bowl. Taste the honey and pour it into the bowl. Add seven drops of the red wine. Place a glass of red wine for the saint next to the spell. Light the candle and say the incantation.

INCANTATION: Say these words:

> I do summon the night, the stars, and the moon above! Bear witness to this rite of love tonight. Oh San Cipriano hear my plea, open the heart of _____ [name of beloved] and return him to me. No one else can fill me with longing and desire as he does. It has to be him who returns to me, with the spark of love burning in your heart. In the name of San Cipriano with the blood of the wine staining the dark velvet night, and the honey roses sweet to entice the senses of _____ [name of beloved]. I lure him back to my embrace.

Allow the candle to burn and petition San Cipriano to open the heart and mind of the one you love. If there is an obstacle preventing the object of your affection from returning to you, San Cipriano will help remove it and inspire your love to return. This spell can be repeated until you have seen the results you desire or a change has come to set you free from the bondage of desire for someone whose will is not to return to you.

LOVE POWER

Love call, for hot nights of steamy sex and fidelity.

PURPOSE: Is your lover playing hide-and-seek with you? On today, off tomorrow? This is a classic symptom of an erratic relationship. Here we are going to summon the very pipes of Pan to send out the love call.

Another purpose for this candle is to reunite a lovetorn relationship. The strong pull of this candle seal will draw a straying mate back to you. If your sex life has gone sour, use this seal to ignite passion and desire. Use Mars to repair your sex life and your marriage. Light this candle to keep someone home and create your own fire.

Love Power

CANDLE COLOR: Red.

CLEANSING: Water, salt, cinnamon oil, crushed red pepper.

DEITY: The God Pan and the nymph Syrinx. A story is told that the great God Pan was about to throw his arms around his favorite nymph, Syrinx, when she was turned into river reeds by one of the River Goddesses she called to for help. The God sighed and music piped out of the reeds. He cut them and fashioned them into a pipe, which has since become known as the Pipes of Pan. He uses his pipes to sway lovers into each others' arms.

OIL: Fire of Love, Come to Me, cinnamon, vetivert, frangipani, and musk.

INCENSE: Come to Me, Love, Attraction, pine, musk, or patchouli.

FEEDING: Iron filings, honey, Dragon's Blood, dirt from your lover's yard.

Love Power Spell

ITEMS NEEDED

A letter written in red ink as
   a petition of your desires
A bowl
Honey
Cinnamon powder

Allspice berries
Myrtle leaves
The petals of a dark-red rose
Red wine

CASTING THE SPELL: Light your incense during the preparation and carving of your candle to call forth your love through the pipes of Pan.

Compose the petition in red ink. It should contain all the things you most desire in your love life with this person. Be brutally honest. Pay attention to detail.

Now fold the letter in half and fit it inside the bowl. Place the candle on top of the letter. Drizzle the honey all around the bowl and over the letter, picturing passion between you and your love. Next add the cinnamon powder and the allspice berries and say, "This is to put excitement and passion to my spell." For fidelity, scatter the myrtle leaves and say, "I add the power of the myrtle for true love." Add the rose petals saying, "Now I cast the flower of Venus for pure love and romance," and finally, pour in the red wine saying, "Bring for me a spell of total abandonment to love and lust."

Now in your mind's eye, envision your innermost secret fantasy with this person taking place. Then chant the incantation nine times while lighting the candle.

INCANTATION: Chant nine times:

> Your lust I feel thrust deep within me. To lay together in love's glow, with passion's embers still burning bright I will make you mine tonight.

Allow your magick spell to take hold. Repeat the incantation nine times in a row once a day in front of your candle spell. Visualize you and your lover being together in this way.

LOVE POWER CONCEPTION CANDLE

Use the "Love Power" seal on page 82.

For the conception of a child.

PURPOSE: This seal can be used in conjunction with the Mother Birth (page 185) seal. Usually I recommend Mother Birth on a yellow candle for conception. When using both the Mother Birth seal and the Love Power seal together, however, I recommend using a red candle. To empower this candle for this purpose, write the man's name in the mars symbol along with the words "divine male seed" and in the receptive moon, write the female's name and the words "the seed is planted."

CANDLE COLOR: Red, yellow.

CLEANSING: Water, sugar, pompeia perfume.

DEITY: Pan and Aphrodite.

OIL: Cinnamon, strawberry, or Aphrodite.

INCENSE: Love, Come to Me, Blessing, rose, strawberry.

FEEDING: Iron filings, honey, cinnamon powder, and lovage.

Love Power Conception Spell

This candle is empowered by offerings to Pan and Aphrodite.

ITEMS NEEDED

A letter of intention and what you want in this conception—a healthy child, personality attributes, appearance, and so on
One bowl

Three teaspoons of olive oil
Honey
Five cinnamon sticks
Plain pumpkin seeds
Anise seeds
Red wine
Fresh mint leaves

CASTING THE SPELL: Pass both the inscribed candle and your letter through the incense. Fold the letter and put it in the bowl. Next, add the three spoons of olive oil. Add the honey, and spread a layer of pumpkin seeds on top. Add the cinnamon sticks and anise seeds for instigation. Pour in the wine, followed by a layer of fresh mint leaves.

Light your candle and say the incantation.

INCANTATION

O thou staff of light, rod of creation, send thy seeds straight in to my receptive moon womb. Here I will house in my soft warm darkness a child to come into the light of this world. So Mote It Be.

Repeat this incantation nine times in a row once a day until your candle has burned out. Nine is a number of power, because it is the last number of the single digits. It means the culmination of the work, all of the process that it took for all of the numbers to work up to nine. This gives you the power to complete your work. This spell works best when started on the new moon.

KEY TO THE HEART

Want to be my valentine?

PURPOSE: This candle makes an excellent valentine. Use it when you want someone to hold the key to your heart, and in exchange you want the key to his or hers. This candle is great when a relationship is at that stage when you're both ready to take the next step—for instance, a commitment for marriage. This also helps instigate that special, intimate bond between two people. When two people are ready to start a life together, there is a time where you learn each other's habits, and this is a very intimate bond. Sometimes, though, getting there could use a little push. For example, do you both shower in the morning? Does one drink coffee, the other tea? The first year is the hardest, and getting used to each other's habits and still keeping the intimacy of your personal life exciting, is an art in itself. This seal will help smooth out the bumps in that road.

Key to the Heart

CANDLE COLOR: Pink or red.

CLEANSING: Water, sugar, rose water or a few drops of rose oil.

DEITY: Erzulie, Venus, Aphrodite.

OIL: Erzulie Love, Bewitching, Voluptuous Venus.

INCENSE: Venus, Erzulie, Bewitching.

FEEDING: Iron filings, honey, pink rose petals.

Key to the Heart Spell

This is to open the doors to love.

ITEMS NEEDED

A letter stating your
    intentions, written in red
    ink to the Goddess of your
    choice
Two red paper hearts

A bowl
Honey
Rose wine
Pink rose petals

CASTING THE SPELL: Light the incense and compose your letter. Then write your name on one paper heart and your beloved's on the other. Place the letter in the bowl, then take the heart with your name on it and place it on top of the letter, and place the other heart on top of yours. Now place your prepared candle on top of this. Pour in some honey, followed by the rose wine. Add the pink rose petals all around the candle in the bowl. Picture the both of you together, becoming more enraptured with one another. Let your imagination run wild, then release the thoughts from your mind—let them flow into the candle by envisioning what you desire while you cast your spell. As you do this say the incantation.

INCANTATION

> Two hearts beat as one, one rhythm of love as the drum beats in the night. The pulse of Mother Earth throbs within my love and me at midnight. Bonding and fusing our love beneath the moonlight. Together we shall grow as one tonight.

As your candle burns, see it as a seed of love that you have just planted in the Universe. Know that the seed is growing and pushing upward as a plant—a living thing growing on the other side of your world. It will soon manifest in your life.

KEY TO THE HEART (WEDDING CANDLE)

Use the Key to the Heart seal on page 86.

Blessing for your Handfasting or wedding day.

PURPOSE: This candle is a blessed announcement to the Universe of your taking of vows, and it will bring a blessing to your union. This candle can be done before the marriage, the day of the ceremony, and for a year after that. During the honeymoon phase or first year of the marriage it is wise to bless your union with loving communication. This candle can be lit at any time in a marriage or relationship that needs more loving talk and understanding. I especially advise this candle to be lit during the ceremony so as to bless the unity of the couple. The purpose here is to have a great time at your wedding.

CANDLE COLOR: White

CLEANSING: White rose water, sugar, cascarilla (powdered eggshells).

DEITY: Erzulie, Juno, Venus

OIL: Marriage Mind, Handfasting, India Bouquet, neroli (orange blossom)

INCENSE: Handfasting, Venus, All Night Long

FEEDING: White sugar, honey, white rose petals, cascarilla, crumbled camphor.

Key to the Heart Wedding Candle Spell

ITEMS NEEDED

  Two white paper hearts cut from parchment paper, linen paper,
    or any white paper, with the names of the bride and groom
    written on them in red ink. (If you can find white paper
    doilies, then cut them into heart shapes.)
  A letter of intention written to the deity of your choice
  A bowl
  White sugar
  White peace powder (or if not available, plain white talc
    or baby powder)
  Seven copper pennies
  White rose water

A small split of champagne
White rose petals

First, light your incense and pass the two hearts through the smoke, saying the names of both the bride and groom seven times. Then say:

> As above so below, as below so above, together these two shall ever be in love.

Fold the letter in half and place it in the bowl. Then place the two hearts on top of the letter, and place the candle on top. Add the white sugar, followed by the white peace powder. Next, put the seven copper pennies in the bowl, add some rose water, and the champagne. Sprinkle the white rose petals all around. Light the candle, and with love, compassion and sincerity, say the incantation.

INCANTATION

> Let there be compassion and strength, joy and prosperity, respect and humility, and holy union between [bride's name] and [groom's name].

STAY AT HOME

To create a love nest they will not want to leave.

PURPOSE: This candle ensures that your mate will stay home and work out problems with you instead of straying. I call this seal "the velvet hammer," which when used appropriately can be a soft domination spell. The purpose here is to create a warm and happy home environment so that your mate will not want to stray, but will instead look forward to coming home.

Many people feel that it is bad karma to use this type of candle. Some folks consider it manipulation magick. If your intention is to dominate someone, then this opinion is correct: you cannot force anyone to do something they do not want to do. That is not the intention that this candle was designed for. With this candle you are putting out a call to the Universe to allow time to see you both through your troubles. If your mate is straying, then you need to see if things can be worked out or if you need to move on. This should be accomplished through communication, honesty, and your determination to find an amicable way to resolve the problems you are having. Do not nag the person about staying home. Instead, start setting up the house to be more comfortable. Make a love nest for you both. Try to discuss the problem without getting angry. Yelling and screaming will only shut down the lines of communication we are trying to open. If your partner has been cheating and you wish to work things out, then you should add a Love Healing seal to this spell. (See Love Healing candle on page 106.)

Stay at Home

CANDLE COLOR: Purple, white.

CLEANSING: Lavender water, sugar, and three bay leaves floating in the bowl of cleansing water.

DEITY: Juno, Erzulie, Sophia.

OIL: Stay at Home, Come to Me, Leather and Lace.

INCENSE: Bewitching, Come to Me, patchouli.

FEEDING: Iron filings, honey, patchouli, Marriage Powder.

Stay at Home Spell

ITEMS NEEDED

A letter of intention	Sugar
Two paper dolls made of red, white, or pink paper	Marriage Powder
	Patchouli
Paper to draw a house on	Iron filings
A bowl	Red wine
Cinnamon powder	

CASTING THE SPELL: Incense should be lit during the preparation of this candle. Write the letter and pass it through the incense smoke. Write the corresponding names and sex signs (♂ or ♀) on each paper doll, saying:

> I name this doll [state name]. It represents this person and the love and soul of our relationship.

Pass both dolls through the incense. Next, draw a house on the paper and write "The love nest of [write both your names]." Pass it through the incense smoke saying:

> This is the heart of the house in which we dwell.

Place the letter in the bowl, and the picture of the house on top of that. Next, place the female doll on the house and place the male on top. (For those in same-sex relationships, add the more domestic partner in the house first followed by the next doll.) Place the candle on top. Now add the cinnamon powder, sugar, Marriage Powder, patchouli, iron filings and red wine to the bowl. Light the candle and say the incantation.

INCANTATION

> Oh [name of deity] I seek your aid in this spell to set our problems right. Inspire loving communication in our home and allow sweet love to radiate its healing light in our hearts.

Couples counseling or therapy is highly advised along with this spell. If this has been impossible to accomplish before, this spell will certainly help push the reluctant partner in that direction.

LOVE'S MESSENGER

To put out an irresistible love call to the one you want.

PURPOSE: To communicate a message of love to someone near or far. When you have a message to send to your lover, whether it be that you miss him or her, or you just want to say "I love you" without repeating yourself all of the time, this candle spell will make your special delivery for you.

CANDLE COLOR: Orange, pink, yellow, white, red.

CLEANSING: Glory Water, sandalwood cologne, a few drops of cinnamon oil.

DEITY: Mercury and Venus.

OIL: Love's Messenger, Dixie Love, sandalwood, or cinnamon.

Across the Miles

INCENSE: Call Me, sandalwood, Black Star.

FEEDING: Iron filings, cinnamon powder, honey.

Love's Messenger Spell

ITEMS NEEDED

Love's Messenger

A letter of intention written to Mercury, Messenger of the Gods, and Venus, Goddess of Love.
A bowl
Cinnamon powder
Vervain
Three clear quartz crystals
Glory water (or if unavailable, use lavender)
Sandalwood cologne
Pink carnation petals

CASTING THE SPELL: Light your incense and write your letter. Remember to be very clear on exactly what you want to say. Fold the letter and pass it through the incense. Place it in the bottom of the bowl, then sprinkle the cinnamon powder and vervain around the candle. Now place the three crystals against the candle in the bowl. Add the Glory water along with a small amount of sandalwood cologne. Scatter the petals of the pink carnation around the candle. Light the candle and say the incantation.

INCANTATION

Mercury, Messenger of All Thoughts, I want you to speak into the mind of [beloved's name]; Venus, Goddess of love, instill in the heart and mind of [beloved's name] that [he or she] may know the truth of my love.

This candle will also inspire your lover to dream about you, and assist you in astral projection to help the flow of communication between you.

LOVE UNCROSSING

To remove unwanted obstacles from your love life.

PURPOSE: This spell is to remove obstacles for couples. It will also help remove obstacles for issues such as trust, so you can allow love in your life. If you have been single a long time and cannot seem to find love, perhaps there is a block that needs to be removed. This spell will open the way to love. This candle spell will also remove any negative magick or bad thoughts others may have sent to you.

CANDLE COLOR: White or pink.

CLEANSING: White lavender water, Florida water, sugar.

DEITY: Erzulie, White Tara, Kwan Yin.

OIL: Love Uncrossing, Kindly Spirit, peach, or carnation.

INCENSE: Love Uncrossing, vanilla, sandalwood, or peach.

Love Uncrossing

FEEDING: Camphor, cascarilla (powdered eggshell), sugar, white flower petals (mums or carnations).

Love Uncrossing Spell

ITEMS NEEDED

A letter of intention
A bowl
Sugar
One tablespoon of milk
White lavender water

Florida water
Fresh basil leaves
White flower petals
    (chrysanthemums or
    carnations)

CASTING THE SPELL: Light the incense, then write your letter of intention and pass it through the incense smoke. When you are done, fold it and place it in your bowl. Put your prepared Enchanted Candle on top of the letter. Now sprinkle the sugar all around the letter, followed by the milk. Next add the White lavender water, and the Florida water. Arrange the basil leaves and flower petals on top. Light your candle and say the incantation.

INCANTATION

From the East to the South, then West to North, I conjure a circle of love and healing light around us two. As the four watchtowers each represent a chamber of our hearts let all ways be clear for love to flow.

As your candle burns, picture in your mind's eye all of the obstacles and blocks being flushed out of your lives and the natural rhythm of love beating through your hearts.

LOVE UNCROSSING (FOR SINGLES)

Initiating Love Magic

Use "Love Uncrossing" seal pictured on page 93.

Moon in Libra

Helps when you feel something is stopping you from finding love.

Full banish

PURPOSE: If you have been unable to meet anyone new and your life is in a rut, then this is the spell for you. Perhaps you have trust issues from being hurt in the past. This spell will remove all negative vibes that remain around you. This candle will open doors so you can get out there and meet the right people.

CANDLE COLOR: Pink or white.

CLEANSING: White lavender water, white rose water, two to three drops of mint oil (mint extract or fresh leaves will do fine).

DEITY: Erzulie, White Tara, Kwan Yin.

OIL: Love Uncrossing, sandalwood, lavender, peach.

INCENSE: Love Uncrossing, lavender, vanilla, or peach.

FEEDING: Camphor, cascarilla, sugar, lavender flowers (dry are fine). ↗ powdered eggshell

Love Uncrossing for Singles Spell

To fling open the doors to love and remove all the nasty frustration of endless days of being in a deadlock. This spell will set you on the way to freedom.

ITEMS NEEDED

A letter of intention
A picture of yourself (a photocopy is fine)
A bowl
Sugar
White rose water
Fresh mint leaves

White lavender water
Pink or white carnation petals (if you wish to be extravagant, use a whole white gardenia in place of the carnation petals)

Light your incense, and pass both the letter and photograph through the smoke. As you do this, picture all the blackness clearing from your life and being replaced with a pure, positive image of yourself. Now place the letter in the bowl with the picture over the letter. Set the candle over your picture, and scatter the sugar all over them. Pour a good measure of both the rose and lavender waters into the bowl. Float individual mint leaves in the bowl along with the carnation petals. (If you are using a whole gardenia, then add it to the bowl.) Light the candle and say the incantation.

INCANTATION

Oh Mother of peace and transcending beauty, I ask that you clear the four chambers of my heart. Relieve me of all sorrows. Replace tears with joy and healthy optimism.

As the candle burns, picture in your mind's eye the serene flow of white water energy sweeping down over your body.

MIDNIGHT

At midnight in the realm of the Goddess, share new delights with your lover!

PURPOSE: Romance, sexual fantasies, long nights of sensuous love-making. If you are already in such a relationship and you want things to evolve into even deeper realms, then this candle spell will take your lovemaking to new heights. If you wish to attract someone with whom to share these wonderful, long, fanciful nights, this can certainly get things rolling. This spell is all about the erotic side of Venus—she is more than just love and romance: Venus is also endless nights of sensual pleasure.

CANDLE COLOR: Red, pink, yellow.

CLEANSING: Red rose water, sugar, a few drops of your perfume. If you are already with a lover, then add a few drops of his or her perfume or cologne.

Midnight

DEITY: Venus, Oshun, Erzulie, Aphrodite, exotic gypsy spirits.

OIL: Passionate Lover's, Voluptuous Venus, Love Me, strawberry.

INCENSE: Venus, Erzulie Love, Oshun, strawberry.

FEEDING: Iron filings, honey, a drop of molasses, sugar, and cinnamon powder.

Midnight Spell

ITEMS NEEDED

> A letter of intention
> A bowl
> Honey
> Whole or powdered orris root (Orris root can be bought from any shop that carries herbal supplies. It is actually the root of an iris flower.)
> Red wine
> Shavings of dark chocolate
> Red rose petals

CASTING THE SPELL: Light your incense, write your letter, and place it in the bowl. Add the honey to sweeten your love life and the orris root to strengthen your love bond. Now take a sip of the red wine in honor of the Goddess, and pour some of it into the bowl. Add the chocolate for decadence, and scatter the red rose petals for romance over the wine. Light the candle and say the incantation.

INCANTATION

> I avail myself to the total abandonment of love, lust, and erotic fantasy. My lover and I will experience passionate and tender devotion. With total magnetism we will court a new dance of passion, making love in endless dreams of delight.

MIDNIGHT (FOR ATTRACTION)

Use the "Midnight" Seal on page 96.

To find that somebody special who feels the same way you do about love, sex, and romance.

PURPOSE: For a single person looking for a new love, Midnight will allow you to meet a person who shares your desire for physical intimacy. If you are looking for a permanent relationship, this candle spell will be helpful as well. The beauty of these spells is that your letter of intention explains the specificities and details of your particular request.

CANDLE COLOR: Red, yellow, pink.

CLEANSING: Water, a few drops of your perfume (if it is a spray then spray it once or twice), and a few drops of the oil you choose to anoint your candle with.

DEITY: Erzulie, Venus, Aphrodite, Oshun.

OIL: Enchantment, Midnight, Goddess of Love.

INCENSE: Erzulie, Goddess of Love, opium, rose, musk, or lilac.

FEEDING: Iron filings, chocolate syrup, sugar, toenail clippings (one will do).

Midnight Attraction Spell

ITEMS NEEDED

  A letter of intention
  A bowl
  Sugar and cinnamon powder mixed together
  White musk powder (Botanicas and some occult shops supply
    this. An alternative would be to use a white sachet powder
    into which you stir a few drops of musk oil.)
  Allspice berries
  Sparkling rosé wine
  Seven whole mini red carnations
  Gold glitter

Light your incense, then write your letter of intention and place it in the bowl. Place your candle on top and sprinkle the cinnamon sugar combination on top of the letter to fire up your attraction. Follow with the white musk powder, for more mystery and allure. Add the allspice berries to bring the power of magnetism. Pour in the sparkling rosé wine, and float the heads of the seven mini carnations in the wine. Sprinkle gold glitter over the flowers and wine and light your candle, saying the incantation.

INCANTATION

I invoke thee, Goddess of Love. Through my sighs I shall raise a song of passion. As the incense smoke rises it carries my moans of delight to inspire a lover unique and rare to find. As we begin our caress, it is the moment that inspires heavenly nights to begin ever onward.

FEMME BLANCHE

To clear karma from love.

PURPOSE: This candle is to help resolve old traumas and karma regarding one's love life. It can be from your recent past (your current lifetime), or perhaps karma from a past life. You can find out if there is bad karma from your past life from a reading done for you by a psychic or a good astrologer. Or it may just be intuition. Either way, there may be old lessons you are having a hard time learning. Sometimes we just keep repeating the same mistakes in relationships. For example, your lover may not call for a few days and you respond by calling him or her constantly. This furthers the problem by letting him or her take advantage of you. Another

Femme Blanche

problem could be incessant jealousy on either person's part. These and other common relationship problems may go deeper than just the current relationship. They could be past life problems, and Femme Blanche can help.

This High Priestess of the High Places, the all-knowing White Lady, will help restore balance to your life. Femme Blanche is a Haitian aspect of Erzulie, or a White Venus. I have found through my work with her that she is more concerned with affairs of the emotions of love that cause problems in the head and then subsequently in your life. This is why when we keep repeating past-life problems and there are mistakes we keep making it is time to turn to Femme Blanche.

CANDLE COLOR: White

CLEANSING: Clear water, a block of camphor or camphor oil, Florida water.

OIL: Femme Blanche, Obatala, White Tara. *carnation*

INCENSE: White Tara, sandalwood, Obatala.

FEEDING: Camphor, cascarilla (powdered eggshell), sugar, honey.

Femme Blanche Spell

This is a special drawing spell that will require two bowls. Its intent is to draw away the old negative patterns that keep resurfacing in your life. One bowl should be twice the size of the other. Femme Blanche will draw all of the bad energy away from you. This will clear the way for a cleaner, more productive personal life.

ITEMS NEEDED

- Two bowls, one large, one small
- Letter of intention
- White sugar
- Clear water
- One block of camphor
- 3 slices from a stick of cocoa butter
- Cascarilla (powdered eggshell)
- White flower petals
- White scarf or handkerchief

CASTING THE SPELL: Incense should be lit during the preparation of this spell. First, to see if you have the proper bowl sizes, place the smaller bowl on your altar (or wherever you will be doing your spell). Now take the larger bowl, and invert it over the smaller bowl. Is there room between the two bowls? Is the bowl on top stable, with its edges on your work surface, rather than on the smaller bowl? Is the~~inverted~~ bottom of the top bowl large enough to place your candle on? If you answered yes to these questions, then your bowls are good, safe tools to use for this spell.

Light your incense and pass both bowls through the incense smoke to purify them. Pass your letter of intention through the incense smoke and place it in the smaller bowl. Next, add the white sugar, clear water, camphor, cocoa butter, cascarilla, and white flower petals. Next, turn the larger bowl upside-down and place it over the smaller one. Place the white scarf over the bowl and put your candle securely on top. Light your candle and say the incantation.

INCANTATION

Oh Mother of high and holy places, Mother whose feet are so holy and unhindered by earthly matters that they do not touch the ground, it is to you whom I come to with my needs. Impart thy high wisdom to my life and clear all matters that restrict me and hold me back.

HYPNOTIQUE

To seduce a passionate lover.

PURPOSE: Use this spell to mesmerize someone you want and to inspire him or her to abandon themselves to passion. I especially recommend this candle for men who want to spice up their love lives. If you are already in a relationship and you want to heat things up, this spell is very potent.

CANDLE COLOR: Red, pink, purple.

CLEANSING: Water, sugar, red rose water, a tablespoon of brandy.

DEITY: Erzulie, Aphrodite, Venus, Sirens.

OIL: All Night Long, Commanding Love, Voodoo Nights, jasmine, gardenia, honeysuckle.

INCENSE: All Night Long, Bewitching, Aphrodite, gardenia.

FEEDING: Iron filings, honey, rose petals, lovage herb.

Hypnotique Spell

ITEMS NEEDED

Hypnotique

A letter of intention
A bowl
Lovage
Seven red-and-white-striped
   peppermints
Water
Brandy
Red and white flower petals
   (like red-and-white-striped
   carnations)

Light your incense during the preparation of this spell. Pass the letter of intention through the incense smoke and place it in the bowl. Put the candle in the bowl. Sprinkle the lovage over the letter. Unwrap the seven mints and place them around the candle. Add the water and then some brandy. Scatter the flower petals around the candle. Now light the candle, saying the incantation.

INCANTATION

Cast the fire into my spell to make your heart burn bright with love for me tonight. As I do say these words my gaze penetrates you and grips you by your very soul, and your heart and mine intertwine.

LOVE OUANGA

A magnetic charm to light your way to love.

PURPOSE: To draw two people closer together. This is a calling spell, which means it is used to appeal to the Gods to bind two people together. This spell has incredible drawing powers. An ouanga is actually a red charm bag that is used to draw whatever the user may want. In this case it is love. My first knowledge of an ouanga bag comes from New Orleans Voodoo. Another name for it is a conjure bag or a gris-gris bag. Since 1971 I have used ouanga bags for spell and herbal charm work.

CANDLE COLOR: Red or pink.

CLEANSING: Lavender water, a few drops of the oil you chose to dress your candle, sugar.

DEITY: Eros and Venus

OIL: Rhea's Love Haunt, Voluptuous Venus, Arabian Nights, strawberry, gardenia, camelia, mimosa.

Love Ouanga

INCENSE: Goddess of Love, Bewitching, Rhea's Love Haunt, musk, rose, lilac, lavender.

FEEDING: Iron filings, honey, lavender flowers, cinnamon powder.

Love Ouanga Spell

ITEMS NEEDED

A letter of intention
A bowl
Two paper dolls, one to represent each of you. Write the names and draw a heart on each doll.
Two lodestones

Whole or powdered orris root	Basil
Cinnamon stick or powder	Lemon balm
Whole chile peppers	Red wine
Lavender flowers	Red rose petals

CASTING THE SPELL: Place the letter of intention in the bowl, and place the two paper dolls face to face on top of the letter. Now add the candle on top. Place the two lodestones at the base of the candle glass inside the bowl. Next to this, place the orris root, cinnamon stick and whole chile peppers. Now sprinkle the lavender, basil, and lemon balm into the bowl.

Add enough red wine to cover, and arrange the red rose petals around the candle. Light the wick and let the magick of love begin. Say the incantation.

INCANTATION

I call thee forth oh love of mine, lips to lips sealed in a passionate kiss spreading desire and thrills throughout our bodies. I cast a spell of love so intoxicating that we cannot bear to be apart.

LOVE OUANGA (TO MEET SOMEONE NEW)

Use the "Love Ouanga" seal on page 103.

To draw a love close to your heart.

PURPOSE: To make a love charm to find a new love. Previously we used this seal to draw a lover and you closer. By changing the spell a little I am going to show you how to use it to attract new lovers to your side. If you choose to work with Oshun in this spell, then the candle color will be yellow. If you choose to work with Erzulie, then the color will be pink. You can also make and light both a pink and a yellow candle if you really want to get the message out there.

CANDLE COLOR: Yellow or pink. Mettalic Gold (Oshun)

CLEANSING: Water, Florida water Cologne, Flor De Naranja (orange blossom cologne).

DEITY: Oshun, Erzulie.

OIL: Cleopatra, Oshun, Erzulie, Voodoo Nights, ylang-ylang, peach, muguet.

INCENSE: Erzulie, Oshun, Aphrodite, Tramp.

FEEDING: Iron filings, honey, Come to Me Powder, five pennies.

Love Ouanga New Love Spell

ITEMS NEEDED

A letter of intention	Rosemary
A bowl	Sunflower petals
A paper heart with your	(for Oshun)
name on it	Pink rose petals
Five small gold safety pins	(for Erzulie)
Cinnamon powder mixed	Honey
with sugar	Champagne

First, light your incense. Place your letter of intention in the bowl. Inside the paper heart, draw a pentagram (a five pointed star *without* a circle around it). This will represent you. With one of your safety pins, pierce the tip of the top point of the pentagram and say:

I pierce my senses with the glow of attraction.

Leave the safety pin in place. Next pierce each of the points, working your way clockwise around the star leaving the pins in place, saying:

These are my five senses, I will reinvent my life to hook the love I want.

Place the heart over your letter of intention and place your candle on top.

Sprinkle the cinnamon sugar over the letter and add the rosemary and sunflower petals or rose petals.

Taste the honey and pour it in the bowl. Add the champagne to the bowl on top of the other ingredients and light your candle. Say the incantation.

INCANTATION

I fill my cup of life with champagne, romance, and the lover of
my dreams.

LOVE HEALING

Love heals all wounds.

PURPOSE: To heal a love relationship that has been ripped apart.
Sometimes there are outside forces that can harm a relationship—
those who would cast dark magick or send you negative energy out of
jealousy or vengefulness with the sole purpose of separating you and
your loved one. But more often the cause of separation is just that too
many troubles have caused a rift. Whether the harm has been done
from the outside or from the inside, work this spell. Sometimes it
will return a relationship to what it was before it went awry. If this
is not possible, the candle will heal your broken heart so that love
may grow anew.

Love Healing

CANDLE COLOR: Pink, white, green, blue.

DEITY: Erzulie, Tara, Venus, Kwan Yin.

OIL: Love Healing, rose quartz, Serenity, carnation, lavender, muguet, or magnolia. Across the miles

INCENSE: Love Healing, Helping Hand, peach, sandalwood, lavender.

CLEANSING: Water, Peace Water, Lavender Water, Rose Water

FEEDING: Pink or red rose petals, sugar, honey, camphor.

Love Healing Spell

ITEMS NEEDED

A letter of intention
A bowl
Sugar
Spring water
Peace water

Rose water
Lavender water
Florida water
Pink or white rose petals

CASTING THE SPELL: Light the incense, and pass your written letter through the smoke. Place the letter in the bowl. Now add the sugar and the spring water, followed by the Peace water, rose water, lavender water, and Florida water. Now add the rose petals. Light the candle and say the incantation.

INCANTATION

Let the healing rays of the Universe extend out to the heavens on high. As it reaches the heart pulse of the Goddess [name of Goddess] may she reply by extending her loving rays back to us who are sad and forlorn, broken with sorrows. Send thy aid of healing love to us who are in disrepair and make our hearts whole again in loving communication.

Love healing can be used for more than bringing lovers back together. I have applied this special magick to many different situations. Children from other marriages often resent a new love coming into your life—they want their parents back together, or they are used to having just the one parent. I include the children on the candle with both of the names of the new couple. I call this family therapy. Having a problem with your boss? If you used to get along and things are going sour, a little love healing may be just the ticket. Parent-child relationships are often difficult. This works great for kids and parents of all ages. If you are having an unresolved issue and the person is no longer reachable, then do this spell for healing and resolve so that you no longer suffer.

Following are some variations of spells you might want to use with a Love Healing Candle. Choose the candle color according to the candle color guide that you feel best suits your needs.

LOVE HEALING NO. 2

Use the "Love Healing" seal on page 106.

To soothe and calm angry tempers.

PURPOSE: Sometimes a person is just angry and needs to be healed. This is also good for couples who are too angry to communicate.

CANDLE COLOR: Blue or white.

CLEANSING: Water, lavender water, sugar, a few drops of Peace Oil.

DEITY: Kwan Yin, Tara, Yemaya, Mother of All Peace.

OIL: Peace, Love Healing, Peace and Protection, Crystal Healing, lavender, carnation, and neroli.

INCENSE: Peace, Love Healing, lavender, Crystal Healing.

FEEDING: Camphor, sugar, cascarilla (powdered eggshell), white carnation petals.

Love Healing for Angry Tempers Spell

ITEMS NEEDED

   A letter of intention
   A bowl

Blue or white Love Healing Candle
Water
Lavender water
Peace water (Peace water is a product sold in botanicas or occult
   shops. If you cannot find Peace water, you can make it
   yourself. Take a glass of water, add a few drops of Peace oil to
   it. Place a white cloth or paper towel over the glass of water.
   Pray to the Mother of All Peace by saying "I banish all heavy-
   hearted hate and unwanted life forms from this water now.
   Let it be a vehicle of the Mother of all Peace, and pervading
   tranquility, as I use it now.")
A few drops of blue food coloring
Camphor
A few eucalyptus leaves
One ice cube
One white flower (a carnation or mum)

CASTING THE SPELL: Light your incense. Take your letter of intention and place it in the bowl. Place the candle on top of the letter.
Add the water, lavender water, and Peace water into the bowl. Add
the blue food coloring till you achieve a shade of blue that is appealing to your eye. This is a spell that requires your own magickal choice
of the right color blue. Now float the camphor and eucalyptus leaves
in the bowl and add the ice cube. If your bowl is fairly large then you
may add more ice. Be careful not to let the bowl overflow. If there is
room, you may float the flower in the bowl. If not, just scatter the
petals on top of the water.

To start the spell take several deep, relaxing breaths and focus
your mind's eye on your subject. Visualize this person surrounded in
the serene blue water you have just created. Light the candle and say
the incantation.

INCANTATION

   Mother of All Pervading Peace, place these souls upon your
   ferry, and carry them across the sea of sorrow. Uplift their spirits
   and quench their anger. Oh merciful mother of us all shine your
   compassionate light upon [names] so that the love-healing rays of
   your heart center may go out to my love.

LOVE HEALING NO. 3

Use the "Love Healing" seal on page 106.

A Love Healing for death and dying.

PURPOSE: To heal someone who has experienced the loss of a loved one and to help the departed soul travel on in a safe journey to the Summerland. It will continue to allow contact with the departed in a structured and healthy manner. The grief process is difficult when someone is getting ready to make that journey across. Love Healing will assist the person who is dying by diminishing fear, as well as help loved ones who are grieving during the transitional period from life to death.

CANDLE COLOR: White, green, pink, blue.

CLEANSING: Lavender water, Glory water, salt, and a few drops of the oil you choose to dress your candle with.

DEITY: Tara, Kwan Yin, Mother of Mercy (Virgin Mercedes).

OIL: White Tara, Obatala (Virgin Mercedes), lotus, sandalwood.

INCENSE: Crystal Healing, amethyst, White Tara, sandalwood, white sage.

FEEDING: White chrysanthemum petals, camphor, one drop of olive oil, teaspoon of salt.

Love Healing for Death and Dying Spell

ITEMS NEEDED

A letter of intention	Water
A drawing of a boat with your loved one in it	Salt
A bowl	White flower petals or any whole flower that floats

CASTING THE SPELL: First a few words about the drawing of the boat—a simple line drawing is fine. Its meaning is symbolic; you don't have to be a skilled artist for it to be effective. The boat represents the ferry of the Goddess of compassion. Think of it as the boat of the Buddha Tara, who carries souls across the waters to safety. The wood of the symbolic boat is an aspect of the triple will of the Goddess. "From me all things come and to me all things return." The triple will of the goddess is to be a maiden which expresses our youth, to be a mother which expresses our age of responsibility, and to be the crone which expresses our years of wisdom and the end of our stage here on Earth. An alternative: if you are good at origami, you can make a paper boat instead.

Pass the letter, the drawing, and the bowl through the incense smoke. Put the line drawing inside the letter and fold it in half. Place this in the bowl, and put the candle on top. Pour in the water, and add three pinches of salt for purification. Add the white flower. Light the candle and blow your breath upon the water in the bowl. Do this nine times to represent completion. Say the incantation.

INCANTATION

I have gone beyond the moon, and I saw the realms of the compassionate shining one. I will not be sad for you because you are free of the fetters that bind and tie. Go beyond the moon to the great one who shines her everlasting light in to our hearts. So Mote It Be.

EMPRESS OF LOVE

To invoke an abundance of love and happiness.

PURPOSE: With this spell, we are aspiring to awaken the Goddess of Love in one of her rare but most opulent forms. When asked, the Goddess of Love can grant many things, including wealth. This seal is used to invoke Oshun in one of her more voluptuous aspects to give you love, money, and blessings. The other Goddesses mentioned are synchronized with Oshun, so you can call upon any one of the names listed without insult to the deity. It's like having a different name depending on where you go. For this spell, the Goddess of Love is manifesting as the glorious beauty of the hosts of the heavens. She is shedding her light, which is pure love and inspiration, on all beings. She can grant love, enhance a love relationship, and bless a marriage. She gives financial blessings to those who ask of her.

CANDLE COLOR: Yellow

CLEANSING: Water, Rose water, honey, one tablespoon of milk, a few drops of sweet almond oil.

DEITY: Oshun, Venus, Aphrodite, Erzulie.

OIL: Oshun, Venus, Ambrosia, rose, peach, neroli, cinnamon, anise, almond.

INCENSE: Goddess of Love, La Flamme, Oshun, honeysuckle, jasmine.

FEEDING: Iron filings, five copper pennies, honey, the petals of a yellow flower.

Empress

Empress of Love Spell

ITEMS NEEDED

A letter of intention
5 sugar cubes
A plate and a bowl (the plate should be larger than the bowl—a large dinner plate and a small cereal bowl, for example)

Honey
Yellow flower petals
Gold and copper glitter
Brandy

CASTING THE SPELL: Light incense and pass the letter of intention through the smoke. Then pass the five sugar cubes through the incense smoke. Place your letter of intention in the bowl and put your bowl in the middle of the plate. Put the candle on top of the letter in the bowl. Taste the honey and pour a generous amount into the bowl as you say: "Oh gracious goddess of love and blessings, I offer you this honey to sweeten the lives of [say the name of the person for whom you are you are doing the spell)." Your candle will burn in a bowl of honey. Scatter the yellow flower petals on top and sprinkle the glitter over it all.

The next part is tricky and I advise you to do it with patience and care. Place the five sugar cubes around the perimeter of the plate. Put a few drops of brandy on each sugar cube—but not too much or it will dissolve the sugar cube. Light your candle, and light each cube of sugar to the glory of the Goddess. This sugar offering can be repeated every day until the candle has finished burning. As you light the candle and the sugar cubes, say the incantation.

INCANTATION

I light up like a candle burning when we make love. Our bodies move in one fluid motion as we harmonize in the night. Together we make this offering to you, oh Goddess of love, romance and blessings from above.

Visualize the lovely Goddess shining above you, shedding her golden rays of loving abundance.

SPELLBOUND

To catch a new love.

PURPOSE: To catch a new love or ensnare one already there. Suddenly you will be able to clearly see the people that are around you. You will have created a web to snare what has been whizzing by you. It puts you in touch with people who may not have noticed you before. This spell will help you weave your own web of love and intrigue. This spell will not bring anyone against their will, but it will draw many possibilities to you. When carving this candle you must remember not to weave deception or ill will for another. In short, if there is someone you wish to attract or hold and they are unavailable, then look for someone else.

CANDLE COLOR: Red, pink, purple.

CLEANSING: Water, red wine, a couple of dashes of Tabasco sauce or red pepper, sugar.

DEITY: Arachne, Erzulie, Love Nymphs, Venus.

OILS: Fire of Love, Sirens, Spellbound, wisteria, jasmine, patchouli, narcissus.

INCENSE: Cleopatra, Leather and Lace, Come to Me, Tramp.

FEEDING: Iron filings, Love powder, sugar, a pinch of cinquefoil.

Spellbound Spell

ITEMS NEEDED

    A letter of intention
    A bowl
    Honey
    Red wine
    Petals from a dark red
       flower
    Wormwood

Spellbound

CASTING THE SPELL: The incense should be lit during the preparation of this spell. Take the letter of intention and place it in the bowl. Put your candle on top and scatter the wormwood over the letter. Add a generous amount of honey and then sprinkle drops of red wine on top. They should be small droplets to represent the sacrifice to your cause. Now place the red flower petals on the honey, light your candle, and speak the incantation, all the while envisioning your new lover ensnared in your embrace.

INCANTATION

    Oh Universal Mother of the Web, spin me a web of love to catch a man/woman who is strong, faithful, single, and secure. I ask thee to send me someone to hold me as I embrace them in my web of love tonight.

COME TO ME

To draw someone you desire.

PURPOSE: The name speaks for itself. The magick helps you attain the object of your desire. Whether you want to call someone to you whom you already know and have desired for a long time, or wish to attract a new love, this seal will have a powerful influence. This candle spell can also reconnect you with a straying mate.

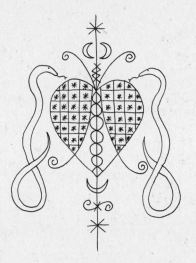

CANDLE COLOR: Red, pink, yellow.

CLEANSING: Red wine, sugar, Red Rose Water.

DEITY: Erzulie, Venus, Aphrodite, Oshun.

OILS: Come to Me, Witch Love, Silk, All Night Long, musk, lilac, honeysuckle, jasmine, ambergris, and gardenia.

Come to Me

INCENSE: Come to Me, Bewitching, All Night Long, musk, patchouli.

FEEDING: Iron filings, honey, musk powder, cinnamon powder.

Come to Me Spell

ITEMS NEEDED

Some of your hair	Honey
A letter of intention	Cloves
Sugar	Allspice berries
A bowl	Red wine
Fresh cherries (optional)	Red cherry wine
A handful of almonds	

CASTING THE SPELL: Light your incense. Take some of your hair and place it on the letter of intention. Add a spoonful of sugar over the hair. Fold the letter and place it in the bottom of the bowl. Put your candle on top of the letter in the bowl. If you were able to get fresh cherries then add them to the bowl. Add the almonds and drizzle honey over everything. Next, add the cloves and allspice berries, and pour in a small amount (about a shot glass full) of the red wine and then the cherry wine. Each day pour a fresh glass of cherry wine in a glass next to your candle as an offering to the goddess. When the last of the wine is offered leave that glass until the candle is done. (If leaving the glass troubles you, the wine may be disposed of the next day with no consequences.)

Light the candle and say the incantation.

INCANTATION

Come to me! Come! Come! Come to me now! Over land or by moonlit sea, answer the ancient call, answer unto me.

COME TO ME NO. 2

Use the Come to Me Seal on page 115, the Love Healing Seal on page 106, and the Sorceress Seal on page 131.

To reunite lovers.

PURPOSE: To reunite two estranged lovers. This seal can be combined with a Love Healing Seal and a Sorceress Seal to add an extra-special message of love that is tough to resist. When you really want to send the message out that you want to repair a torn romance, this candle packs a lot of power. As I've mentioned before, you cannot force someone back against their will, but this sends a strong message of your desire to work things out.

CANDLE COLOR: Red, pink, yellow, purple.

CLEANSING: Water, vetivert, Red Rose Cologne, sugar.

DEITY: Erzulie, Venus, Aphrodite, Oshun.

OILS: Come to Me, San Cipriano, Rhea's Love Haunt, jasmine, musk, patchouli, camelia, gardenia.

INCENSE: Come to Me, Aphrodite, Venus, strawberry, rose.

FEEDING: Iron filings, Commanding Powder, honey, vetivert.

Come to Me Reuniting Spell

ITEMS NEEDED

A photocopy of a picture of your lover
Commanding powder (if you can't find commanding powder at a
    botanica or occult shop, then make your own by adding a few
    drops of Commanding oil to some orris root powder or talc)
A letter of intention
A bowl
Honey
Coriander seeds
Star Anise
Myrtle
Cinnamon sticks or powder
Red wine

CASTING THE SPELL: Incense should be lit while preparing for this spell, as well as during the ritual. Take the photocopy of your lover and draw the Come to Me Seal right over the picture; sprinkle the Commanding Powder over it. Carefully fold the picture in quarters and place it on top of your letter of intention. Now fold the letter of intention over the picture, and pass the packet through the incense smoke. Place it in the bowl and put your candle on top. Add the honey to the bowl—pour a nice amount, covering the packet. Add the coriander seeds, star anise, myrtle, and cinnamon, and sprinkle in some more Commanding powder. Finally add some red wine. Next to the bowl, place a glass of red wine with honey and cinnamon sticks as an offering to the Goddess of Love. (When the candle is finished you may dispose of the red wine offering by pouring it into the earth.)

When lighting the candle say the incantation.

INCANTATION

    I conjure thee, my love, to come to me now; I command you by the forces of Erzulie, to return to me, whose arms await to embrace you in my circle of love. Do not let others turn you away from our love. Return to me. Come abide by my side. I, who love you without question, bid you come back to me.

SAPPHO'S LOVE

For divine lesbian love.

PURPOSE: This is to draw lesbian love to you. Love, sex, and fantasy are a part of the magick here. The other intention of this candle is to find a companion and mate who can share a life with you.

CANDLE COLOR: Red, pink, yellow, purple.

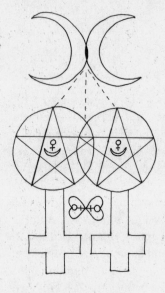

Sappho's Love

CLEANSING: Water, wine, and a few drops of the oil you use to dress your candle.

DEITY: Sappho was a living woman who was the first woman to openly praise lesbian love in poetry. She lived on the Island of Lesbos. Other deities who I have also found to be sympathetic to lesbian love are the Yoruban Goddess Oya, Oshun, Aphrodite, Britomartis, Kwan Yin, Lakshmi, Venus, and of course Erzulie. I have invoked their aid for different lesbian clients over the years and they have always responded quite favorably.

OIL: Sappho, Venus, lotus, wisteria, lavender, camelia, carnation, muguet, almond, and ambergris.

INCENSE: All Night Long, Venus, lotus, lavender, honeysuckle.

FEEDING: Iron filings, sugar, rose petals.

Sappho's Love Spell

ITEMS NEEDED

A letter of intention
  describing what you desire
A bowl
Sugar
Bay leaves

Passion flower herb
Periwinkle herb
Two orris roots
Rosé wine
One pink carnation

CASTING THE SPELL: Incense should be lit during the casting of this spell. Write your letter. Fold it and put it in the bottom of the bowl. Now place your candle on top of the letter. Pour some sugar on top of the letter, and place a few bay leaves around the candle. Add the passion flower herb, periwinkle herb, and the two orris roots. Take a sip of the wine and pour it in the bowl. Lastly, pull the carnation apart and sprinkle the petals all around your candle.

Light the candle and allow your magick to flow. Speak the incantation.

INCANTATION

Sappho, I ask of you to bring love here, I am lonely and forlorn. A sister of a kindred spirit is what I desire. To embrace me in her arms and to share love's glow with one that I know.

LOVE HEALING WITH SAPPHO

Use the Sappho's Love Seal on page 118 and the Love Healing Seal on page 106.

Love healing for lesbians.

PURPOSE: To restore love and heal a lesbian relationship. This spell is designed with focus on the special needs in a relationship between two women. Carve the Sappho's Love Seal on one side of the candle, and on the other side draw the Love Healing Seal. Write both of your names on both seals.

CANDLE COLOR: Pink or white.

CLEANSING: Water, carnation oil, sugar.

DEITY: Sappho.

OILS: Love healing, carnation, ylang-ylang, camelia, gardenia, chamomile.

INCENSE: Love Healing, Blessing, or carnation.

FEEDING: Iron filings, pink carnation petals, white sugar.

Sappho's Love Healing Spell

ITEMS NEEDED

Your letter of intention
A bowl
A camphor block, crumbled
Cascarilla or (powdered
    eggshell)

Rosemary leaves
Sugar
Pink champagne
White or pink carnation
    petals

CASTING THE SPELL: Write your letter of intention and light the incense. Place the letter in the bowl. Sprinkle the camphor, cascarilla, rosemary leaves, and sugar on top of the letter. Pour in the pink champagne and add the carnation petals. Light your candle and envision healing energy emanating from your candle. Speak the incantation.

INCANTATION

Oh Sappho, I ask that your wisdom act as a healing balm of love and compassion to reunite us in body, heart and soul.

SAPPHO'S WISDOM

Use Sappho's Love Seal on page 118.

For courage in coming out of the closet

PURPOSE: Sometimes we need guidance on understanding our lesbian lives. This candle is very beneficial for gay women who are just coming out. No matter how old you are this can be a tough time in your life. Change is never easy. For those of you who are already out but still have troubles with being gay or just need some help in your lesbian lifestyle, this will help. Even though laws are changing very often, and more and more people have come to accept the gay community, there are still those who don't. If they have any influence over your life then it is sometimes hard to be who you are. I have personally known many gays and lesbians who have been disowned by their families, and many of today's runaway youths are tragically unwanted. Sometimes employers find out you are gay and suddenly everyone at work treats you differently.

CANDLE COLOR: White

CLEANSING: Water, sugar, and a few drops of the oil you chose to dress your candle.

DEITY: Sappho

OIL: Ancient Wisdom, lotus or sandalwood.

INCENSE: Blessing, sandalwood, or lavender.

FEEDING: Iron filings, honey, lavender flowers.

Sappho's Wisdom Spell

ITEMS NEEDED

A letter of your intention
A bowl
Honey
Crumbled camphor

Lavender flowers
Water
One to two drops of red food
  coloring.

CASTING THE SPELL: Light the incense and place your letter in the bowl. Place your candle on top of the letter. Pour the honey over the letter, and add the camphor and lavender flowers. Pour the water in and add enough food coloring to turn the water pink. Light your candle and let the wisdom of compassion and patience be your guide. Then say the incantation.

INCANTATION

Oh Sappho, I implore of you to lend your ancient wisdom to help me with my cause. To be free as the wind blows without any restrictions upon my choices whatsoever. Let those who do not understand not impede me in my natural process of love.

BOYS' NIGHT OUT

For gay men who want to draw a new love to their lives.

PURPOSE: Male mysteries—the special magick that two men can share—are of a very unique nature. This seal has been used to invoke the companionship between two men with love, lust, and a lasting relationship.

If you are a gay man, are currently not in a relationship, and wish to attract a lover then this seal is great for you. You can also use any one of the other love attraction seals along with this. Boys' Night Out is also helpful if you are just coming out. It can help give you clarity, confidence, and protection from those who are less understanding than you'd like them to be.

Boys' Night Out

CANDLE COLOR: Red or pink.

CLEANSING: Water, red wine, cinnamon oil, pinch of iron filings.

DEITY: Pan, Satyrs, Dionysus, Hyakintos (the Lily Prince).

OIL: All Night Long, La Flamme, hyacinth, musk, patchouli, vanilla, peach, strawberry.

INCENSE: All Night Long, La Flamme, Love Attraction.

FEEDING: Iron filings, cinnamon powder, honey.

Boys' Night Out Spell

ITEMS NEEDED

A letter of intention to your
  deity of choice
A bowl
Honey
Damiana

Master of the Woods herb
  (can be found in many
  occult or herbal shops)
Red wine

CASTING THE SPELL: Light your incense. Let the smoke surround you and fill you as you write your letter of intention. When finished, place your letter in the bottom of the bowl and place the prepared candle on top of the letter. Taste the honey and pour it over the letter while saying your love's name (or while envisioning the type of person you would like to bring into your life). Add the damiana and Master of the Woods herb to honey. Take a sip of the wine to commune with the great god Pan, and pour the wine into the bowl. Say the incantation and light your candle, letting the magick of lust and love vibrate out to the universe and answer your love call.

INCANTATION

Oh Lord of Lust, Love and yearning, hear my plea and answer unto me, oh Lord of the Magickal Dance. So that my love and I may become entranced in your sacred rituals of masculine mystery.

BOYS' NIGHT OUT NO. 2

Use the Boys' Night Out Seal on page 122.

A coming-out spell for gay men.

PURPOSE: To help alleviate some of the pressure of coming out of the closet. This can be a difficult time for gays or lesbians of any age. Announcing your sexual preference to family and friends can be stressful, painful, and confusing. This spell not only helps give you the courage you will need, but also helps heal those around you so a smoother transition can be made. This spell can also be done on behalf of a gay friend who is having trouble coming out.

CANDLE COLOR: White or pink.

CLEANSING: Water, white lavender water, a few drops of hyacinth oil.

DEITY: Hyakintos, Dionysus.

OIL: Hyacinth, Love Healing, Delight Oil, strawberry, gardenia, musk, allspice.

INCENSE: Love Healing, Blessing, lavender.

FEEDING: Camphor, honey, white chrysanthemum petals.

Boys' Night Out Coming Out Spell

ITEMS NEEDED

A letter of intention	White sugar
A bowl	White lavender water
Camphor	White chrysanthemum petals

CASTING THE SPELL: Take your letter and place it in the bottom of the bowl; place your candle on top. Now add the camphor and white sugar. Pour in the white lavender water, and finally, scatter the white mum petals around the bowl. Light your candle and let the healing transformation begin. Say the incantation.

INCANTATION

Oh Lord Dionysus, I humbly ask of thee thy assistance in this, my deed: To come out and be free of all restraints and fears. So that I may walk with my face held high up in the sun and receive your grace.

CHAMPAGNE

To make your love life sparkle and dazzle!

PURPOSE: This seal has been named after the rejuvenating effects of romantic champagne. This candle will help to restore a relationship that has gone stale and will add renewed romance. If your mate is not willing to accept that changes need to be made, then this candle will help entice him or her to seek that new spark you are trying to ignite.

CANDLE COLOR: Red or pink.

CLEANSING: Water, rose water, and a few drops of rose or musk oil.

DEITY: Venus, Aphrodite, Erzulie.

OIL: Venus, La Flamme, rose, gardenia, musk, muguet, wisteria, jasmine.

INCENSE: Venus, musk or rose.

Champagne

Champagne Spell

To recapture the joy of that first blush of love is the intention of this spell. It would help if you also committed some Venusian acts of self-indulgence—change your hairstyle, get a manicure or pedicure, take a long luxurious bath—whatever makes you feel goddesslike. Now, start planning some romantic time alone with your lover. New, sexy lingerie will definitely help set the mood. This is something you can be creative with. Take your time and execute the plan wisely.

ITEMS NEEDED

A letter of intention	Sugar
A bowl	A small split of champagne
Coriander seeds	Red or pink rose petals
Mistletoe	

7 foil-wrapped chocolate confections of your choosing. (I suggest chocolate-covered cherries, Rocher, Baci, or whatever is available. What is important is that both you and your lover like the candy you choose, as you will share this candy on your romantic evening alone.)

CASTING THE SPELL: Place your letter of intention in the bowl and put your candle on top of the letter. Sprinkle the coriander and mistletoe on the letter, add the sugar, and gently pour in the champagne. Let the foaming subside and add the rose petals. Place the seven chocolates around the outside of the bowl. Light your candle, and say the incantation to empower the spell.

INCANTATION

Oh lovely Goddess Venus, you who know all answers to love, rekindle the heart of [your beloved's name]. Speak of our love with passion and joy. Open the doors to love's desire so that we may find our hearts united in love again!

When you have your romantic evening in place, share six of the seven chocolates with your lover—three for each of you. Open a good bottle of champagne as well. The extra chocolate and a glass of champagne should be offered to the Goddess Venus by placing them next to your candle spell and announcing that the offerings are for her.

LADY SILK

Flirt and seduce a new love into your life!

PURPOSE: This spell is all about flirting. In the illustration of the seal is a fan in the center. In Victorian times, fans were commonly carried by ladies and had a language all their own. Women from many cultures used fans as a way of discreet communication for flirting. Fans can veil the face so just the eyes speak, or when a gentleman comes close, a woman can flutter her fan to indicate that he is making her hot with desire. To make this spell most advantageous for you, your desire must be to get out there and start shopping for a new love! Be open to all possibilities of networking and meeting people. If you have been tired, unmotivated, and are suffering from low self-esteem in social settings, then this candle is great for you.

Lady Silk

This candle and spell are meant to inspire you and allow you to change your life and get out there and be positive and vivacious!

CANDLE COLOR: Yellow, gold, pink.

CLEANSING: Water, a few drops of honey, and cinnamon powder.

DEITY: Oshun. She corresponds with the Virgin Mother Caridad Del Cobre.

OIL: Oshun, Lady Silk, Tramp, Spellbound, cinnamon, anise, musk, honeysuckle.

INCENSE: Oshun, jasmine, cinnamon.

FEEDING: Iron Filings, five copper pennies, honey, cinnamon powder, anise seeds.

Lady Silk Spell

This is a perfect candle if you already have someone in mind and you want to fan his or her desire. If you haven't met that right someone, then this will most certainly draw lovers to your side.

ITEMS NEEDED

A letter of intention to
   Oshun
A bowl
Unsalted pumpkin seeds
Star anise seed pods
Lovage

Deer's tongue
Cinnamon sticks
Honey
Yellow rose or
   chrysanthemum petals

CASTING THE SPELL: Light your incense and write your letter of intention to Oshun. Be respectful but be honest about your desires. She is known to grant love many times over, but if she deems your lover unacceptable for you she will not help you. Oshun holds her graces in very high esteem; she chooses her lovers with much consideration. She will treat you the same way.

Place the letter in the bowl, and place your candle on top. Scatter the pumpkin seeds, star anise, lovage, deer's tongue, and cinnamon sticks around the candle, then pour a generous amount of honey in the bowl. Place your flower petals on top, and light the candle, saying the incantation.

INCANTATION

I invoke the mysterious goddess Oshun, to use her magickal powers to fan the desires and intentions of [person's name] to see only me. Let the flame of this candle burn bright in the heart of [person's name] so that he/she is drawn to me only.

To meet someone new, follow the same recipe as above. When lighting the candle say this invocation:

> Oh lovely Goddess Oshun, mistress of love and passion, bring to me a love worthy of my heart, body, and soul. Fan the passions within so that we may be drawn to one another.

Keep your confidence high, as confidence is an important part of the spell. Know that you have much to offer and are worthy of someone very special to share yourself with. This inner knowledge is just as important an ingredient as the herbs and offerings. If you show the Goddess you lack this ingredient, then the first thing she will do is try to give you the ability to gain confidence and self-reliance so that you are truly ready for love.

SCARLETTE'S SEDUCTION

For total abandonment to your sexual fantasies.

PURPOSE: This candle is not about love; rather, it embraces primal lust, sex, and total fantasy. There are times in life where you may be feeling sexually frustrated. This could be for a number of reasons: personal inhibitions about sex, or perhaps the inability to discuss your intimate fantasies with your lover. This spell will unlock those doors and guide you to fulfilling your dreams. If you want to attract someone to help you make your fantasies real, Scarlette's Seduction will assist in that, too. If your intention also includes love, then you may want to carve a love seal on the other side of the candle.

Scarlette's Seduction

CANDLE COLOR: Red, purple.

CLEANSING: Water, red wine, one tablespoon of brandy, sugar.

DEITY: Venus, Aphrodite, Erzulie, Red Tara (Kurukula)

OIL: Scarlette's Seduction, Tramp, Leather and Lace, musk, gardenia, strawberry, cherry, jasmine, narcissus.

INCENSE: Scarlette's Seduction, Bewitching, All Night Long, musk, patchouli.

FEEDING: Iron filings, honey, cinnamon powder, and Vetiver herb.

Scarlette's Seduction Spell

ITEMS NEEDED

A letter of intention	Yerba mate
A bowl	Dry Hibiscus flowers
Honey	5 to 7 Cinnamon sticks
Red wine	White musk powder
Brandy	Sexy lingerie to wear during
Vetiver, cut into strips	this ritual (optional)

CASTING THE SPELL: Light your incense. Pass the letter through the incense smoke and place it in the bottom of the bowl. Put the candle on top. Now taste the honey and slowly pour it over the letter, saturating the letter with your decadent thoughts as you do so. Scatter the vetiver over the honey and add the cinnamon sticks, yerba mate, and hibiscus flowers. Sprinkle the white musk Powder over the herbs and honey. Next, take a sip of the brandy, swirl it around in your mouth, and think of the taste of your lover. Pour some over the honey. Add the red wine, tasting it with relish as you pour the rest into the bowl. Light your candle, and say the incantation.

INCANTATION

Darksome night and shining moon, take me to another room. Feel the passion in my soul, take me ever so bold, to my lover's waiting arms ever to enfold in rapture, bliss, and with a stolen kiss. Awaken in the Red Witch's Lair with your hands entwined in my hair. Braced against each other tight where we will love throughout the night.

Allow your candle to burn and picture the passion flowing from your body into your candle spell. Repeat this incantation and visualization every day until the candle is finished burning. Be honest with yourself and do not feel ashamed of your sexual fantasy. Let it flow and explore your own inner sanctums of lust and seduction.

SORCERESS

To reunite lovers.

PURPOSE: To return a straying mate, or reunite a separated couple through gentle domination magick. St. Martha Dominadora once saved a child caught in the mouth of a giant anaconda by tying up the snake's mouth with the ribbons from her dress. In the tarot, the Strength card is often depicted as a woman who has dominion over a lion through her sweetness and intelligence. Domination magick does not have to be about controlling another against his or her will. Instead it can be used as a gentle push toward healing.

Anyone who has suffered a setback or breakup in a marriage or relationship can tell you how painful it is. That is why this spell calls for real love from both of the couple to work best. Why real love? Without it the spell really will not work—I've said it before and I'll say

Sorceress

it again: *You cannot force anyone to do anything they really do not want to do.* You may be thinking, "If the couple really loves one another, then why would they need a spell at all?" Sometimes real love is just not enough to keep couples together. Each couple has a reason for separating. With St. Martha's help you may be able to work it out.

CANDLE COLOR: Green, red, or purple.

CLEANSING: Water, wine, vetiver cologne (Kolonia 1800 Con Vetiver can be found in most botanicas), Gardenia Cologne (Kolonia 1800 Gardenia), and sugar.

DEITY: Saint Martha Dominadora.

OIL: St. Martha, Bewitching, Call Me, Commanding, Leather and Lace, Witch Love, vetivert, gardenia, musk, and honeysuckle.

INCENSE: St. Martha, All Night Long, Gardenia.

FEEDING: Iron filings, cane syrup (melao), a teaspoon of brandy, one drop of menstrual blood or Dragon's Blood Powder.

Sorceress Spell

ITEMS NEEDED

A large plate
A letter of intention
A bowl
Cane syrup
Amansa guapo leaves or
   patchouli leaves
Garapata extract

Yohimbe extract
Do As I Say oil or narcissus
   oil
Plum or red wine
Purple flower petals
81 sugar cubes
Brandy

CASTING THE SPELL: First decide where you will be burning your candle for the next few days, and set the plate there. Place your letter of intention in the bottom of the bowl and place the bowl on the plate. Place the prepared candle on top of your letter of intention. Next, drizzle a small amount of cane syrup over the letter. Add the amansa guapo leaves (these may be hard to find, but a good botanica will usually carry them—if you cannot find them, patchouli leaves or root are just as good). Pour some garpata over the letter. (*Garpata* means "extract of a tick" because it "sticks" to you in a magickal sense.) Then sprinkle the yohimbe extract or powder onto the letter as well. (Yohimbe can usually be found in a health food store; it is an herbal sexual stimulant.) Add nine drops of the Do As I Say or narcissus oil, and repeat your lover's name nine times. Nine is the sacred number to St. Martha, and it represents accomplishment or completion in numerology. Add the wine, followed by the purple flower petals.

Place nine sugar cubes in a circle on the plate around the candle. Add a few drops of brandy to each cube, just enough to saturate the sugar, while saying your lover's name. Add a separate glass of wine next to the spell for the Goddess. Then light your sugar cubes, one at a time, while saying the incantation nine times.

The incantation and the burning of the sugar cubes should be repeated daily for the next nine days. If the candle is finished burning and you want to rid yourself of the spell you may dispose of it but continue to leave the sugar cubes on the plate as an offering to the Sorceress.

INCANTATION

Holy Mother Martha, Goddess of All Seduction, for the oil which you will consume today, for the oil which nourishes this candle lamp. For the wick, which burns away all impurities, I dedicate this candle and spell so that you may relieve me of my miseries and help me to overcome all difficulties. As you dominated the beast at your feet, give me health and work so that I may provide for my needs.

My Mother grant me that [name of beloved] may not live in peace until he/she comes to stand at my feet. This way, my Mother Goddess, for the love of my life, grant my petition and eliminate my miseries. So Mote It Be.

Oh Sorceress Martha, who entered the mountain and tied up the beast with your ribbons, I beg you to tie up and dominate [name of beloved].

Martha Dominadora, let them not sit in a chair nor lie in a bed until they are lying at my feet. Love's Mistress, hear me, help me, for the love of my life and the passion of my soul. So Mote It Be.

The original version of this prayer is available in Marc Benezra's *Helping Yourself With Selected Prayers*, Original Publications, 1995.

There can be any number of reasons why a couple may be separated. Besides the use of magick to help reunite lovers, I suggest couples counseling. If your mate or lover refuses to go for counseling with you, then go by yourself. You cannot change another person, but you can learn to change how you respond to that person. This is not an immediate cure, but if you are in the relationship for the long haul then it's worth taking the time to work things out. In the long run it will pay off.

SORCERESS (LOVE, BONDAGE, AND DECADENCE)

Use the Sorceress Seal on page 131.

For those who have a fondness for the darker side of love.

PURPOSE: Do you want to bring decadence to your life? Do alternative sexual lifestyles secretly thrill you? Then the Sorceress, who is actually another aspect of St. Martha, is here to help you find the right partner or bring more excitement and adventure to your current relationship. To find a safe partner for sexual relations that can include lasting love or not, we turn to her. This "darker side of love," as I call it, can be extremely fulfilling if you find the right partner. If you are already in a relationship but have been unable to explore this side of intimacy with your lover out of fear of rejection or shame, then this candle can help you to find the courage to explore it. Whatever your situation is, this candle will enhance the openness of a decadent sexual relationship.

CANDLE COLOR: Red, purple, black. (Caution: I suggest only experienced magick practitioners use black. You need to visualize this color as sexy black lingerie, not as a tool to mentally dominate someone, or to blacken out his or her will. Using a black candle can backfire terribly if the wrong intention is behind it. For example, you can end up in a bad relationship where harm can be done both to you or your partner. Many a sorrowful situation can arise when you seek total control over another's will. Bad breakups, psychological damage, and in some extreme cases physical harm can result. If a black candle is used in the right frame of mind to explore a sexual fantasy, then there may be a lot to gain from using it, but the other candle colors work just as well.)

CLEANSING: Water, patchouli, musk, amansa guapo perfume.

DEITY: St. Martha Dominadora, Oya, Pacha Mama.

OIL: St. Martha, Commanding, Delight, Cleopatra, La Flamme, Leather and Lace, narcissus, gardenia, honeysuckle, jasmine, vetivert, musk.

INCENSE: La Flamme, All Night Long, St. Martha, Fire of Love, patchouli, musk.

FEEDING: Iron filings, cane syrup, patchouli leaves, a pinch of Dragon's Blood, a few grains of black pepper.

Sorceress Dark Love Spell

Be very clear during this spell about what you want, and be precise on boundaries. It's your sexual fantasy, so set up clear lines of distinction. State very clearly what you will accept and what you will not, and do not expect your lover to be a mind reader. Explain what is acceptable when writing your letter of intention. Most of all, it is important to trust the person with whom you are getting involved.

ITEMS NEEDED

A clear letter of intention
A bowl
Cane syrup
Honey
Sugar
Allspice berries
Cloves
Wormwood

Strega liqueur. (If you want a nonalcoholic version, then steep wormwood herb in hot water and use the tea instead. *Do not drink this tea!* It is extremely toxic.)
Purple statis flowers

CASTING THE SPELL: Light your incense and pass the letter of intention through the smoke. Place the letter in the bottom of the bowl and put your prepared candle on top. Add a drizzle of cane syrup, followed by the honey, and sprinkle the sugar on top. Now add your allspice, cloves, and wormwood. Pour the golden Strega liqueur over everything, and scatter purple statis flower petals in the bowl.

Light the candle and say the incantation.

INCANTATION

> *Come and play one, twice, three*
> *Into a game for you and me.*
> *Enthrall your mind with me tonight*
> *Where love's dark whispers seduce my fright.*
> *Anticipation is a scented aphrodisiac*
> *That makes all my lovers want to come back.*
> *Behold the moment to wait and dare*
> *The Sorceress beckons us to her lair.*

A final word about the lifestyle you are choosing. There is a quote that says, "Who is the master and who is the slave?" This means that it takes as much slavery to dominate someone as it does to be the submissive. After all, the dominator has to do all the work keeping the slave in place. Try to acknowledge that there are both dominant and submissive sides on both ends of the leash, so to speak. Revel in that balance!

LOVE AND HAPPINESS

Add sunshine to your life!

PURPOSE: The title of this spell says it all—add happiness, love, and a lack of complications to your life. This spell brings more than general uplifting; it brings us love in all respects. If you are already with someone and you are happy, then consider this spell an enhancement—an insurance policy that good things will continue. This spell will bring love to your life with family, friends, and loved ones. The love and happiness invoked in this spell will help heal a broken heart and give the subject inspiration to meet someone new.

CANDLE COLOR: Yellow, white, pink, orange.

CLEANSING: Orange water, rose water, lavender water, sugar.

DEITY: Aurelia (Roman Goddess of the sun's golden rays), Iris (Roman Goddess of the rainbow), Amaterasu (Japanese Goddess of the sun), Apollo, and the Three Graces.

OIL: Kindly Spirit, Rainbow, Enchantment, Faith, Hope, and Charity, frankincense, jasmine.

INCENSE: Happy Times, Special Favors, honeysuckle, frankincense, frank and myrrh.

FEEDING: Iron filings, honey, chamomile, sugar.

Love and Happiness

Love and Happiness Spell

For blessings in life, to promote self-love and love of family and friends, and to increase happiness in a relationship.

ITEMS NEEDED

A letter of intention
A bowl
Honey
Chamomile
Marigold flower heads (fresh or dry)

Basil
Rosemary
Orange water
Yellow flower petals

Incense should be lit both during the preparation and while saying the incantation. Place your letter in the bottom of the bowl; put your candle on top of it. Pour the honey in first; scatter the chamomile, marigold, basil, and rosemary over the honey. Add the orange water. Scatter the yellow flower petals on top. Light the candle and incense and say the incantation.

INCANTATION

By the restorative beauty of the sun and its golden rays do I invoke thee to come and shed your blessings upon [person's name]. Bountiful blessings of love and rainbows come to shower resurrection in the life of [person's name]. By the adoration of pure love pouring upon thee shall you walk free and easy in this life. As I do say So Mote It Be.

In these times of many people walking with a troubled heart and feeling so lonely, I find that a dose of happiness and sunshine mixed with love will behave like a healing tonic.

6.

Enchanted Money Candles

It has been is said that money is the root of all evil. Well, the pursuit of it can certainly bring out the dark side of some people. But I have my own saying: *Ignorance* is the root of all evil. More financial problems come from ignorance than from money itself. Still, money is tricky. Not only do we need it to survive, it is inextricably connected to our sense of self-worth, our self-esteem, and our judgment of others. Money is something everyone wants, whether we like to admit it or not. Yet it is not easy to get. Thank goodness we have money spells!

FAST LUCK

To bring about a change of luck.

What is *luck* anyway? A windfall, an advantage over the odds, a triumph over the evil fates that are looking to make you miserable? So often I hear the words "I need some luck." In fact, this phrase is like a universal mantra. I hear it just about every day, in relation to all problems in life. Whether it's about money, love, apartment hunting, employment, bills piling up, family troubles . . . it all boils down to the same thing: We are always looking for a break.

The obvious reason we need luck is because it is so hard to catch. Luck is never

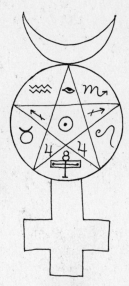

Fast Luck

easy to find, and it's even harder to hold on to. One minute you see it peeking around the corner, and the very next moment it's gone. The power directives—the lightning-quick mental powers of Mercury—inherent in this seal are meant to give us a better chance of letting luck find us, and maybe even getting it to stay a while. The goal here is for luck to come and better our situation for the long run, not just for a moment.

There are other magickal uses for this seal besides attracting luck. Being a seal of Mercury, it will also open doors to the mental realms of communication. This can mean communication within yourself (as in soul searching, or seeking answers from within) or with other people (as in networking).

PURPOSE: To obtain luck, a change of fortune, to turn your luck around. Use this spell to empower all other spells that require extra luck. Great for money drawing and gambling luck.

CANDLE COLOR: Orange, white, purple, green, yellow.

CLEANSING: Water, sandalwood cologne, orange water, three bay leaves (float them in the bowl of cleansing water), a few drops of cinnamon oil or perfume.

DEITY: Mercury, Elegua, Ganesha, Thoth, Hermes, Fortuna, and all spirits of good fortune.

OIL: Fast Luck, Mercury, Special Favors, Horn of Plenty, sandalwood, cinnamon, coconut, and rose geranium. Come to Me Arabacca Soudager

INCENSE: Double Fast Luck, Drawing, Elegua, Chinese Luck, bayberry, sandalwood.

FEEDING: Iron filings, honey, Three Kings incense, cinnamon powder, three pennies.

Fast Luck Spell

This spell will be directed toward changing one's general luck and helping to open the doors to financial benefits. Incense is a very strong component here, as Mercury is a planet ruled by air. Incense and vapors are an important part of contacting Mercury.

ITEMS NEEDED

A very clear and precise letter of request
A bowl
Honey
Fresh clover (a four-leaf clover is an excellent luck talisman)
Fresh or dried peppermint
A few grains of gum mastic (optional)
Three tonka beans
White wine
Three crystals: one clear quartz, one hematite, and one carnelian
  or citrine, all about the same size

CASTING THE SPELL: Light the incense while preparing your candle and writing your letter. Pass both the candle and the letter through the incense smoke while announcing your desires. Place your letter of intention in the bottom of the bowl. Pour in the honey to make life nice and sweet. Now add the clover and peppermint.

Add the gum mastic and the three tonka beans. Pour in the white wine as an offering to the God Mercury. Take your three crystals and place them around the outside of the bowl, touching against it. These will help act as a catalytic projector pulsing the powers of your spell out to the Universe.

Light the candle and more incense if you need it, and say the incantation.

INCANTATION

I conjure thee, oh Mercury, to come with speed unto my heed. A change, a change, a change of luck is what I need. Bring me the key that unlocks all doors that would not open for me before. Opportunities knock and the doors fly open as these words are spoken. So Mote It Be.

This spell is great in an emergency situation when you are really desperate for some luck to help transform something bad to something good. There are other seals that can be safely used along with Fast Luck in your candle. Some examples are Lakshmi, Road Opener, and Tara, to name a few. It can also be used to enhance one's luck in games of chance or in opportunities that require being in the right place at the right time.

FAST LUCK (NETWORKING SPELL)

Use the Fast Luck seal on page 139.

To create networking opportunities.

PURPOSE: To create more opportunities for networking, communications, and well-being. This could include help in studies, research, meeting people for business or pleasure, attracting clients, and so forth.

CANDLE COLOR: Orange, white, purple, yellow.

CLEANSING: Orange water, sandalwood cologne, Florida water, sugar.

DEITY: Mercury, Ganesha, Elegua, Thoth, Hermes, and Hermes Trismegistus, Master of Masters.

OIL: Mercury, Ganesha, Elegua, Crown of Success, sandalwood, mastic, styrax, cinnamon, coconut, and allspice. Attraction

INCENSE: High John the Conqueror, Success, Van-Van, sandalwood, cinnamon.

FEEDING: Iron filings, honey, cinnamon, three bay leaves, three pennies.

FAST LUCK NETWORKING SPELL

ITEMS NEEDED

A letter of intention
A bowl
Honey
Fennel seeds
Sesame seeds

Cinnamon sticks
Fresh or dried orange peel
White wine
Purple flower petals

CASTING THE SPELL: Light incense during the preparation and invocation of this spell. Pass both your candle and letter through the smoke. Place the letter in the bowl and put your candle on top. Pour in the honey, asking for all communications to come through nice and sweetly. Sprinkle the fennel and sesame seeds over the honey. Add the cinnamon sticks and orange peel for success. Pour in the white wine as an offering to the deity, then add the flower petals to help inspire the communication process. Light the candle and say the incantation.

INCANTATION

The success of my life is in this key that will open all doors for me. Mercury, Elegua, Ganesha rule the door, open all roads to me who is poor, lonely, and forlorn. I will dance to my success in three times three because that is the charm of Mercury.

There are times when some luck in communications is just the ticket you need for successful networking. Instead of dead or dry leads that amount to nothing, this will help you connect with people who can help you along the path to your goals.

MONEY PYRAMID

For building a stable financial structure.

PURPOSE: To build a structure of financial success, money drawing, and general wealth and well being.

CANDLE COLOR: Green, yellow, orange.

CLEANSING: Orange water, cinnamon oil, frankincense oil.

DEITY: Venus, Lakshmi, Tara, Ganesha, Apollo, Jupiter, Earth Mothers and Earth Gods.

OIL: Money Drawing, Jupiter, Lodestone, sandalwood, honeysuckle, cinnamon.

Money Pyramid

INCENSE: Money Drawing, Nine Fruits, Prosperity, coconut, vanilla, jasmine.

FEEDING: Iron filings, a few grains of Frankincense, honey, three bay leaves.

Money Pyramid Spell

ITEMS NEEDED

A letter of clear intention
  written in black ink
A bowl
Honey
Sarsaparilla root

Chamomile
Bay leaves
Fresh basil leaves
Red wine

CASTING THE SPELL: Light the incense during the preparation of this spell, and pass your letter through the smoke. Place the letter in the bowl. Put the candle on top of your letter and pour the honey on top as you ask for sweet success. Add the pieces of sarsaparilla root to bring financial blessings. Sprinkle in the chamomile flowers and place in the bay leaves. Add the red wine as an offering to the deity. Now layer the fresh basil on top to represent money. Light the candle and say the incantation.

INCANTATION

A strong foundation is what I need to build a cash flow that will always succeed. Bring me success, give me wealth, give me the wherewithall to do it all.

This is actually the first seal I ever used to make an enchanted candle. Over the years, it has helped me build a pyramid of power and stability. After all, from that day in 1979 onward I have made, sold, and taught about enchanted candles! They have brought me a wealth of experience, and have helped me financially as well.

MONEY DRAWING

For creating cash flow.

PURPOSE: To obtain money through all means available to us, whether it be gambling, working, or just a lucky windfall.

CANDLE COLOR: Green, gold, yellow, orange.

CLEANSING: Water, Kanaga water, a few drops of the oil you chose to dress your candle with.

DEITY: Venus, Lakshmi, Jupiter, Mercury, Apollo.

OIL: Money Drawing, Prosperity, bayberry, frank-incense, bay, benzoin, sandalwood, Gold, and Silver. Attraction, Come to Me

INCENSE: Money, Helping Hand, Jupiter, Venus, frankincense.

FEEDING: Iron filings, honey, sugar, eight pennies, bay leaves.

Money Drawing

Money Drawing Spell

ITEMS NEEDED

A letter of intention
A bowl
Honey
Dry yellow corn kernels
Cinquefoil (also known as
   five-finger grass)

Benzoin
Three whole nutmegs
Red wine
Fresh mint leaves

CASTING THE SPELL: Light your incense during the preparation of this spell. Pass both the letter and the candle through the incense smoke. Place the letter in the bowl and put the candle on top of the letter. Now add the honey, and sprinkle in the yellow corn for money blessings, the cinquefoil to grab and hold onto that money, and the benzoin for Venus, because she rules cash flow in astrology.

Place the three nutmegs in the honey for special luck. Add a good measure of red wine and float the mint leaves on top. Light this candle and say the incantation.

INCANTATION

Money, money that flies through the air come down to me who is in despair. Oh great Goddess, fill my coffers with some cash so that I may help others—in a flash! To circulate that flow is how I will go, good fortune are the seeds that I will sow. So Mote It Be.

Cash flow to me is like blood flow—without a good circulatory system things get clogged up and you end up with a metaphorical heart attack. This is why the incantation for this spell includes the desire for money to circulate to others as well as yourself.

COLLECT DEBTS

Pay me what you owe me!

PURPOSE: To collect money or favors that are owed to you. Are you one of those great people who are always doing good for others, but when you need a favor nobody seems to be around? If so, this spell is for you. Use it if someone has borrowed money from you and you need it returned. My father's wisdom about loaning people money has always held true for me: Never loan what you cannot freely give. I've found that most people who borrow money aren't going to have it later if they didn't have it in the first place. But thank the Goddess what goes around comes around—your money can come back from other sources.

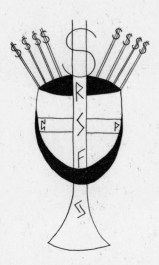

Collect Debts

CANDLE COLOR: Green, yellow, orange, red.

CLEANSING: Water, sugar, sandalwood cologne.

DEITY: Jupiter, Lakshmi, Mercury, Thor.

OILS: Jupiter, Mercury, Money Drawing, juniper, bay, basil.

INCENSE: Money Drawing, Jupiter, frankincense and myrrh, sandalwood.

FEEDING: Iron filings, sugar, basil, and a drop of the oil you chose to dress your candle with.

Collect Debts Spell

ITEMS NEEDED

A letter of intention (you may note in your letter who owes you what, but do not limit yourself as to how it should be returned)
A bowl
Iron filings
Two lodestones

Honey
Eight pennies
Yellow dock
Fresh dandelion flower heads or dry dandelions. (If using fresh flower heads, use eight)
Red wine

CASTING THE SPELL: Light your incense and pass both the candle and the letter through the smoke. Place the letter in the bottom of the bowl and put your candle on top. Add the iron filings over the letter and place the two lodestones on top of the iron filings so that they are leaning against the candle. Pour the honey into the bowl on top of your letter to bring you sweet success. Make a circle with the eight pennies around the candle on top of the honey; then sprinkle the yellow dock and dried dandelion on top. (If using fresh flower heads, do not add them yet—first add the wine, and then float the flower heads in it.) Light the candle and repeat the incantation eight times in a row.

INCANTATION

Maybe you have forgotten [name of person who owes you], when I was there for you. But now its time to give back what was given to you. And if you are without during my time of need, then let the Universe provide me for my good deed. So Mote It Be.

People should not borrow money irresponsibly, never expecting to pay it back. Debts should always be repaid, but often things come up, and even the best of intentions get lost in piles of bills, mortgages, car payments, and so on. At its very best, this candle will get the money you lent returned to you. At the very least it will get your money or favor returned some way other than financially.

MONEY MIST

To attract wealth and financial blessings.

PURPOSE: To draw money through any means possible. This seal can help get you a new job, win a contest, or generally open your scope of financial drawing power. It helps you to be receptive to what the Universe provides.

Money Mist

CANDLE COLOR: Green, yellow, orange, gold.

CLEANSING: Water, sugar, a few drops of the oil you chose to dress your candle, one tablespoon of orange juice.

DEITY: Venus, Lakshmi, Green Tara, Jupiter, Fortuna, and nature spirits.

OIL: Come to Me and Money Drawing mixed together, Jupiter, bergamot, frankincense, honeysuckle. Attraction

INCENSE: Money Drawing, Fast Luck, Jupiter, frankincense, honeysuckle.

FEEDING: Iron filings, Money Drawing powder, honey, anise seeds.

Apartment Hunting

Money Mist Spell

ITEMS NEEDED

A letter of intention (be specific but don't limit yourself. Express your financial needs, but do not assume to know through

what path they will come. To do so will limit your roads
of opportunity.)
A bowl
Grains (Whole wheat, birdseed, dry beans, rice, barley, corn,
or cracked cornmeal can be used. Any one or a combination
is fine.)
A small package of trail mix
Dry figs
Honey
A good dry red wine (hey, we *are* going after luxury here)

CASTING THE SPELL: Light the incense and pass the candle and the
letter through the smoke. Wave the incense smoke into the bowl. The
more fragrant and luxurious the smoke, the more prosperous the outcome. Place the letter in the bowl and put the candle on top. Around
the candle, pour the grains, the trail mix, and the dry figs. Pour the
honey over the mixture, and add a nice measure of good red wine.
The grains, figs, nuts, and golden honey represent wealth and abundance. Wine is an offering to the gods.

Visualize yourself in the life you want. Do not allow a single negative image to enter your mind. It may take time to get there, but stay
steadfast to your visualizations and what you want will come. Look
at it this way—you can spend all of your time griping about being
poor and how nothing goes your way, and life will surely continue
that way. Or you can spend your time seeing a positive image of yourself—you'll be surprised at what happens.

Light the candle and some more incense. Say the incantation three
times a day until your candle has burned out.

INCANTATION

Oh Bona Fortuna! Goddess of wealth and mother of all abundance, shine your favorable side on me. Hail Jupiter, God of expansions, luck and fortune, send your beam of jovial light to me. Oh
Mother Lakshmi! Victory to thee, victory to thee! Wealth has shed
its light on me. As I walk in light, it is my right to have my needs
met. On this day I see myself set.

When you say "I see myself set," you are affirming that you are not
only going to change your way of thinking, but also your actions.

Often our actions cost us the very thing after which we are striving. This seal is to help venerate the way you think and act in order to change your financial lifestyle, hence the name "Money Mist." It means to be literally misted all over your body with moisture that nourishes wealth, and makes things grow lush and abundant.

EMPLOYMENT PYRAMID

Empower your career and financial earnings.

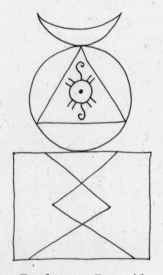

Employment Pyramid

PURPOSE: This candle is all about getting a good job. Sometimes this spell will send a job that is a stepping stone to your ultimate destination. This candle and spell are also great for free-lance workers, including psychics, professional motivators, artists, and people who work selling their services, but can be used whether you are being paid by a company or creating your own salary.

CANDLE COLOR: Orange, white, yellow, green, gold.

CLEANSING: Water, Florida water, orange water, rose water.

DEITY: Mercury, Apollo, Ra, Jupiter, solar energy. My personal vision is of a three-headed god: The Sun's face is shining in the center, Mercury is to the right, and Jupiter's to the left. In this we have the magnanimous spirit of the Sun, the communications of Mercury, and the luck of Jupiter all working together.

OIL: Jupiter, Sun, Mercury, Mastic, peach, frankincense, heliotrope, juniper, pine, chamomile Joy

INCENSE: Lucky Job, Steady Work, Jupiter, frankincense, mastic, vanilla.

FEEDING: Iron filings, Steady Work powder, sassafras bark, honey.

Employment Pyramid Spell

ITEMS NEEDED

> A letter of intention (Be careful not to limit yourself. You may list preferences, but be sure to state that you are open to all possible positions.)
> Your résumé (If you do not have one, then create one. We want all of your potentials magnified.)
> A bowl
> A larger plate on which to fit the bowl
> Iron filings
> Frankincense
> Sassafras bark
> Star anise
> Acacia
> Honey
> Honey mead or red wine
> Eight orange slices
> Gold glitter
> Sunflower petals (girasol) or any yellow flower petals

CASTING THE SPELL: Light the incense. Pass the candle, letter of intention, and resume through the incense smoke, followed by your bowl and plate. Place your résumé on the plate and place the bowl on top of it; put your letter of intention in the bowl. Place the prepared candle on top of the letter in the bowl. Sprinkle the iron filings (for attraction) into the bowl; add the frankincense, sassafras bark, star anise, and acacia. All of these herbs are sacred to the divinities whom we are petitioning for success. Pour on the honey for a sweet position to come to you. Now add the wine. I prefer honey mead for sweetness and a heady response for this (after all, if we get the boss in a good frame of mind on the astral plane then we have a foot in the right direction), but a good red wine is just as acceptable.

The next step is to arrange your eight orange slices around the perimeter of the plate. This will represent a circle of the sun surrounding you. Drizzle honey over the slices and sprinkle them with gold glitter. You are sitting in the center of the sun with a golden glow all about you. Cast your yellow flower petals upon the wine and get ready to light your candle.

For general job hunting say the following when you light your candle:

INCANTATION

Positions, positions from which shall I choose, be they scarce or be they rich. Today I have found my niche.

I ask of the three to see me, Mercury to seek and find the job, Jupiter to give me the luck and abundance I need, and the Sun to shine his magnanimous face on me with grace so that I may be employed and no longer carry this burden of woe and sorrows.

In exchange I agree to be the best employee, ever diligent in my work, and I will strive to excel in my career so that I may have finances to support my home.

If you are a freelancer, say:

Phone calls with offers of work I receive.
Now I pick and choose as I please.

If you are having a difficult work situation try this incantation to improve your working condition:

I cast a spell upon all I see to set things right with no cost from me. Improvements, cooperation, and harmony are the three magick ingredients I need. Put them in the cauldron and stir it up well, set them free now to work my spell. No strife, friction, or malediction can continue here, for all that are not right shall put themselves to flight.

An alternate incantation to use is:

Let all that I am manifest for good times three. Oh dear Mercury, in alchemical light I transform; away with this dark and ugly storm. In its stead open the doors to Apollo, to cast his golden glow upon my brow. Beam on me, oh Jupiter, I no longer despair when thy smile is with me.

Too often people find themselves in a situation where they keep needing to find a new job. This candle is to help you internalize your thought process to recognize what the pattern is that causes you to pick these unsuitable jobs. This seal will help you recognize the root of the problem and put you on a path to a more permanent and fulfilling job. If you have been at your job a while and the situation is ugly—not enough pay, or your job has just lost its growth potential for you—then this candle will assist in helping you find better opportunities.

For a promotion, try this incantation:

Let no one stand in my way,
This promotion is mine today.
My hard work and dedication
Create an indication
That I should be recognized
And my talents properly prized.
May those in charge be helped to see
That no one deserves this promotion more than me.

To help in networking for business and success, try:

I weave a web to ensnare a wealth of contacts
So I and others can exchange facts.
To grow and inspire a new job that abounds
with success, and fulfillment and more cash all around.

A successful career requires a good attitude about your work. I have met many people who hate their jobs and only make things worse for themselves by acting miserable at work. Keep a positive attitude, and over time you will see your life improving. Networking also requires that you be very upbeat and believe in yourself. The candle will bring you the opportunities, but it is up to you to make the most of them.

WINNER'S CIRCLE

A gambler's luck charm.

PURPOSE: If speculation and ventures are your game, then this is a great spell for you.

CANDLE COLOR: Green, yellow, gold, orange.

CLEANSING: Water, Gambler's Perfume, Drawing Perfume, Abre Camino Perfume (Open Road).

DEITY: Jupiter, Lady Luck, Fortuna, Ganesha, and all lucky earth spirits.

OIL: Lady Luck, Lucky Thirteen, Gamblers, Lucky Lotto, sandalwood, bergamot, frankincense, bay.

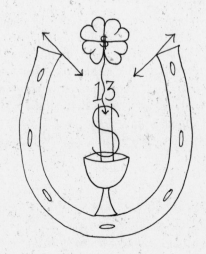

Winners Circle

INCENSE: Lady Luck, Gamblers, Nine Fruits, Coconut, Sandalwood, Pine.

FEEDING: Iron Filings, mace, Fast Luck powder, honey.

Winner's Circle Spell

ITEMS NEEDED

> A letter of intention (include favorite numbers you may play or systems of gambling you use)
> Old lottery tickets, racing forms, a picture of a slot machine, cards, or anything made of paper that relates to gambling and that you are willing to sacrifice for the spell's sake. Photocopies are fine.

A bowl	Allspice berries
Two lodestones	Cloves
Nutmeg	Seven cinnamon sticks
One gingerroot	Champagne
Honey	

CASTING THE SPELL: Light your incense. Put all of the paper you have (tickets, forms, and your letter) in the bowl. (Don't make it too bulky or the candle will tip over.) Place your prepared candle on top of the paper. Lean the two lodestones on the candle in the bowl. Add a nutmeg on one side of the candle, and on the other put your ginger-root. Pour the honey over everything, and scatter the allspice berries and cloves on top. Put seven cinnamon sticks halfway into the honey—they should look like spikes. Pop the cork of the champagne and celebrate, visualizing your success. Slowly pour the bottle of champagne into the bowl. Light the candle and say the incantation.

INCANTATION

Spinning wheel of fate is turning, the dice are tumbling, and my hands are burning. My new luck is turning with every second that this candle is burning. Three times three, fate is lady luck for me, it brings me a happiness I just can't shake when lady luck makes my fate.

According to Webster's dictionary the word *gamble* means "To take a chance on an uncertain outcome as a contest or a weekly lottery number. Any risky venture." Any of the luck of gambling spells will help increase your odds. Much success to you and I hope you win!

CASINO

When you're off to Vegas, Rio, Atlantic City, or the Mohegan Sun!

PURPOSE: A Gambler's Luck seal is for winning at games of chance related to professional gambling. Slot machines, dice games, the big wheel, roulette, blackjack, bingo, keno, and lottery games. Your chances of winning any game you can play in a casino or state lottery are increased with this seal and spell. You should begin this candle and/or spell a week before you go gambling. This way the candle and spell will be finished a day or two before you leave.

CANDLE COLOR: Green, orange, yellow, and gold.

CLEANSING: Water, Luck perfume, a few drops of the oil with which you dressed your candle

Casino

DEITY: Fortuna, St. Expedito, Jupiter.

OIL: Gamblers Luck, Lucky Seven, sandalwood. *Attraction Come to Me*

INCENSE: Jupiter, Lady Luck, and bayberry.

FEEDING: Iron filings, honey, and chamomile

Casino Spell

ITEMS NEEDED

A letter of intention (express your desire for abundance, but with no specific amounts listed)
A bowl
Sugar
7, 11, or 13 bay leaves

Bayberry bark
Oak bark or three acorns
Chamomile
Honey
Thirteen pennies
Champagne

CASTING THE SPELL: Light your incense. When composing your letter, write it this way: "I will soon be traveling to (list location) and I ask that the laws of abundance be open to me. In this case this kind of law is like a rule that resides in the universe. It pays each place we go.

We ask the Law Of Abundance to recognize me where I am likely to play (list game) and ask that Lady Luck smile on me." This is just an example—be creative and specific, but remember to stay away from amounts. When you limit the amount you can win, it usually does not happen.

Once your letter is written, place it in the bottom of the bowl and put your prepared candle on top. Now sprinkle the sugar around the candle over your letter. Add the bay leaves, bayberry bark, oak bark or acorns, and chamomile next. Pour the honey on top of this herbal mixture. All around the honey, add the thirteen pennies. Pour in the champagne and light your candle while saying the incantation.

INCANTATION

> I have a special friend; she's sitting next to me. The odds are in my favor, for it's lady luck, you see. Tonight she's tipped the scales of good fortune for all to see, and money and luck rain down on me.

Gambling seems like a great risk to me—if you cannot afford to lose the money you are playing with, don't do it! Too often I have seen people blow their rent money, then frantically spend more money trying to make up the loss. Play to entertain yourself, not to survive.

WHEEL OF FORTUNE

The Gods of Fortune smile on you!

PURPOSE: To change destiny or fortune when things just keep going bad and we want to get off that cyclic wheel of bad luck. Change your fate with Fortuna and open up new opportunities with this spell.

CANDLE COLOR: Yellow, gold, green, orange, purple, seven colors.

CLEANSING: Florida water, Kananga water, and a few drops of almond oil.

DEITY: Fortuna.

OIL: Helping Hand, Horn of Plenty, Special Favors, vanilla, and almond.

INCENSE: Three Kings, sandalwood, Special Favors, vanilla, Prosperity.

FEEDING: Iron filings, three pennies, honey, trefoil (a three-leaf clover—if at all possible get three of these).

Wheel of Fortune

Wheel of Fortune Spell

ITEMS NEEDED

A letter of intention written to the Goddess Fortuna	Juniper berries
A bowl	Fresh or dry mint
Seven pennies	Fresh or dry basil
Honey	May wine or white wine
Lavender flowers	Carnation petals in any color you choose

CASTING THE SPELL: Once you have carved the candle and before you oil it, imagine your luck suddenly becoming good. For example, see yourself receiving something good from the negative situation that you are in. Take a deep breath. Hold that thought and breathe for ten seconds then release it by blowing out onto your carved candle seal. Do this three times. Now oil your candle and proceed to glitter it or dress it in any manner you have chosen.

In your letter of intention, be explicit with the Goddess Fortuna about your need to have fortune change for you. Do not tell her how to change it or what to change it into. Just express the situation or situations that need changing. Put the letter in the bowl and place your prepared candle on top. Add the lavender flowers and juniper berries. Pour in the honey and put the seven pennies in it. If you are using dry mint or basil add them, along with the lavender and juniper berries. Add the wine. If you are using fresh mint or basil, scatter it and the carnation petals on the wine.

Light your candle and more incense, and say the incantation.

INCANTATION

Spiraling, spinning wheel of fate, change my fortune from sadness to joy. I've shed enough tears of sadness, it's time for happiness to balance my life. So let fortune smile upon me now. So mote it be.

I was once told by an old man that when he was in the service during wartime he was in Italy. There, in a museum in a small town he saw a statue done in solid gold of the Goddess Fortuna. It wasn't very large—maybe eighteen inches tall—but the detail he described was beautiful. He said the front of the body of the woman was perfect right down to her pubic hair, but her back was monstrous—it showed all of the degradations of life: images of skeletal people begging or starving, being tortured, and so on. The lesson here is when fortune turns her back on you things can get pretty ugly.

SEAL OF SUCCESS

For success as a way of life.

PURPOSE: To attain success in any endeavor. This is a terrific candle for any project you are working on that needs a little extra assistance to be a stunning success. Maybe a job you applied for can use an extra push to help you not only succeed in getting it, but to help you shine once you have it.

CANDLE COLOR: Orange, yellow, gold, purple.

CLEANSING: Water, salt, a few drops of frankincense oil.

DEITY: Apollo, Ra, Nike (goddess of victory), Libertas (goddess of liberation), Ganesha, Chango, Zeus for Olympian might.

OIL: Sun oil, Success, Crown of Success, frankincense, bay oil, heliotrope.

INCENSE: Frankincense, Sun, Success, Chango Macho, Van-Van, Three Kings, Jerusalem, and copal.

FEEDING: Iron filings, frankincense, three bay leaves, honey.

Seal of Success Spell

ITEMS NEEDED

A clear letter of intention listing
    your goals and things you'd
    like to achieve
A bowl
Ten star anise
Honey
Bay leaves
Fresh orange peel (dry is fine)
Frankincense
Sassafras bark
Cloves
White wine (preferably in a deep golden color)

Seal of Success

CASTING THE SPELL: Pass the candle, the letter, and the bowl through the incense smoke for added solar power. Solar power is the ability to attract the good fortune that the sun brings into any endeavor. By passing the letter and bowl through incense, which is solar in nature, we are communicating to this deity that we have left no stone unturned when looking for our success. Place your letter in the bowl and put the candle on top of it. Add the honey. Sprinkle the anise, bay leaves, orange peel, frankincense, sassafras bark, and cloves on top of the honey. All of these herbs are for success and the attraction of opportunistic actions. Add the wine, the golden color of which is an appropriate offering to a solar God or Goddess of victory, as it emulates the sun. Light your candle and say the incantation.

The sun thrusts upwards into the sky, and I see the birth of a new day before me, heralding to me that success is on the way. I will grasp that scepter of power so to change my world to benefit all that I do.

LAKSHMI GODDESS

To invoke abundance.

PURPOSE: To change oneself from destitution, sorrow, and poor finances. Wealth and prosperity is what Lakshmi loves to give. She is also helpful in networking and bringing people together. Lakshmi is excellent for business and always provides a lot of customers. She has personally saved me more times than I can count. I am a devotee of Mother Lakshmi and honor her every chance I get.

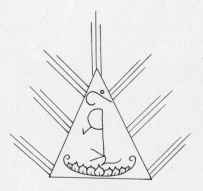

Lakshmi Goddess

To invoke the presence and auspicious properties of Lakshmi one must be of clear mind—without malice or jealousy—and only focused on oneself and what is needed for personal achievements and to better others. You may include as many people in your thoughts as you like. Lakshmi loves people as well as all animals. No sharp implements should be placed near her work, except your carving tool, of course. No offerings of meat of any kind should be placed near her altar. This does not mean that you cannot eat meat while working with her, although I usually refrain from eating it an hour or so before I recite her mantra. The worshippers of Lakshmi in India never eat meat or animal products of any kind. She is a mother of all living creatures, and therefore the flesh of any creature would not be an appropriate offering. There will also be no alcohol offered in this ritual—she doesn't like drugs or stimulants of any kind. Being sober here is important, as it makes for a better connection to the presence of this Goddess.

Lakshmi is a wonderful household Goddess for whom to establish an altar. Work with her to bless your home with wealth, health, and well-being. Mother of all fertility, she also blesses those who ask for children. A spell for Lakshmi for financial blessings, fertility, love, and happiness is a little more elaborate then the other spells—instead of everything being placed in a single bowl, I suggest a separate vase of flowers and many offerings of herbs and fruit.

CANDLE COLOR: Green, yellow, red, pink.

CLEANSING: Water, honey, rosewater, sandalwood cologne or oil.

DEITY: Lakshmi, Hindu Goddess of wealth and all blessings, consort of Vishnu and premiere Mother Goddess of India.

OIL: Lakshmi, Lotus, sandalwood, honeysuckle, gardenia. *Attraction Come to Me*

INCENSE: Prosperity, Money Drawing, Nine Fruits, Coconut, Sandalwood.

FEEDING: Iron filings, honey, shredded coconut, a few grains of rice, dirt from a bank (a pinch is plenty).

Lakshmi Goddess Spell

ITEMS NEEDED

A letter of intention stating your needs
3 bowls, one for your spell work and two smaller ones to hold pennies
Dates
Dry rice
Shelled almonds
Shredded coconut
Jasmine flowers (dry are usually what you will find, but fresh would be great)
Honey
Coconut milk (you can either use the real milk, which is thin like water, or coconut cream)

A clear bowl of water for
  refreshing her mouth
  (this will be changed
  daily)
Flowers in a separate vase

A small bouquet of fresh
  basil, preferably in flower,
  is especially prized by
  Lakshmi.
108 pennies

CASTING THE SPELL: Incense should be burned during the entire procedure. Pass the candle, letter, and bowls through the incense smoke. Place the letter in the spell bowl and add your prepared candle on top of it. Put the dates, rice, almonds, shredded coconut, and the jasmine flowers all around the candles. Doesn't that look lovely? Now slowly pour the honey over the ingredients you have placed in the bowl, followed by the coconut milk; praise Lakshmi for her abundant gifts of life. To invoke her presence, place the clear bowl of water to the right of the candle bowl, and to the left, place your flowers and a small bouquet of basil. If you don't have enough flowers for a separate vase, then float a fresh flower in the bowl with the milk. Take the two small bowls and place one hundred and eight pennies in one bowl. Place the other bowl next to this one. Each time you say the mantra, cast one penny into the empty bowl. This way you will have kept count to make sure you have said the mantra the appropriate amount of times. Light your candle and incense, and say the incantation 108 times.

INCANTATION

Om Sri Maha Lakshmi Yai Namah.

Another more complicated version is:

Om Kamala Vasini, Kamale Maha Lakshmi, Raja Me, Dehi Dehi Varaday Swaha.

Say it as well as you can—it's okay if you don't pronounce everything perfectly. She knows that even if you are saying it incorrectly, the merit is the same. I have even found that after reciting this mantra for a while, miraculously someone who knows of Her comes along to teach the correct pronunciation. If you prefer an English version, then say this:

Oh Mother Lakshmi, victory to those who praise your honor. As you raise your arms, let showers of golden wealth fall upon me.

The full bowl of pennies represents the deity with all to give. The empty bowl represents the subject, waiting to be filled. Copper is a metal of Venus, a Goddess similar to Lakshmi, and is a great conductor of wealth. Many blessings for both a more prosperous and spiritual you!

GANESHA (REMOVER OF OBSTACLES)

To remove obstacles and open doors to success.

PURPOSE: Ganesha removes all negative barriers that block your good opportunities. He stamps his mighty foot and dispels all terrifying evils and plagues and opens all roads. He is the scribe of the gods and ruler of the intellect. He gives great wealth. His vessel is a mouse, which is of course at home in the granaries. He rules the wealth of the earth and has dominion over these areas. Often you will find pictures depicting Lakshmi, Ganesha, and Saraswati, Goddess of intellect and poetry, together. This is to show what a powerful force the three of them are combined.

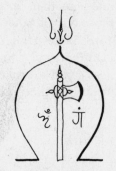

Ganesha

CANDLE COLOR: Red, orange, white, yellow, purple, seven colors.

CLEANSING: Water, drops of coconut oil, sugar, one tablespoon of milk.

DEITIES: Ganesha, Thoth, Elegua, Mercury, and Hermes.

OILS: Ganesha, sandalwood, Road Opener, Elegua, coconut, and cinnamon. King's Perfume

INCENSE: Ganesha, sandalwood, coconut, Road Opener, jasmine.

FEEDING: Iron filings, honey, shredded coconut, three pennies.

Ganesha Spell

ITEMS NEEDED

A letter of clear intention
3 bowls—a large one for the spell work and two smaller ones
Unshelled peanuts
Shredded coconut or fresh chunks (keep the milk from the nut)
Grains, such as wheat, barley, and rice, mixed.
Betel nut (optional—not always easy to find but if you can get it, great)
Coconut milk or coconut cream
Honey
Flowers (either a separate vase, or one to float in the candle bowl)
Bowl of water
108 pennies

CASTING THE SPELL: Light your incense. Write your letter and pass it through the incense smoke. Place the letter in the bottom of the spell bowl and put your prepared candle on top of it. Surround your candle with a healthy handful of peanuts, and add the coconut, grain mixture, and betel nut. Pour honey over everything, and gently add the coconut milk. Add a flower if you are not setting up a separate vase of flowers. To the right, place a separate bowl of water for refreshing Ganesha's mouth. To the left, place either the fresh flowers or the incense. In front of all this, place the two smaller bowls; place the 108 pennies in one, and leave the others empty. Each time you say the incantation, take one penny from the full bowl and place it in the empty one. Repeat this until all 108 pennies have been transferred from one bowl to the other. As you count, say the incantation.

INCANTATION

Om Sri Ganesha Yai Namah

Or you can recite the English version:

Om Ganesha, keeper of the gate, open all doors to me of luck and fate.

As you are passing the pennies from one bowl to another, visualize all of the obstacles that have been blocking you from attaining success being removed. See your life as the empty bowl filling up with all good things.

TARA

For rescue in desperate times.

PURPOSE: Calling upon Tara invokes the compassion of the primordial mother of all the Buddhas. Her name means "she who saves."

Tara

Tara's sole purpose is to answer people in times of need; to ferry them from danger and deprivation across to safety and abundance. She, like Lakshmi, loves to give wealth and prosperity. She removes without exception all sorrows and fears, poisons, disputes, and black magick. Invoke her compassion not only for finances but also for the removal of all negative forces that block progression in life. When I first read about Tara and how she saves people in dire need, I realized that she is the 911 of Goddesses. People cry out to her in terrible moments in their lives and she saves them. She is the mother of all compassion. There are twenty-one aspects of Tara in all, but Green Tara or White Tara will both work for our purposes. I tend to use White Tara for more spiritual workings to unblock finances. For instance, if you have a supervisor who is causing you trouble, and you see no way around the situation, White Tara, who has the power of pacifying, can be invoked to calm things down and take this person out of your way so that he or she stops bothering you. It's a temporary solution, like a Band-aid, until the root of the problem can be worked out. Green Tara is invoked for more physical needs. This aspect of Tara gives financial blessings. For example, you can ask her to remove the obstacles that stand in your way of getting a job.

CANDLE COLOR: Green or white.

CLEANSING: Water, few drops of Lotus oil, honey.

DEITY: Green Tara, White Tara. Other aspects of Tara are Kwan Yin, Saint Clara, and Virgin Mercedes.

OIL: Green Tara, White Tara, Spiritual Cleansing, Lotus, sandalwood, peach, carnation, gardenia.

INCENSE: Moon, Prosperity, Money Drawing, sandalwood, peach, lotus, and gardenia.

FEEDING: For Green Tara: Iron filings, honey, crushed almonds. For White Tara: Camphor, honey, and white flower petals.

Green Tara Spell

ITEMS NEEDED

Letter of clear intention
3 bowls: one large enough for the spell work and two smaller ones
Shredded coconut
Almonds

Honey
A clear glass bowl filled with water
Three carnation, mum, or daisy heads
108 pennies

CASTING THE SPELL: Light the incense and envision rainbows in the smoke. Visualize happy pictures of what you desire, and the incense will carry your messages to Tara. Pass your letter through the incense smoke and place it in the bottom of the bowl; place your prepared candle on top of the letter. Sprinkle a layer of the coconut around the candle and scatter the almonds on top. Pour a generous amount of honey over the nuts. To the right of the candle, place the clear glass bowl, and float the three flower heads in it. In front of this, place the two smaller bowls. Fill one with the 108 pennies, and leave the other one empty. Each time you say the incantation, cast one penny into the empty bowl. Repeat this until all the pennies have been transferred. As you light your candle and say the incantation, envision her symbol (it's in the center of the triangle on the seal).

INCANTATION

Om Tara Tut Tara Ture Swaha

An English version is:

Oh supreme and noble Tara, protect us from all fears and suffering.

WHITE TARA

Use Tara seal on page 166.

To remove negativity and make way for clarity and positive change.

PURPOSE: For transposing all financial and spiritually negative and confining situations.

In reality, people harm one another, both intentionally and unintentionally. When someone has been harmed by another person, he or she often feels that protection magick is necessary to prevent further harm.

If you are angry when performing a protection spell, the idea of revenge may be circulating in your mind. For example, let's say your boss yells at you in front of people that you know hate you because they think you are the boss's favorite. You want to do a spell to protect yourself from further harm, but you're still totally humiliated and angry about her behavior. And rightly so!

It's in cases like this that I recommend Tara. She will help remove the bitterness that can seep into a protection spell. Black magick can ride on the waves of unchecked human emotions. White Tara will remove severe emotions so that clarity and positive energy can be the driving force in your spell work.

White Tara is called the All-Seeing One. Another thing often said about this goddess is that she sees in all directions. Pictures of White Tara often depict her as having seven eyes—two in the normal place, one in the center of her forehead, one in each palm, and the last eyes in each of the soles of her feet. She is seated in the center of a lotus, which in Buddhist practice means perfection and purity that is self-created. She saves one from all dangers. She is pacifying calmness and all-pervading peace. She also gives financial aid when asked. I call her the Mother of Peace. When we are financially in a good state, life is a lot more peaceful. Picture her symbol (in the center of the triangle, in her soul) for the most positive effects while chanting.

DEITY: White Tara.

CANDLE COLOR: White.

CLEANSING: Florida water, water, sugar.

OIL: White Tara, Obatala, Virgin Mercedes, sandalwood, lotus, carnation. Most Powerful Hand,

INCENSE: White Tara, Nag Champa, Tibetan Soul, sandalwood, lotus, and rose.

FEEDING: Camphor, white flower petals, sugar.

White Tara Spell

ITEMS NEEDED

A clear letter of intention	Sugar
3 bowls: One large enough for the spell work, and two smaller ones	Water
	Seven camphor tablets
	Three white flower heads
A small handful of rice	108 pennies

CASTING THE SPELL: To prepare the spell, light the incense and pass the letter through the smoke. Place your letter in the bottom of the large bowl. Cast the rice over your letter for financial gain. Sprinkle sugar all around the candle over the rice to make life sweet. Now slowly pour in the clear, cold water. Add the seven camphor tablets to the bowl for clearance from all directions. Float the three flower heads in the bowl as a lotus offering to Tara. In front of this, place your two bowls; fill one with the 108 pennies, and leave the other one empty. Light your candle and say the incantation, each time transfering a penny from the full bowl to the empty one.

INCANTATION

Om Tara Tut Tara Ture Swaha

The English version is:

Oh supreme and noble Drolma Tara, protect us from all fears and suffering.

7.

Enchanted Healing Candles

*H*ealing *is a wonderful gift* to give. Whether it is the act of healing a person or healing Mother Earth, it is an act of pure kindness that perpetuates good energy in all involved. When someone is physically ill, people come to me for a healing candle. I always ask about how the person was before he or she got sick. Was he tired? Was she stressed out? Overwhelmed? You can do a healing for someone even if he or she is not sick. In the case of illness, keep a clear mind, add a double shot of compassion, then take a deep breath and begin. Ask the healing deities to come and remove all illness from the person's body, mind, and soul. Know that you are performing a sacred act by looking to ease another's pain.

AESCLEPIUS HEALING

For general healing and well-being.

PURPOSE: The imagery of this seal represents Aesclepius, the Greek God of healing. In ancient Greece, the sick and infirm could come to the temples of Aesclepius. Through the use of hypnosis and potions, the patient was put into a healing trance and was healed.

The healing effects of this candle happen on the physical plane, but the healing itself is accomplished through the spiritual plane. Its purpose is to heal the auric body of light. The auric body is the astral or twin self. It goes through changes just like you do physically. When the auric body is healed, it manifests healing of the physical self as well.

Long-distance healing can be accomplished with this spell. Visualize the body well, healthy, and free of all dis/ease while you are

Aesclepius Healing

working your spell. Notice how I spelled dis/ease? *Dis/ease* means that the body is not at ease. Your job as a healer is to restore ease to the body, to remove anything causing it distress.

The first thing to remember when faced with a difficult illness is not to panic, as it only heightens the negative assent of trouble. When I was diagnosed with cancer, my first response was to cry, drink, and ask "why me?" After about a week of drowning and speaking to friends I began to realize, "why not me?" Cancer is not a punishment—it's an illness. I recognized that I was not going to beat it by crying or by burying my head in the sand. I spoke to my doctors, chose a plan, and then went straight for my candles and got to work. I have been in remission for thirteen years, and if cancer ever rears its ugly head again, I know what plan of action I will take.

Most important, remain positive. The level of healing work cannot be judged by whether a miraculous recovery occurs so much as by the personal effect it has on the whole person. One of the best medicines is laughter. Helping to put someone in a better frame of mind can be what is needed to help recovery.

CANDLE COLOR: White for general healing and cancer; yellow for respiratory disease, melancholia, stress, depression, and ulcers; red for all muscles, blood disorders, heart, liver, kidneys, major organs; green for all physical disorders such as chronic pain, wounds, and recovery from surgery; blue to strengthen the body to fend off disease.

CLEANSING: Spring water, lavender water, Florida water.

DEITY: Aesclepius, Greek God of Healing

OIL: Healing, Blessing, St. Lazarus, carnation, chamomile, and lavender.

INCENSE: Healing, Sun, Moon, lavender, rose, lily, and sage.

FEEDING: Camphor, Healing powder, Life Everlasting, sage.

Aesclepius Healing Spell

ITEMS NEEDED

A bowl	Sage
A letter of intention	Lavender
A picture (or photocopy of one) of the person to be healed, if available	Juniper berries
	Mint
	Clear cold water
Salt	Carnation or mum petals

CASTING THE SPELL: Pass the bowl, letter of intention, candle, and photo through the incense smoke as you repeat the patient's name. This will help disperse any negativity around the person. Place your letter in the bottom of the bowl and put your candle on top of it. Pour a ring of salt around the candle. Add the sage, lavender, juniper berries, and mint all around the candle. Slowly pour in the cold water, and then float the petals of your flower in the bowl.

Light the candle and say the incantation while visualizing healing light surrounding the person entirely in the color of the candle you chose.

Healing light surround [person's name] with life-healing energy. Be they near or far, may Aesclepius shine on him/her like a healing blue star, to imbue his/her body with love and light all through the day and through the night. Aesclepius, let your powers of healing walk with him/her as a talisman emblazed on his/her soul to cleanse away all illness and allow the healing to unfold. Wrap his/her body securely in your arms, so that his/her soul and body will be free from all harm.

HEALING WAND

For health and well-being.

PURPOSE: For healing on both the physical and emotional levels of the body. After a time of distress, the emotional body often creates dis/ease. This will cause the physical body to become ill. If there is emotional trauma going on in your life or in the life of a loved one, I always recommend a Healing Wand candle to stabilize and heal the emotional trauma and all ill effects it may cause later. This works on all aspects of physical healing as well.

Healing Wand

You will notice that the symbol in this seal is found often in the medical world. Why the serpents? Most people have the misconception that the serpent is evil. Yet when we are sick and a medical office carries that symbol, we rush in with no fear of snakes. Why is the serpent on the emblem of the medical profession? Why did Aesclepius carry a serpent in a chalice? Because the serpent represents the spine in the human body, and the ancients knew that the spine supports the body, the nerves, and the role of communicator between the brain and the body.

DEITY: Panacea, Hygeia, Rhea, Isis, Morgan Le Fey, Apollo, White Buffalo Calf Woman, Hermes, Hippocrates.

OIL: Crystal Healing, Healing, carnation, basil, lavender, rosemary, hyssop.

INCENSE: Isis, Healing, lavender, white sage, sweet grass.

FEEDING: Camphor, honey, white flower petals.

CLEANSING: Water, lavender water, few drops of hyssop oil.

CANDLE COLOR: White, yellow, green, red, blue

Healing Wand Spell

ITEMS NEEDED

A letter of intention
A bowl
A wineglass full of water
Camphor
A photocopy of a picture of
   the person to be healed
   (optional)
Flowers as an offering
   (optional)

Honey
Life Everlasting flowers
   (a dry herb)
Lavender flowers
Hyssop
Five clear quartz crystals
   (optional)

ITEMS NEEDED: To set this spell into action, incense should be lit both during the preparation and every day the candle burns. Place your letter in the spell bowl and put your candle on top. On the right of the bowl place the wineglass filled to the brim with water, and float your camphor in it. Place your photo of the person to be healed underneath the wineglass; To the left place your flowers. Pour the honey into the bowl over the letter and sprinkle in the healing herbs. If you are going to use the crystals, place them outside the bowl in a circle with the points touching the bowl like the five points of a pentagram. The goblet shape represents the head, the water the spirit and mind, and the camphor cleanses the auric debris—the negative muck that clings to the aura, which in turn feeds the illness. Each day, take the camphor out of the wineglass and change the water. As you pour the water out envision the psychic debris leaving; the fresh water represents a clear mind. The spiritual cleansing removes all of the bad energy so that nothing remains to fester and impede the well-being of the patient.

Light the candle and say the incantation.

INCANTATION

First, before the holy ones that I invoke, I [your name] declare that I have compassion for this person for whom I request this healing. I beseech in your infinite loving souls to reach down and cleanse (name of patient) of his/her sorrow. When he/she feels that he/she walks alone in this desolate world, be a comfort and healing balm over his/her injured body. Remove all afflictions and cleanse the wounds in both the auric and physical body. Let the shining face of the God and Goddess illuminate the heart, body, and soul of [patient's name] while he/she is in a dark time of this world.

UNCROSSING

To remove spiritual stumbling blocks.

PURPOSE: People speak of having a cross to bear. This candle will get rid of the negative burdens that other people have bestowed on you. Uncrossing is for defending against psychic attack or black magick, and for eliminating the spiritual debris of other people's jealousy, anger, or negative thoughts. It is to unburden the user of all the spiritual garbage hanging around and making a mess of life.

A *psychic attack* is when someone is engaging in a battle with you through the power of thoughts directed by will. Its intent is to cause you harm. This could be intentional or unintentional, and the person doesn't have to be a magick practitioner to do it. For example, say someone is jealous because you are dating a person they have been trying to seduce for years. He or she treats you coldly and then starts thinking about how you should disappear, or even that something bad might happen to you. Those negative thoughts they are throwing at you can do some serious damage to your auric body, which in turn can manifest physically.

Black magick is performed through a psychic attack combined with spell work. Someone purposefully arranges a hateful spell against you with the intent to really cause you harm. What do you do if you find out someone has cast a black spell against you? Do you panic? Absolutely not! Take a nice, cleansing bath by using

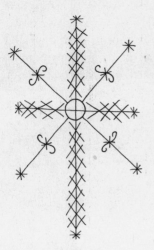

Uncrossing

salt in a tub of water, make an uncrossing candle spell to remove all the trauma someone is bothering to send you and, proceed to any one of the protection spells in this book, such as White Tara.

When I suggest to people that they do this candle once a month, they are often surprised and wonder at the frequency. I call it "spiritual hygiene"—it's like washing your face or brushing your teeth. You do not necessarily have to be under psychic attack to do this candle spell. Which time of the month you choose is really up to you; waning moon, waxing moon—there are arguments for and against both. I say mark your calendar once a month and just do it. Clean auras make for fewer complications in life.

CANDLE COLOR: White, blue, gray.

CLEANSING: Water, Florida water, salt.

DEITY: Elegua, Mercury, Ganesha, Legba.

OIL: Uncrossing, Spiritual Cleansing, lavender, coconut, basil, sandalwood. Reversing

INCENSE: Uncrossing, Banishing, lavender, frankincense and Myrrh, sage.

FEEDING: Iron filings, honey, basil.

Uncrossing Spell

ITEMS NEEDED

A letter of intention
A bowl
Salt
Water

Florida water or any clean-
    smelling perfume.
Basil, fresh or dry

CASTING THE SPELL: Burn incense during the preparation of this spell. Before carving the candle, pass it through the incense smoke. Do the same for the letter of intention and the bowl. Everything should be purified.

Once the candle is prepared, place the letter in the bottom of the bowl and put the candle on top. Pour a good measure of salt around the candle over the letter. Next add the ice-cold water. Pour in the Florida water or perfume. If you were able to get fresh basil, add the leaves and float them in the bowl. If you are using the dry herb, scatter it over the water.

Light the candle and more incense and say the incantation.

INCANTATION

I ground myself to the Great Mother upon which I stand. Roots grow from the soles of my feet, attaching themselves to the earth. I feel the pulse of the Great Mother's heartbeat rushing up through my body, cleansing me of all weariness. She that sustains me sends electrifying jolts of loving support through my body so that I may stand tall and fortified with the strength of the mighty oak. I ask thee oh Elegua [or deity of choice] to be my guardian spirit and see that no harm comes across my path. May all the sender of this negativity see a mirror reflection times three. So Mote It Be.

HOUSE BLESSING

Cleanse your home of all negative spiritual vibes.

PURPOSE: To cleanse your home of all negative spiritual energy. This candle will also bless a new home and help heal the energies of the one you are presently in. It will bless the home with an overall sense of peace, clarity, and happiness. House blessings should be done when you have noticed that things are getting unruly, if there have been too many arguments, or whenever you sense that things are not spiritually fit in your home. For example, you may find that you are happy outside of your home, but when you get home you feel depressed or tired, and have no energy.

House Blessing

This candle spell should be performed before moving into a new space. Even if you cannot burn the candle in your new home before you move in, carve your new address into the candle and light it. Let it burn for the week before you move. Then dedicate another candle upon moving in.

CANDLE COLOR: White, blue, yellow.

CLEANSING: Water, Florida water, lavender water, and salt.

DEITY: Diana, Yemaya, Selene, Juno, Athena, Artemis.

OIL: House Blessing, Banishing, Peace, Moon, cucumber, camphor, lavender, and carnation. Moving, Neptune, Peace & Protection, Apartment Hunting

INCENSE: House Blessing, Peaceful Home, St. Clara, lavender, sage, frankincense and myrrh, Three Kings.

FEEDING: Camphor, honey, white flower petals (mums or carnation are fine).

House Blessing Spell

ITEMS NEEDED

A letter of intention	Blue food coloring
A bowl	Camphor
Sugar	Fresh mint leaves
Clear cold spring water	One white carnation

CASTING THE SPELL: Burn incense while preparing this spell. Pass the letter through the incense smoke and place it in the bowl, then put your candle on top. Add sugar all around the candle and over the letter to make your place "home sweet home." Slowly pour the water over the sugar. Wait a few minutes for the cloudiness to dissipate, then add a few drops of the blue food coloring. Stir the water, and add more drops until you have a color you like. Add the camphor for clearance of all negative forces. Float a few fresh mint leaves along with the white carnation in the bowl for spiritual blessings.

For a total clearing of the house, take your incense and go through the house censing all of your space, especially in corners. Visualize neon-blue light flowing with the incense smoke. When you are done, light the candle and say the incantation.

INCANTATION

Oh Goddess of silver crescent pale moonlight, arch your bow over Yemaya's ocean waves, skirts ruffling along the surface, reflecting all blessings to our home, and our lives. Be thou a protectress of our home from all harm. I invoke the living divinity of [Goddess's name] in this, our sacred space.

MONEY HOUSE BLESSING

Cancer

Use "House Blessing" seal on page 178.

To cleanse and give financial blessings.

PURPOSE: Sometimes we need to have another avenue of income in order to keep our homes healthy, worry-free, and full of abundance. Money House Blessing is designed to bless the house with both finances and spiritual blessings. This can come in a multitude of ways. For example, negative spirits can cause mischief in the house by causing things to break, adding to expenses. This candle will stop these problems from happening. This candle can also be used as a money drawing spell. My grandmother had a saying—"When money flies out the window, the love flies right behind it." I learned early on to cleanse my house of negative spirits and bless it with abundance so that all who live under its roof are free of financial worries and able to enjoy life.

CANDLE COLOR: Green or blue.

CLEANSING: Water, salt, glory water, Florida water.

DEITY: Yemaya with Elegua, Diana and Pan, Rhiannon, Gaia, Rhea, Pomona.

OIL: Money House Blessing, Nine Indian Fruits, a blend of carnation and mint, gardenia, or vetiver.

INCENSE: Money House Blessing, any type of fruit blend like cherry or peach, frankincense and myrrh, sandalwood, wisteria.

FEEDING: Iron filings, sugar, honey, cane syrup.

Money House Blessing Spell

ITEMS NEEDED

A large bowl
7 or more apples (any kind, any color)
A letter of intention
A wineglass filled to the brim with fresh water

CASTING THE SPELL: To prepare this spell, waft incense smoke through the entire house, finishing at the front door. Walk the incense through the open doorway of your home. After the initial cleansing, pass the candle through the incense smoke. Place the letter in the bottom of the bowl and put your prepared candle on top of it. Place the apples in the bowl around your candle. Place a glass of water next to this. (The water should be changed every day the candle is lit until it is finished burning.) Light the candle and say the incantation.

INCANTATION

God and Goddess, bless this home with abundance, health, and wealth. Give me all that I may need. Let no one leave my home in hunger, poverty, or thirst. My home shall be a sanctuary to me and all that that enter herein. So Mote It Be.

Allow the candle to burn. As you are leaving your house the next day, take an apple to your front door. Pass the apple from the bottom left corner, up the frame, across the top, down, and across the bottom. Wave the apple down the center of the door. This is a spiritual cleansing. The fruit will pull away all negative vibrations from your front door and at the same time bless it with prosperity.

Go outside, lock the door, and find a tree so that you may leave the apple with the Gods. Give them thanks for cleansing your home and blessing it with prosperity. Repeat this action until all of the fruit is gone. If someone accidentally eats one of the apples do not despair. It is the Gods' way of having one of them.

METROPOLIS (THE HOME FINDER)

Use "House Blessing" seal on page 178.

Find that perfect new home!

PURPOSE: To find a new home or apartment these days can be pretty tough. This candle spell can really land you a sweet deal. The key is to be patient and trust in the Universe to provide. This candle can also be used to find a new roommate. The names of all the members of the household that will be moving should be carved into this candle. I usually include all my pets, too.

CANDLE COLOR: Orange, white.

CLEANSING: Water, orange water, Florida water.

DEITY: Mercury and Vesta.

OIL: Metropolis, House Blessing, a blend of sandalwood and allspice, bergamot, orange oil.

INCENSE: Mercury, House Blessing, Nag Champa, sandalwood, cinnamon, copal mixed with lavender flowers.

FEEDING: Iron filings, honey, and cinnamon powder.

Metropolis Spell

ITEMS NEEDED

A letter of intention that includes the location where you want to live, the price range you can afford, and the amount of

rooms you need. Be realistic, and do some research on your
desired area.
A bowl
Honey
Oak wood or bark (acorns are also acceptable)
Mugwort
Lovage
Three tonka beans
White wine

CASTING THE SPELL: Once the candle has been prepared, light the
incense. Pass your letter of intention through the incense smoke and
place it in the bowl. Pour honey over your letter. Add the oak for a
strong home and protection and the mugwort to assist in astral travel
to find your home. Add the lovage so there is always love in your new
dwelling as well as the three tonka beans for luck and money. Pour
in the white wine as an offering to Mercury and Vesta. Light your
candle and say the incantation.

INCANTATION

> Home sweet home, I seek a safe and happy house. Oh Mercury,
> oh Vesta, aid me in my search, help me find a place to light my fire
> and dwell in harmonious bliss. Ruler of the keys, oh Mercury open
> the door for me. The perfect place that is right for me is what I
> seek, and there to live in peace.

BANISHING

To banish heavy-hearted hate.

PURPOSE: The function of this seal is to eliminate problems of any
kind, be they spirits, ghosts, negative energy, or just troublesome
people. This hermetic seal is designed to neutralize any trouble so
that a smooth path will follow. This seal aligns the malfunctions in
your body and your life, so that healing is done on both a physical
and spiritual plane. Another use for this seal is calming, soothing,
and cooling down angry tempers, fights, and arguments. I tend to
use it in conjunction with other candles like Uncrossing, Tara, Love

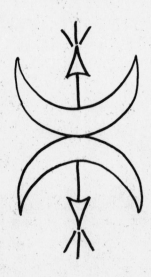

Banishing

Healing, Love Uncrossing, Divine Protection, House Blessing, Solar Blast, and Healing.

CANDLE COLOR: White, gray, and blue.

CLEANSING: Lavender water, Peace water, spring water.

DEITY: Yemaya, Diana, Artemis, Isis, Luna, Maat, Obatala, and all calming influential beings.

OIL: Banishing, Cast Away, Moon, camphor, mint, wintergreen, basil. *Bend Over*

INCENSE: Banishing, Uncrossing, Moon, Peace, lavender, frankincense mixed with lavender and chamomile.

FEEDING: camphor, cascarilla (powdered eggshell), salt.

Banishing Spell

ITEMS NEEDED

A letter of intention
A photocopy of the person to be healed or banished (optional)
A bowl
Ice cubes (to be replenished daily)

CASTING THE SPELL: Light the incense and pass all of the items through the smoke. Place both the picture and letter in the bowl. Place your candle on top of this message of banishment and peace and cover all of it in ice cubes. Light your candle and say the incantation.

INCANTATION

To the sea you are banished, on a solitary ice raft you will float far, far away. No hot and angry words, thoughts, or deeds can touch me, as you float away from me. I am free. All discord has been put to rest, your dark clouds are gone from me. I walk in balance, without fear of you.

As the candle burns, visualize whatever problem torments or plagues you floating away from you on a chunk of ice in the Arctic Ocean. See the situation itself neutralizing into a calm, harmonious outcome. The magick will work as the ice melts and the candle burns. Each day you burn this candle, empty the melted ice into the sink and watch your troubles go down the drain. Add fresh ice to your spell bowl and repeat your incantation each day until the candle finishes burning.

MOTHER BIRTH

PURPOSE: I first created this seal for the conception of my daughter, Tara. After invoking every childbirth goddess I'd ever heard of, and doing numerous spells for conception, I still wasn't conceiving and I felt very frustrated. So I created a conception candle. Nine months after I burned it, I gave birth to Tara.

Whether you are seeking to conceive or are due to give birth, you are about to give, and at the same time receive, the greatest gift of all: life. Take good care of your body, for it is a temple housing the miracle of creation that only you can perform. No child comes with a set of instructions, but each child comes with its own unique gift to this world. It is our job to help them find it and not try to mold them with our own ideas of what that gift might be. Patience and communication are the keys to opening the door for finding that gift.

Mother Birth

CANDLE COLOR: Yellow, red.

CLEANSING: Water, orange water, Florida water.

DEITY: Oshun, Yemaya, Cerridwen, Rhea, Gaia, Danu, Lakshmi, Freya, Ishtar, Amatartsu.

OIL: Cinnamon, cucumber, wisteria, jasmine, lotus, Oshun, Moon, Joy, Adam and Eve.

INCENSE: Oshun, Caridad del Cobre, Milagrosa, Yemeya, cinnamon, Earth, Protection, lotus, jasmine.

FEEDING: For conception: iron filings, honey, cinnamon powder, sunflower petals; for protection: iron filings, honey, fennel seeds, hyssop.

Mother Birth Conception Spell

ITEMS NEEDED

A letter of intention	Motherwort
A bowl	Mistletoe
Honey	Champagne
Dry or fresh red clover	Yellow flower petals

CASTING THE SPELL: Pass the letter through the incense smoke; place it in the bottom of the bowl. Put the candle on top and add the honey. Add the red clover for a strong womb, the motherwort as a sacred herb, and the mistletoe for fertility and magick. Add the champagne to make this a child of love, and sprinkle with the yellow flower petals to fashion a child of joy and sensitivity. Light your candle and say the incantation.

INCANTATION

> I ask for a little one inside of me, my rightful claim a mother to be. To mirror a reflection of the Mother Goddess, ripe with seed that will grow from the slender crescent to the full blown moon, heavy with life. My desire to hold, love, teach, and nurture the dear little child, for this I ask—as I understand it is a lifetime task.

MOTHER BIRTH (FOR A SAFE BIRTHING)

Use the "Mother Birth" seal on page 185. All corresponding elements remain the same.

PURPOSE: Carol Burnett once said that "labor is like taking your lower lip and pulling it back over your head." It is no secret that birth is a difficult transition for mother, child and father. Men have their own difficulties during the childbirth process—nervousness, feelings of helplessness, anxiety. This candle will help give the mother have a safe and easier birth, ease the father's anxiety, and protect the child.

This candle is for more than a safe birthing—it is for a happy pregnancy as well. It still amazes me how difficult people can act when a woman is with child. Families may not approve of a child having been conceived—then when the baby arrives, everyone is cooing around it and fighting to have a chance to hold it. This candle will help family and friends be supportive and compassionate to the expecting mother.

CANDLE COLOR: Blue, white, green.

CLEANSING: Water, orange water, Florida water.

DEITY: Oshun, Yemaya, Hathor, Isis, Rhea, Demeter, Kore, Morgan Le Fey, Aradia, Rhiannon, Mary.

OIL: Protection, Love and Protection, Milagrosa, lotus, acacia, carnation, gardenia.

INCENSE: Oshun, Caridad del Cobre, Milagrosa, Yemaya, cinnamon, Earth, Protection, lotus, jasmine.

FEEDING: For conception: iron filings, honey, cinnamon powder, sunflower petals; for protection: iron filings, honey, fennel seeds, hyssop.

ITEMS NEEDED

A letter of intention	Juniper berries
A bowl	Rowan
Sugar	Water
Camphor	1 to 3 white carnation heads
Hyssop	

CASTING THE SPELL: Light incense during both the preparation of the candle and its lighting. Place the letter of intention in the bowl and place your candle on top. Add the sugar, followed by the camphor, hyssop, juniper berries, and rowan. Gently add the water and float the carnations in the bowl. Light the candle and say the incantation.

INCANTATION

Mother of All Creation, be here with me. For in loving sacrifice do we both share the dual rites of life: to bear in pain torn from our side, to give life to a small one so dear. Guide me in your loving light so that I bear with little strife, a child into our arms.

If there is a difficult birth and someone wants to say an incantation to help you deliver more easily, have them try this:

Full moon waters flow, expel from me [or name of woman giving birth] the seed that has been sowed. Ease the way for a child bright coming out into this world with no strife.

CRYSTAL HEALING

To heal all negatives afflicting your life.

PURPOSE: The image of this seal is a luminous crystal ball supported by a triad, representing the triple will of the goddess in all her forms—Maiden, Mother, and Crone. She will support healing in her sacred circle. The moon floats upright in the center to support the psyche. From its center blooms a perfect lotus, from which emerges a wish-fulfilling gem. In the heart in its center, the symbol of infinity counsels us that universal love and compassion always surround us, for there is no end to this source.

Crystal Healing

There may be more than one trauma that is the cause of ongoing stress and negativity in your life, the effects of which can weigh heavily on different levels of your psyche. For instance, something may have happened that causes you to feel irrational fear whenever you see a spider, and you have no idea why. Something is affecting the subconscious level of your psyche. Or, you may be fully aware that you received a terrible spider bite as a child, which caused an allergic reaction, which almost killed you. In this case, your fear of spiders is completely conscious. This candle is designed to heal hurts on all levels of the psyche.

CANDLE COLORS: White for mental clarity, quitting smoking, and to stop bad habits; green for healing trauma, childhood trauma, past-life karma and sorrows carried over; blue for peaceful meditation, psychic protection, tranquility, calming and soothing the nerves; yellow for opulence, joy, balanced equilibrium, to ease depression or anxiety; orange to bring personal success, achievement, gratification for a job well done; pink for self-love, confidence to go ahead and love again; red for courage, stamina, and as an aid in becoming more assertive.

CLEANSING: Water, salt, fresh or dry basil leaves.

DEITY: All twenty-one Taras, Kwan Yin, and all Mothers of Compassion, healing, and eternal love.

OIL: Crystal Healing, amethyst, Healing, Uncrossing, carnation, chamomile, lavender, heliotrope, rose, sandalwood.

INCENSE: Banishing, Uncrossing, Healing, Nag Champa, lotus, lavender, sweet grass, white sage, sandalwood.

FEEDING: Camphor, sugar, sage.

Crystal Healing Spell

ITEMS NEEDED

A bowl
a letter of intention
Additional items listed under each candle color below, according to the purpose of your spell

CASTING THE SPELL: Burn incense during the preparation of the candle and while casting the spell. Place the letter in the bowl with the candle on top. The additional ingredients will then be placed in the bowl. The candle should be lit as the appropriate incantation is recited.

White (for mental clarity or to end bad habits):

ITEMS NEEDED

> Sparkling water
> Three camphor tablets
> One white carnation

INCANTATION

> I am free of all debris, nothing holds me. My mind is clear and unchained. No worries and no regrets—my life is now free of pain.

Green (for healing past traumas):

ITEMS NEEDED

> Water
> Green food coloring
> One pink carnation
>
> Honey
> Fresh or dry basil leaves.

INCANTATION

> *I see the past, I see the pain—*
> *I see that from which I no longer gain.*
> *Each time I relive the agony,*
> *It's as if it's haunting me.*
> *This leaves a stain on my soul,*
> *And another inner battle then unfolds.*
> *Yet now I see a brand new day! The sun has risen,*
> *And all those who hurt me, I have forgiven.*
> *I am free of the chains of the past!*
> *And shall live unplagued by its horrors at last.*

Blue (for psychic protection, tranquility):

ITEMS NEEDED

Water

Blue food coloring

Sugar

Camphor

One white carnation

A few drops of spearmint oil

INCANTATION

Tranquil blue seas of compassion engulf me. They wash over my mind, body, and soul. Peace has become my new fashion. I wear it like a crown of victory that sheds its healing light over me. No longer do I feel discord. Peace reigns outward and inward. Love and light live in my heart, and I shed some of that light on those I touch.

Yellow (for joy or to ease depression or anxiety):

ITEMS NEEDED

Sparkling water

Honey

One yellow flower

A few drops of jasmine oil

INCANTATION

As I climb to the rooftops and I sing,
Joy has moved in and removed the sting.
No more sadness is in my life,
I am no longer filled with strife.

Orange (for personal success):

ITEMS NEEDED

Orange water

Honey

Sage

Lavender

INCANTATION

> *Success, success is all I see.*
> *This is what is coming to me.*
> *For I have worked so very hard*
> *And now I shall get my reward.*

Pink (for self-love or confidence to love someone else):

ITEMS NEEDED

Rose water
Lavender water

Honey
Pink rose petals

INCANTATION

> *Healing love pours through me,*
> *Clearing my heart center of all debris.*
> *The sadness I've captured inside me shall flee.*
> *Making me whole, and setting me free.*
> *Love flows replacing the pain from before.*
> *I shall be healed ever more.*
> *I open my eyes and now I will see*
> *Just what love has in store for me.*

Red (for courage, stamina):

ITEMS NEEDED

One cup of cooled black
    coffee
Sugar

Red pepper
Peppermint leaves

INCANTATION

> *Onward charge to the battle cry*
> *Banners of sweet victory fly.*
> *Courage is my shield*
> *While on the field*
> *And my fiery stamina shall never die.*

8.

Enchanted Protection Candles

Protection plays a very important role in and out of the magickal life. Some of you may believe that if you are not magickal practitioners you do not require protection. People's negative thoughts can bring harm to your life. Once in a while it's good to light a protection candle just to keep all harm from you and your family. I always say "an ounce of prevention is worth a pound of cure." (Actually, Benjamin Franklin said it first.) If, however, it is evident that you are under attack psychically or physically, then these candles and spells will surely put a stop to all harm.

DIVINE PROTECTION

For psychic protection while performing magick.

PURPOSE: This seal was designed by Lord Hermes, one of the original priests and brothers of the Minoan Brotherhood. The Minoan Brotherhood is a tradition of Wicca created by my High Priest Edmund Buczynski (Lord Gwyddion) in the mid-1970s. It was one of the first all-male Wiccan traditions here on the East Coast and still survives today. The Minoan Sisterhood was created by Ed and me soon after that. This was the compliment coven to the Minoan Brotherhood. Later on, Phyllis Curott would join the first male and female Minoan groups together. Today they are known as the Minoan Fellowship. The three traditions have similarities, yet each is different. They each honor the same gods, but in various ways.

Lord Hermes was my partner in spirit channeling; we worked the Ouija board together, and we learned some of the most amazing

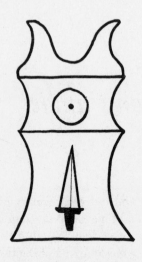

Divine Protection

things. He was powerfully in tune with the spirit world, and was often given wonderful gifts of insight. This seal was one of them.

When he gave it to me, his original title for this seal was "Magus." Its purpose is for calling forth the higher mysteries, or the magick of the God from the Minoan tradition. While creating enchanted candles together in 1982, Lord Hermes and I began to see that invoking this God taps into a very strong protective power. The clients we crafted this candle for later came back to us with marvelous reports of the candle's ability to protect. For example, the first person we gave it to was having a horrible time with some neighbors in his apartment building. They would bang on his door at night then run back down the hall and into their apartment, trying to instigate a fight. The neighbor's nightly visits stopped soon after the client performed this candle spell.

This seal is also for preventing psychic takeovers, repelling psychic vampires, and discouraging psychic attack. It will protect the magus, witch, pagan, and magickal practitioner, as well as any non–magick user.

CANDLE COLOR: Blue, white, red, brown.

CLEANSING: Water, salt, a few drops of mint oil or extract.

DEITY: Asterion, Minos, Kronos, Ouranos, Zeus.

OIL: Divine Protection, Blessing, Protection, musk with a few drops of pine oil, ambergris, frankincense, cedar, mastic, cypress, basil.

INCENSE: Protection, Blessing, Fiery Wall of Protection, frankincense, frankincense and myrrh, cedar, pine, mastic, Dragon's Blood, rue.

FEEDING: Iron filings, honey, cedar chips or powder.

Divine Protection Spell:

ITEMS NEEDED

A letter of intention	Honey
A bowl	Beer
Witches grass herb	Fresh or dry mint leaves
Solomon's Seal herb	

CASTING THE SPELL: Incense should be lit for the God while you are preparing the candle. Once the candle is ready, place the letter of intention in the bowl and put the candle on top. Layer the witches grass around the base of the candle, and sprinkle the Solomon's Seal over it. Pour in the honey, and add the beer—it has a head and will foam up when you first pour it. As you pour the beer, say the first part of the incantation. Add the mint leaves, and say the second part as you light the candle.

> I offer this libation of Beer to the God [deity's name].

Add the mint leaves and say:

> Protection from all harm is the shield I carry around me, from the protective force of the God's light, no baneful one can see me. So Mote It Be.

PEACE AND PROTECTION

For peace and protection from all ill intent.

PURPOSE: For total peace and protection from all malevolent beings, whether they be human or spiritual. Note that the seal from "Banishing" is included in this seal. In addition, the two swords are erect, which is a gesture meaning peace, not war. The symbolism of the two swords also works like giant scissors, ready to cut any discordant strand of negative energy. All together, they represent you and your family living in peace and protection.

CANDLE COLORS: Blue, white, red.

CLEANSING: Water, lavender water, three drops of camphor oil (or some camphor broken up into small pieces and steeped in water).

DEITY: Athena, Artemis, Hecate, Themis, Nemesis, Demeter, Ares, Erinyes (triple will of the goddess)

OIL: Peace and Protection, Peace, Egyptian Protection, Banishing, a blend of camphor and carnation, lavender, basil, frankincense, Dragon's Blood, mint, myrrh.

INCENSE: Protection, Banishing, Uncrossing, Dragon's Blood, frankincense, lavender, rue.

FEEDING: Iron filings, honey, Dragon's Blood, rue.

Peace and Protection

Peace and Protection Spell

ITEMS NEEDED

A letter of intention	Black peppercorns
A bowl	Red wine
Salt	Fresh or dry mint
Dragon's Blood	Fresh or dry basil
Fresh or dry rue	

Burn your incense as an offering during the preparation of this spell. Pass the candle, letter, and bowl through the incense smoke for purification. Place the letter in the bowl and put your candle on top. Pour a ring of salt in the bowl around the candle's base, followed by the Dragon's Blood, rue, and peppercorns. Offer your libation of red wine to the deities so that they will protect you from all harm, and add the mint and basil leaves on top of the wine to cleanse and protect and offer peace to your family and home. Light the candle and say the incantation.

INCANTATION

With this wick I do light a candle of protection. No longer sick with fear we will have peace without shedding tears. No matter what section of our home they try to touch, we will live without fear. Praise be to the mighty ones who protect us. So Mote It Be.

JUSTICE

For calling on the forces of karmic law.

PURPOSE: There is no hiding from karmic law. In time, all things come to be weighed and balanced. When you feel it is necessary to put this force into action because you have been wronged or harmed in some way, then this seal is definitely for you. This is a magickal call for the score to be evened.

The seal itself represents the Egyptian Goddess Maat, weigher of souls. On one side of the scale sits the red feather of truth, on the other side an earthen vessel, which houses the soul of the one being judged. It is said that although she weighs the soul, it is Osiris who judges its cleanliness. The earthen vessel contains water, which is considered the life source.

Justice

If the vessel of water is clear, it will balance with the feather. However, if the water is unclear and it contains "mud"— a heaviness in the soul—then the scales will not be balanced and judgment must be passed.

The balancing of karmic debt requires putting all anger and emotions aside and allowing karmic law to decide what is to be done. This is perfect for a situation when someone has done something really bad to you, or brought you into very sad circumstances. Everyone says, "Don't worry they'll get theirs," or "What goes around comes around." Well, this just speeds things up a bit and helps heal your anger so you can let go and get on with your life.

CANDLE COLORS: Red, blue, brown, black (black should only be used in extreme cases).

CLEANSING: Water, red wine, salt.

DEITY: Maat, Anubis, Osiris, Saturn, Justo Juez (Just Judge, the Crucifixion), Hera, Moerae, Erinyes, Oya.

OIL: Justice, Osiris, Saturn, Just Judge, basil, myrrh, rue, Dragon's Blood, and pine. Bend Over

INCENSE: Saturn, Just Judge, Justice, Dragon's Blood, frankincense and myrrh, Three Kings, pine.

FEEDING: Iron filings, Dragon's Blood, myrrh, and honey.

Justice Spell

ITEMS NEEDED

A letter of intention	Mustardseed (black or
A bowl	yellow)
Salt	Graveyard dirt (optional)
Dragon's Blood	Red wine
Myrrh	

CASTING THE SPELL: To set up this spell, the first thing you must do is to take several deep breaths. Let go of the anger, and get focused on allowing Universal karmic law to handle what needs to be done. The responsibility for any judgment is now out of your hands. Light your incense and pass the letter of intention through the smoke. Place it in the bowl and put your candle on top. Pour a ring of salt in the bowl around the candle base, and add the Dragon's Blood, myrrh, and mustardseed. Sprinkle the graveyard dirt all over the mixture to bury the perpetrator in his or her fate.

Pour in the red wine as an offering to the Goddess or God of your choice and say his or her name aloud as you do so, saying the incantation.

INCANTATION

Oh, hear me [deity's name], I ask that you hold court and the power of your justice treat me well. I ask that [name of enemy] be judged by you for what has been done to me. I ask for your intercession here as no court of the land can satisfy me, and no judgment here can rectify what was done. I put my fate in your hands, for only the higher court of karmic law can withstand the test and put this sad situation to rest. Please give me peace. So Mote it Be.

Now light the candle and with all of your will empty out each and every ugly little scenario that has been replaying in your mind. Let it go into the candle and to the judgment of a higher authority than we have here on Earth.

WIN AT COURT

Moon in Sagittarius

For bringing a favorable verdict in court.

PURPOSE: Court matters are never easy—even if you are clearly in the right, a simple thing can create delays or cause things to go awry. Sometimes you can be right and still lose! This candle is for all types of lawsuits, custody battles, and support issues. It also works for cases that are not necessarily going to court but require hearings. Use for workmen's compensation issues, social security in any of its forms, or any type of discrimination in the workplace. If you are forced out of a company for any unfair reason and you are taking your employer to court, this candle will most definitely help you in your case. If you are too young to retire and wish to continue to work, then I suggest you do an employment pyramid candle as well. There are so many different legal circumstances that this seal covers. It will help keep you protected from an unbalanced justice system.

Win at Court

CANDLE COLOR: Purple, blue, white.

CLEANSING: Water, Bay Rum, Florida water, head of a white carnation.

DEITY: Jupiter, Zeus, Odin, Osiris, Ra, Maat, Themis, Athena, Libertas, Obatala.

OIL: Win at Court, Jupiter, High John, sandalwood, lavender, juniper, violet blended with three drops of mint oil, vervain, hyssop, amber, clove.

INCENSE: High John, Success, Jupiter, a smudge blend of sage and juniper, white sage, lavender, frankincense, Three Kings, frankincense blended with a few bay leaves and one or two cloves on a hot coal.

FEEDING: Iron filings, anise seeds, cinquefoil, hyssop.

Win at Court Spell

ITEMS NEEDED

A letter of intention or copies of any legal document that pertains to your case.
A bowl
Honey
Star anise
Hyssop
Juniper berries
Red wine
One red felt bag

One lodestone
One hematite
One High John the Conqueror root
One Low John root
One whole nutmeg
Bay leaves
Basil
Cloves
Book of matches

CASTING THE SPELL: This spell has two parts to it. One is the candle bowl spell; the other part is to make a charm bag to carry with you. Pass the letter of intention through the incense smoke. Place it in the bowl and put the candle on top. Add the honey and the star anise, hyssop, and juniper berries. Pour in the wine and say the incantation.

INCANTATION

To you oh sword of justice, I ask of thee, in good faith to be with me.

Now light the candle and say:

Oh Goddess of Justice, hear my call, and speak for me. Jupiter, oh God of Wisdom and Insight, let your powers of clarity be with me. Stand by my side and answer my call. See liberty and justice come once and for all.

Once the spell is set up, gather the rest of the ingredients. You will be creating a charm bag in front of the candle spell. Light more incense and pass the red bag through the smoke first, then follow up with the rest of your ingredients. Put the lodestone in the bag—this is the magnet that will attract forces to your side. After that, add the hematite, the High John root, the Low John root, the nutmeg, bay leaves, basil, and cloves.

Here is the trick that seals the spell tight: Take a match from the book, strike it, and drop it lit into the bag. Quickly spit into the bag to put out the match, and then blow into the bag. Pull the strings tight and close it.

You have just added the four elements to your charm bag and empowered it with your own essence. The match represents earth, since it is made from a tree, the lighting of the match represents fire, the spit from your mouth is water, and blowing into the bag is air. Plus both the saliva and breath are your own essences, which ties the charm to you. Now place the charm bag in front of your candle bowl and leave it there until the spell is done. You will carry it to court with you, and you may keep it always as a charm to overcome troubles.

DURGA

To invoke Mother Durga for protection.

PURPOSE: Mother Durga is the slayer of demons and negative forces that bring sorrows and sufferings to humankind—greed, avarice, hatred, spite, jealousy, envy, corruption, and violence, just to name a few. According to Hindu legend, demons brought these negatives to earth and infected all of Mother Earth's children with them. Even the gods themselves became defeated by these demons, no matter how hard they tried to repel them. As a last resort they called to Mother Durga. They were hesitant to do this because whenever she got upset she would go into a frenzy, and it was next to impossible to calm her down. Near the end of the war, there was only one demon left to face. He was the fiercest of all the demons and Mother Durga fought him and slayed him. So intense was her frenzy that she transformed into the fierce warrioress Kali Ma and continued her fury. It was only Shiva, Kali's beloved consort, who was finally able to abate her bloodlust.

Durga

This does not mean if you call her up she is going to go crazy—as long as you are not embodying the power of the gods at war with demons! She gets angry when the demonic forces still inspire people to be cruel to one another. If you are the victim and are not doing harm to another, she will attack the ills that cause people to harm you, but will leave you unscathed. So it is extra important not to use this spell or call this Goddess to harm others.

Mother Durga rides on the back of a tiger or lion. She has ten arms, and in each one she carries a weapon or magickal instrument. Reasons for invoking Mother Durga are simple—to slay those aspects of your enemies' power that are harming you. We have no wish to harm them but only disarm them from harming us further.

CANDLE COLOR: Red.

CLEANSING: Red wine, Dragon's Blood.

DEITY: Durga

OIL: Durga, Banishing, Mars, Dragon's Blood, rue, myrrh, vetivert, patchouli. Bend Over

INCENSE: Banishing, Protection, Mars, Dragon's Blood, myrrh, patchouli, Nag Champa.

FEEDING: Iron Filings, honey, red cayenne pepper, Dragon's Blood.

Mother Durga Spell

ITEMS NEEDED

A letter of intention	Dragon's Blood
3 bowls: one large bowl for the candle spell and two smaller ones	Black pepper
	Honey
	Red wine
Salt	Red rose petals
Red cayenne pepper	108 pennies
Myrrh	

CASTING THE SPELL: Light incense as an offering to Mother Durga. Pass the letter of intention through the incense smoke, imploring Durga to come and read your letter and set matters right. Put the letter in the large bowl and place the candle on top of it. Pour salt into the bowl around the candle, followed by the red cayenne pepper, myrrh, Dragon's Blood, and black pepper. Pour on the honey as a food offering to Durga to please her. Add the red wine as an offering and scatter red rose petals to compliment her beauty.

Place the two smaller bowls in front of your spell bowl. Put the pennies in one bowl and leave the other empty. Light the candle. Recite the incantation one hundred and eight times, each time moving a penny from one bowl into the other. Repeat this until all the pennies have been transferred. While chanting the prayer, visualize Great Mother Durga riding on the back of a tiger. In each one of her ten hands she bears a weapon and is bristling with ferocity as she comes to battle for your safety.

INCANTATION

> Om hrim dum Durga Yai Namah

Say it phonetically as best you can. Have no fear—she will respond, even if your pronunciation isn't a hundred percent correct.

If you prefer an English version:

> Oh supreme and fearless Mother Durga, destroy all evils without exception that my enemies send to me.

KALI MA

For invoking the fierce mother goddess, Kali Ma.

PURPOSE: This seal is for the destruction of enemies through the invocation of Kali Ma, for life-and-death situations, the salvation of self and family, where danger abounds, Kali Ma comes to defend you with a wrathful expression. In the Hindu legend of the battle of the demons, Durga lusted for blood and turned into Kali Ma. In Hindu mythology as with many myths from different cultures one aspect of a God or Goddess can easily transmute into another. I have been told that Lakshmi, Mother Goddess of Compassion, Wealth, and Abundance is an aspect of Kali Ma. In the Hindu belief system, all Goddesses are one—they just change faces when the need presents itself. In essence, they are all just different aspects

Kali Ma

of the divine mother. This makes a lot of sense to me. It's just like when I watch Mother Moon go from shy young virgin quarter to full mother to dark crone. What's interesting about Kali Ma is that if you are essentially a good person she can be a benefactor to you, and can also be your enemy's worst nightmare. She gives gifts and wealth to her devotees. She offers protection from harm and help to those who need it. Kali Ma, it should be added, is a fierce protector of women. Women offer a natural blood sacrifice every moon period. This is one of her offerings—blood. For the purposes of this book, however, I substitute red wine, and from my experience she finds that perfectly acceptable.

It is said that Kali Ma generally does not like men. I find this to be untrue. She just does not like the aggressive nature that many men tend to allow to rule them. You may be thinking that for a Goddess who does not like violence and aggression, she does not exactly set a good example. Or does she? I will give you an analogy of mine to try and explain why people are devoted to this mother goddess who is so dark with blood and rage that she is called the Black Queen of Death and Destruction, or the Black Mother.

Kali is described as naked and wearing a necklace of skulls and a girdle of arms and legs. She tramples on the burial grounds in India, doing her ecstatic bloodlust dance. She has anywhere from four to ten arms. Although this image of her, which was the first one I ever saw, is pretty horrifying, I found myself powerfully drawn to her. And I met many people who were devoted to her the same way I was devoted to Lakshmi. It was upon research that I discovered the greatness of Kali Ma and I have myself been a devotee ever since.

The dual nature of Kali Ma can be looked at this way: Let us for a moment picture ourselves in a fictitious high school. We have three kinds of kids: the very tough ones, the ones who are in the middle striving to become like the toughest ones, and then we have the meek. The ones in the middle are trying to prove themselves, so they attack one of the meek ones. The tougher ones see this, and knowing that it is no challenge to pick on a person with no aggressive tendencies, they step in to stop it. Kali Ma is the same way. As long as both parties can fight their own battles, she is fine. What she does not like is a bully. What she stamps out with her feet doing her dance are all the ills that plague human nature in unevenly matched battles.

I have made an attempt to try to simplify Kali Ma. Make no mistake—she is fierce. Do not invoke her unless all other avenues have been exhausted. She will not bother to settle petty arguments or disagreements.

If you are under siege by some dark magick or being verbally or physically attacked, and it is really compromising your life, then it is appropriate to invoke her. I myself only invoke her to give prosperity and offer protection. This you can do with her freely. Invoke her to prevent and protect. My first suggestion when there is trouble is to refer to one of the other deities, such as Tara for pacifying, or Durga to slay those ills that plague you (remember, Durga is an aspect of Kali Ma). Other seals that can be used are Uncrossing, Peace and Protection, Divine Protection, and Justice.

CANDLE COLOR: Black, blue, red.

CLEANSING: Red wine, salt.

DEITY: Kali Ma

OIL: Myrrh, Dragon's Blood, patchouli. Bend Over

INCENSE: Dragon's Blood mixed with myrrh.

FEEDING: Iron filings, Dragon's Blood, guinea pepper.

Kali Ma Invocation Spell

ITEMS NEEDED

A letter of intention
A book of matches
Three bowls: one large one
    for the candle spell and
    two smaller ones.
Guinea pepper
Black pepper

Myrrh
Dragon's Blood
Sulfur
Salt
Cemetery dirt
Red wine
108 pennies

CASTING THE SPELL: Burn your incense as an offering to Kali Ma in preparation for this ritual. Gather everything together once the candle has been prepared and the letter of intention has been written. Please be very careful in this next step. Strike a match and burn your letter in the bowl. Kali Ma will read your letter among the ashes. Place your candle in the bowl on the ashes. Around your candle, add the guinea pepper, black pepper, myrrh, Dragon's Blood, sulfur, salt, and the cemetery dirt. Add the red wine as a substitute for blood.

Light the candle and place the two small bowls in front of the large one. Put all of the pennies in one bowl and leave the other one empty. Each time you recite the incantation, one penny should go from the full bowl to the empty one. Repeat until all the pennies have been transferred from one bowl to the other.

INCANTATION

Om Hrim Hram Hrim Hrum

English version:

Oh Mother Kali, oh Lady of the Gods, destroy all evils that plague me in my hour of suffering.

9.

Enchanted Self-Improvement Candles

Self-improvement is such a *wonderful* gift to give to yourself. Sometimes it is just the ticket you need to get your life back on track. When you go get a haircut or a makeover or shop for new clothes, you not only feel better, but people notice you. Doing something for yourself is a healing act of unconditional love, a gift to a very important person—you.

SONG OF THE ELDER GODS

To bring inspiration in all phases of the arts.

PURPOSE: This seal came from the astral realm of the creative arts and will work for all people in the arts and entertainment fields. It will help in your creative flow, and to bring recognition and honors. It was sent as a Druidic symbol of the Lyre from the Gods of the forest. It is stylized from an early harp that bards played while telling their stories traveling from town to town. Their stories would be told while playing music for everyone from kings to tavern patrons. Bards also used the harp for magickal purposes to coax the faery folk from their realm in order to enchant and make magick. The elder earth Gods still respond to this symbol. Use this candle to find a woodland muse to come to your aid and inspire you in any form of creativity and the arts.

CANDLE COLOR: Purple, yellow, orange, red. Purple is recommended for inspiration, psychic creation, and helping to put you in tune with astral entities, muses, and musical spheres. Yellow is good for music, literature, documentaries, and all forms of writing because it is the color that represents air and communication—it can help to open you to receive thoughts as well as project them out. Orange is for success, achievement, and accomplishments. Red is for personal drive and initiative and will help you get past that lethargic state when you seem to have no motivation. It also helps break through writer's block.

Song of the Elder Gods

CLEANSING: Spring water, honey, a few drops of any floral perfume.

DEITY: Pan, woodland muses, wood fairies, ancient bardic spirits.

OIL: Mercury, Jupiter, Inspiring, mimosa, honeysuckle, sandalwood, a blend of pine and musk.

INCENSE: Ancient Wisdom, Success, Dream, Earth, pine, sandalwood, honeysuckle, jasmine, lily.

FEEDING: Iron filings, honey, fresh flower petals. If the season allows, they can be gathered from your local neighborhood; wildflowers like clover, buttercups, daisies, or whatever grows in your region are great.

Song of the Elder Gods Spell

ITEMS NEEDED

A letter of intention
A sample of your art
  (optional)
A bowl
Honey

Cinnamon sticks
Mugwort
Elderflowers
Red wine

CASTING THE SPELL: Once you have prepared your candle, light your incense and write your letter of intention. If you have any writing that you have already done, place a copy of it underneath the bowl. Put the letter in the bowl and put your candle on top. Pour on the honey to make the muses sweet on you. Add the cinnamon sticks, mugwort, and elder flowers. Now pour in the red wine as an offering so the Elders can drink to your success. Light some more incense, light the candle, and say the incantation.

INCANTATION

> *Muses of the old ones come to me,*
> *For inspiration is what I need.*
> *Help me tap into the Creative Well,*
> *For in my heart is a story to tell.*
> *Come around me, my muses*
> *and infuse my heart and mind*
> *with inspiration, passion, and creativity—*
> *O, make the magick mine.*

SOLAR BLAST

To overcome illness, depression, or a general lack of life luster.

PURPOSE: This spell is for a person overcoming illness, depression, despair, or a life that needs to be refilled with new goals and insights.

This seal will replace sorrow with joy and will replace fear with courage. Emotional well-being will turn the wheel of fortune to where you are being met with open encouragement from yourself. This is an anti-anxiety candle. Let the joy of the sun blast away all of those dark clouds like a murder of crows taking flight. Sow seeds of joy where sorrow once lived as a rainbow falls upon you. Inscribe your name in

Solar Blast

the cauldron of rebirth and you will emerge a person appreciating the dawn of a new day and a new you.

CANDLE COLOR: Yellow, white, orange.

CLEANSING: Water, orange water, two tablespoons of orange juice, bay leaves or Bay Rum.

DEITY: Dawn, Iris, Aurelia, Amateratsu, Apollo, Aurora, Sophia.

OIL: Rainbow, Joy, Sun, frankincense, orange, heliotrope, rue, amber, carnation, acacia. Come-to-Me

INCENSE: Sun, frankincense, amber, copal, mastic, cedar, or a blend of frankincense and chamomile.

FEEDING: Iron filings, honey, yellow or orange flower petals.

Solar Blast Spell

ITEMS NEEDED

    Music that makes you want to jump up and down, inspires you,
        and makes you happy
    A letter of intention
    A bowl
    Honey
    Dry rose hips
    Damiana
    Chamomile
    Dry or fresh sunflower petals
    Dry or fresh marigold flowers
    A libation: sparkling white wine, white wine, champagne, honey
        mead, sparkling water, or orange water.
    A hand mirror in any size or style

CASTING THE SPELL: Light your incense. For this spell, I particularly like to use a bowl with a rainbow cut into the glass, or any bowl with a rainbow hue. A yellow glass bowl, or one in any color that reminds you of sunshine is also good. (This is not a requirement for the spell to work; I just like it.)

Put on the music. Pass the bowl through the incense smoke. Listen to the music, and look deep within yourself and write about what would make you personally happy. This is your letter of intention, and it will allow you to come out of your blue mood without involving anyone else. This is only about you! Pass the letter through the incense to cleanse and purify it.

Place the letter in the bottom of the bowl and put the candle on top of it. Pour the honey on top of your letter and sprinkle in the rose hips, damiana, and chamomile. Slowly pour the liquid over these. Add the marigolds and the sunflower petals. Place the mirror in front of the candle bowl. Light the candle and say the incantation.

INCANTATION

> *Showers of gold rain down upon me.*
> *Happy colors float all around me.*
> *From the tears that rained down from my eyes,*
> *The Goddess Iris casts a rainbow across my dreary skies.*
> *I awaken to the Goddess's call:*
> *"It is time to stand erect and tall."*
> *The Goddess's Dawn brings a new day*
> *And Aureila sheds her golden light beams to send me on my way*
> *To happiness. So mote it be.*

The following day, light incense to the morning sun, then take your mirror and pass it through the incense smoke. Go to the window where there is the most sun. If it is a cloudy day, do not fret; the light outside tells you the sun is still out. Hold the mirror up to catch the sun's rays and feel the power of that light being captured in the mirror. When you are ready, turn the mirror around and look at the sun's reflection in the mirror and smile. Yes, you must smile for the spell to work. Now get busy, and fill your life with catching up on what you have neglected, and do something good for yourself at least once a day. Take yourself to a movie that makes you happy. Or buy yourself a little gift. Or take some time to take a nice hot bath. Or walk in a garden and smell some flowers. Repeat the mirror spell daily until the candle is finished burning.

HIGH PRIESTESS INITIATION

For the initiation ceremony to high priestesshood.

PURPOSE: This candle serves two purposes. It was created for the elevation of a high priestess in any tradition of the Craft. This seal is open to any tradition that chooses to use it. Initiation is a sacred and holy moment in a priestess's life and this candle is to inspire a doorway to the Gods so that she may be blessed on this special night.

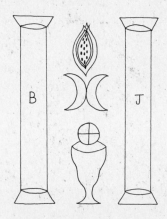

High Priestess Initiation

The other purpose for this candle is to open up your psychic abilities. This is done through entering the sacred portals between the two pillars of the seal. These pillars represent the dual forces of the universe. Their kabalistic meanings are Severity and Mercy. For you they are the pillars of darkness and light, black and white. They represent the dual forces of nature, the dark and light side of the moon. Unveiling the psychic world and piercing the mystic vapors that protect it from outsiders is what this candle is designed for. If you are truly ready to enter deep into the psychic realms, then this candle will help light the way. When the Goddess of Wisdom is invoked, she will help open the doorway to your inner mind and allow a natural flow between the worlds of the physical and the psychic. Do you read Tarot cards or practice any other form of divination? This seal will help you to get more from your divination work.

The eloquent beauty of this seal is designed with the High Priestess card of the tarot in mind. It vibrates with the nature of that card. Therefore, the seal can be used to invoke the essence of all that card represents—namely, enlightenment through the subconscious mind releasing hidden mysteries and awakening the Goddess to live and breathe within you. If you invoke her wisdom, she will provide you with knowledge and surround you with people offering wise council, both from the physical world and the psychic realm. The High Priestess card in the tarot also represents hidden forces at work behind the scenes; this seal will invoke that divine intervention.

The High Priestess Initiation candle is also good for Drawing Down the Moon rituals and as a devotional offering to the new or full moons.

CANDLE COLOR: Blue, white, purple.

CLEANSING: Rose water, Kolonia 1800 cologne, a few drops of the oil you will anoint the candle with.

DEITY: Diana, Rhiannon, Isis, Sophia, Athena, Artemis, Gaia, Selene, Aradia, Inanna, Rhea, Themis, Iris, Yemaya, Persephone. Your personal coven Goddess name is best, of course.

OIL: High Priestess Initiation, Goddess, Black Star, a blend of camphor and lily, ambergris, rose, violet, sandalwood, lotus, gardenia.

INCENSE: Moon Goddess, Lunar, Black Star, sandalwood, lotus, gardenia, rose, vanilla, peach.

FEEDING: Camphor, mugwort, rose petals, honey.

High Priestess Initiation Spell

ITEMS NEEDED

A letter of intention	Wine or spring water
A bowl	Camphor
Honey	A mirror large enough to fit
Calamus root	under your bowl and
Lavender flowers	reflect your magick spell
Vervain	(optional)

CASTING THE SPELL: Burn incense during the preparation of this spell. Pass all the objects through the incense smoke for purification, including the tool you will use for carving the candle. Place your letter of intention in the bowl, and put your carved candle on top. Add the honey, and add calamus for psychic inspiration and communication, lavender flowers for purification, and vervain for loving inspiration.

Now add your water or wine slowly and float the camphor in the liquid. If you are using a mirror then it should be placed under the bowl. Light more incense, light your candle, and say the incantation.

INCANTATION

> *On a moonlit night*
> *My soul takes flight,*
> *To temples that exist beyond the starry night.*
> *Into the heavens I soar*
> *Past destiny's door*
> *To descend between two pillars—one is black the other white*
> *Before me stands a chalice clear,*
> *As I drink of it my reason for being here is suddenly very dear.*
> *That which I seek is surely near.*
> *Images swirl and leap about me telling me tales of wonders*
>   *and delights.*
> *A luminous moon above glows softly with veiled light,*
> *Parting the ways of the mysteries I seek tonight.*
> *"Soul flyer"—a voice from the mist begins to speak,*
> *"you are now a seer."*
> *A voice for the Goddess here on earth:*
> *"Tell my children of my mirth.*
> *I am Mother of the Spiral, I am the path from where you all come*
>   *and you all go*
> *And as you travel so,*
> *You are protected in my light."*

ASTRAL TRAVEL AND LUNAR DEVOTION

Use the "High Priestess Initiation" seal on page 213.

For assistance in astral projection, and lunar Goddess devotion.

PURPOSE: For assistance in astral projection and unlocking your psychic doorways. You will also be praising the moon for its gift of intuitive guidance and its mothering ways. Ask for her guidance with any problems you might have and answers will come to you. The changes you manifest in your life will come from dreams. I always describe the High Priestess card in the tarot as "hidden forces at work for you." This means that the Goddess and her retinue of muses and attendants are always around us. Some call them guardian angels. By whatever name, this candle will invoke assistance from the Goddess in psychic ways .

CANDLE COLOR: White, blue, purple, red.

CLEANSING: Spring water, salt, Florida water.

DEITY: Isis, Ishtar, Inanna, Persephone, Aradia, Maia, Gaia, Juno, Freya, Diana, Athene, Lakshmi, and all lunar goddesses.

OIL: Moon Goddess, Ocean Mother, Vervain, Ambergris, Mint, carnation blended with three drops of camphor oil, lily, rose, cucumber, gardenia, mimosa, geranium, lilac.

INCENSE: Moon, Dream, mastic, gardenia, rose, lily, vetivert, lavender.

FEEDING: Camphor, vervain, mint, honey.

Astral Travel and Lunar Divination Spell

ITEMS NEEDED

A clear bowl
A letter of intention asking
    for a safe journey and clear
    answers to your questions
Sugar

Clear spring water
Three white flower heads
    (carnations, mums,
    gardenias)

CASTING THE SPELL: Light the incense and pass the candle and bowl through the smoke. Write your letter, place it in the bowl, and put your prepared candle on top. Sprinkle the sugar over the letter. Add the water, and float the flowers in it. Light your candle and some more incense, and say the incantation.

INCANTATION

> *Mystic moon ever so bright,*
> *Guide my astral travel on my flight.*
> *Goddess, oh wondrous dream of my heart,*
> *May the threads of our connection never part.*
> *Split the veil for me to see*
> *The answers that I seek from thee.*
> *See the candle, feel the fire*
> *Help me find what I desire.*

HIGH PRIEST INITIATION

For the initiation ceremony to high priesthood.

PURPOSE: This seal was born out of Necessity—a student of mine was getting ready to go to a castle in Ireland where he was going to receive his third degree initiation (the rite that would make him a Wiccan high priest). He said to me, "You know, Lady Rhea, I was going through the enchanted candle book and I noticed there is no separate seal for the initiation of a man entering the Wiccan priesthood." I replied that some of the other candles could be used for that purpose as well as their main purpose.

"Yes," he replied. "I know, but still it's not the same. The women have their own special seal to open those portals, the astral doorways to the Gods." He had made an excellent point, so we immediately set to work to create a high priest seal. I came up with a design, and the student loved it. We carved the seal onto a candle for

High Priest Initiation

him, and packed it up to carry off to Ireland. This priest, who became Lord Apollo, said that the profound magick he experienced on the night of his elevation to third degree, priesthood has continued to be part of his life. So for all of you men out there waiting to enter the priesthood, or seeking the male mystery I give you this seal to open doors to the inner sanctum of the Great Father.

Women, too, can use this seal as a devotional magick to the God and consort of the great mother. It will also help women get in touch with the god Within.

CANDLE COLOR: Green, brown, gold, white.

CLEANSING: Water, wine, bay leaves, salt.

DEITY: Cerrnunos, Apollo, Mabon, Poseidon, Neptune, Balder, Jack in the Green, Kronos, Zeus, Saturn, Thor, Ra, Pan, Osiris, Chango Macho, Shiva, Vishnu, and others.

OIL: Pan, Earth, Saturn, Sun, patchouli, musk, pine, sandalwood, frankincense, myrrh, ambergris, bay.

INCENSE: Earth, Sun, Saturn, Pan, musk, frankincense, sandalwood, pine, cedar, sage, mastic.

FEEDING: Iron filings, dirt from a strong tree, honey, sage.

High Priest Initiation Spell

ITEMS NEEDED

A bowl	Dittany of Crete (Optional—
A letter of intention	it has lately been very hard
Honey	to find)
Frankincense	Red wine
Hawthorn	A glass of brandy
Cedar	A fine cigar (optional)

CASTING THE SPELL: Light the incense for the God. Pass the candle through the incense smoke before you carve it, and again after it has been prepared. Then pass the bowl and letter of intention through the smoke. Put the letter in the bowl and place your candle on top of it. The God delights in the sweet taste of honey, so pour it on generously. Add the frankincense, hawthorn and cedar to the blend to awaken the god within. Add a libation of red wine, and toast to the God that you adore. Place the glass of brandy next to your sacred bowl. Light the cigar and take a few puffs, then lay the length of the cigar over the brandy glass and leave here as an offering. Tobacco is a sacred offering to the God, and he really does enjoy a good cigar. Now, light some more incense and light the candle and say the incantation.

INCANTATION

> *Oh lord of the dance upon you we prevail*
> *Come and meet the maiden and pierce her veil.*
> *Oh ancient one whose secret name I call upon this sacred altar,*
> *Come ye with thy rod, reflecting thy strength that does not falter*
> *Hoof and horn, your passage is near*
> *The realm of the Goddess has held you dear.*
> *The charm is made onto this flight,*
> *You have come, oh Horned Hunter of the Night.*
> *In sacred union as nature calls*
> *The mystery of infinity is its cause.*

PURPLE WISDOM

To exceed in wisdom and align yourself with knowledge.

PURPOSE: To seek ancient wisdom, and perhaps find answers from the very akashic records themselves. This seal is for students of the occult sciences, astrology, and especially math. I also use this candle for helping people come to a conclusion or make a difficult decision; I also use it if people need help to accept a trying phase in their lives.

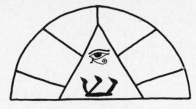

Purple Wisdom

CANDLE COLOR: Purple, white.

CLEANSING: Water, sandalwood, jasmine perfume.

DEITY: Sophia, Athena, Maat, Zeus, Jupiter, Mercury, Hermes, Thoth.

OIL: Jupiter, Ancient Wisdom, Purple Wisdom, acacia, sage, sandalwood, frankincense, juniper, cedar, lavender, jasmine, hyacinth, lilac, wisteria.

INCENSE: Purple Wisdom, Jupiter, Smudge, sandalwood, white sage, frankincense, lavender, juniper, cedar, and jasmine.

FEEDING: Iron filings, honey, sage.

Purple Wisdom Spell

ITEMS NEEDED

A letter of intention	Cedar
A bowl (clear is preferable, but any will do)	Star anise
	Cloves
White sage, fresh sage, or dry sage.	Honey
	Red wine
Juniper berries	

CASTING THE SPELL: Light your incense. Place the letter of intention in the bowl, and put the candle on top of it. Mix the sage, juniper berries, cedar, star anise, and cloves, and scatter them all inside the bowl around the candle. Pour the honey over the herbs; add the wine libation. Light the candle and say the incantation.

INCANTATION

Proverbs 8: 1–9, The Gifts of Wisdom

Does not wisdom call, and does not understanding raise Her voice? On the heights, beside the way, at the crossroads, she takes her stand beside the gates in front of the town. At the entrance of the portals she cries out "To you people, I call, and my cry is to all that live. O simple ones, learn prudence; acquire intelligence, you who lack it. Hear, for I will speak noble things, and from my lips will come what is right; for my mouth will utter the truth. Wickedness is an abomination to my lips. All the words of my mouth are righteous; there is nothing twisted or crooked in them. They are straight to one who understands and right to those who find knowledge.

Are you surprised that I included a Biblical passage? It is Lady Wisdom speaking directly to us! This is one of the few passages in the Bible where the Goddess speaks.

BAST, EGYPTIAN CAT GODDESS

To call upon joy, love, and beauty.

PURPOSE: The goddess Bast brings joy, love, and happiness to the heart. She rules over music, celebrations, parties, and festivals. She has a woman's body and the head of a cat, and wears an earring in one or both ears. Sometimes she is just depicted as a cat with an earring. Like Venus, she loves beauty, joy, and a good time. If you are a devoted cat lover then she will be especially happy to answer your petition. She will give an exotic air to any magickal undertaking. Her realm is of such intense

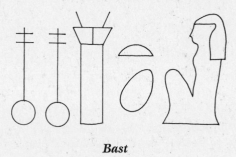

Bast

beauty that when you invoke her presence she transforms a simple ritual into a time and place of unearthly enchantment and wonder. One can actually feel the music, laughter, and joy that she brings. *Lavish, beautiful,* and *independent* are words that define her powers. Holding a social function and want it to be a success? Just invite Bast!

CANDLE COLOR: Yellow, red, pink, and white.

CLEANSING: Orange water, Florida water, water, sugar.

DEITY: Bast, Bastet, Venus.

OIL: Bast, Venus, Showers of Gold, honeysuckle, jasmine, musk blended with a few drops of civet oil, neroli, lotus, sandalwood, vetivert, patchouli. Core to Me

INCENSE: Venus, Joy, Bast, honeysuckle, jasmine, musk, patchouli, sandalwood, frankincense.

FEEDING: Iron filings, honey, one small feather, catnip (the latter is a request from my six cats)

Bast Spell

ITEMS NEEDED

A letter of intention
A bowl
Catnip
Master of the Woods
Mint
Honey
Gold glitter
White wine

Yellow or red flower petals
A small bowl of milk or
   cream (to be changed
   daily)
Happy upbeat music
   (drumming and pagan
   music seem to work well)

CASTING THE SPELL: Seducing the lovely Cat Goddess to our aid is not difficult since unlike her earthly felines she is eager to make all that ask happy. Laughter, love, and joy are like incense to her. The more joy she hears the more she responds.

Incense should be lit during the preparation of this spell. Write your letter of intention and place it in the bowl, and put the prepared candle on top. Add the catnip, Master of the Woods, and mint all around the candle in the bowl, and pour the honey generously on top to make life nice and sweet. Sprinkle gold glitter over the honey like showers of golden happiness raining down on your spell. Pour in the wine.

Strew the flower petals over the wine, and for added festivity sprinkle more gold glitter on top. Place the small dish or bowl of cream to honor the cats that are special attendants to Bast. Change this daily. If you happen to have a feline and it drinks from the bowl, it means double the luck for you!

Light more incense, and play the music to welcome Bast. Light the candle and say the incantation.

INCANTATION

The sound of golden symbols are tinkling in the air,
Saying no longer shall you despair,
For the great Goddess Bastet is here.
Goddess of beauty astonishing fair,
Before the dawn of civilization you were there
Waiting to give the world your gifts of joy, love, and happiness.
Shimmering light falls upon my madness
Bestowing happiness where there was once sadness.
A procession of dancers cast petals before thy feet,
And carry you perched majestically in honor's high seat
I look upon your golden face
And sense the wisdom of joy in my heart taking place.

EMPEROR

To expand on the best of life.

PURPOSE: This is a seal of Jupiter, God of expansion, generosity, bounty, and luck. He is king of the Gods, bearer of thunderbolts, the one who makes the heavens roar. His power totem is the eagle, his weapon the lightning, and for those in his graces, his generosity is abundant. This is an excellent candle for business, negotiations, networking, and overall confidence. You know the expression "By Jove"? Jove corresponds with Jupiter—when someone uses this expression, they are swearing by fortuitous luck. This candle corresponds with the Emperor card of the tarot. When I lecture about the Emperor card, I always

Emperor

define the figure presented as "ruler of all that he surveys." He also shows us he has a magnanimous heart and is merciful. So not only do we invoke Jupiter for luck, but also for his mercy when we are down on our luck.

CANDLE COLOR: Purple, blue, white.

CLEANSING: Water, a few drops of anise oil or extract, lavender water.

DEITY: Jupiter, Jove, Zeus, Odin, Chango Macho, Heavenly Father, Father of the Gods, Ruler of Olympus.

OIL: Jupiter, Ancient Wisdom, Amethyst, High John the Conqueror, sandalwood, juniper, lavender, anise, sage, clove, amber, frankincense, frankincense and myrrh. Kings Perfume

INCENSE: Jupiter, Obatala, Smudge, Nag Champa, sandalwood, lavender, amber, frankincense and myrrh, white sage, Three Kings, mastic, copal.

FEEDING: Iron filings, honey, anise seeds, a few juniper berries, a few cloves.

Emperor Spell

ITEMS NEEDED

Red wine	A bowl
Allspice	A letter of intention
Star Anise	Brown sugar
Cinnamon sticks	Honey
Cloves	Fresh orange slices

CASTING THE SPELL: First, make mulled wine. Heat the red wine, allspice, star anise, cinnamon sticks, and cloves on the stove (do not let it boil). Set it aside; allow the mixture to cool for at least five minutes.

Light the incense and pass the bowl, letter, and candle through the smoke. Place your letter in the bowl and put your candle on top of it. Scatter the brown sugar over your letter; add the honey. Pour in the mulled wine and add the orange slices. This makes a rich warm spicy libation to the God of Plenty. Light the candle and say the incantation.

INCANTATION

In Jupiter's good fortune my soul shall shine;
Luck and abundance shall soon be mine.
My life is as fine as any wine in Jupiter's cellar.
His presence has made all become stellar.
So with this raised glass I do say hail to thee, Lord of Lofty Spaces,
Thy presence is acknowledged, with all of your graces.

ROAD OPENER

To open all roads to success and remove obstacles.

PURPOSE: Just as an uncrossing candle removes spiritual blocks, the Road Opener removes physical blocks. This is a great candle to use if something or someone is standing in the way of your getting a new job, promotion, finding a house, getting customers, and so on. For all situations where your road seems to be blocked, this is the candle for the job. Are you in a rut, uncertain of which direction to go? Then this is the candle for you. It's also great for promoting something new—a project, a business, a new job, studying for school, or just to keep lots of new possibilities coming your way.

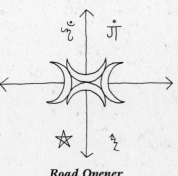

Road Opener

CANDLE COLOR: White, orange, yellow, red, purple, and green.

CLEANSING: Water, sugar, a few drops of coconut oil.

DEITY: Ganesha, Elegua, Hermes, Thoth, Mercury.

OIL: Ganesha, Elegua, Mercury, sandalwood, coconut, rue, honeysuckle, frankincense, a blend of cinnamon and Bergamot.

INCENSE: Elegua, Mercury, mastic, cinnamon, sandalwood, coconut, honeysuckle, frankincense.

FEEDING: Iron filings, honey, cinnamon powder, shredded coconut.

Road Opener Spell

ITEMS NEEDED

A letter of intention
A bowl
Dirt from a crossroads (Any four corners will do. The dirt
could be gravel from a city street, as long as it comes from
four different corners that intersect. Just a pinch from each
is sufficient, but they must be kept separate and not together
for the spell. When you collect your soil, mark the bags
1 through 4.)
Honey
Shredded coconut
A handful of rice
Dry Jasmine flowers
Quassia wood chips (abre camino)
Cinnamon powder
Sweet white wine

CASTING THE SPELL: Once you have gathered your dirt and your
candle is ready, the rest is easy. Light the incense and pass the letter
of intention through the incense smoke. Place the letter in the bowl,
then put the candle on top of it. Open bag number one and sprinkle
the dirt over your letter, saying these words:

Spirits of the east, open the doors to the feast.

Add the soil from bag number two and say:

Door of the south, there will be no doubt.

Do the same with bag number three, saying:

Passage to the west will see to it that there is no contest.

Finish with bag number four, and say:

Guardian of the north will see that I have my way.

Now pour on the honey, because all Mercurial Gods—all Gods
that rule over communication—are drawn to sweet offerings. Add

the shredded coconut, the rice, jasmine flowers, quassia wood chips, and cinnamon powder. Then, to intoxicate life add the sweet white wine to the bowl. This is to make the four guardians of the world happy—they will open doors for you so that good things can materialize in your life. All your paths will be open. Light the candle and smile, knowing that good things are on their way!

WEIGHT LOSS

To help shed those extra pounds and get healthy.

PURPOSE: What can I say about weight loss? You have to eat to live, not live to eat. Unfortunately, for most this is easier said than done.

Weight Loss

I have one friend who claims that a certain ice cream company must put drugs in their product—which would explain why he is so addicted! Lucky for him, he doesn't seem to have gained an ounce. If you are like him and have a metabolism faster than Hermes' chariot, then this candle is not for you. But if you are like a mind-boggling percentage of this country, weight loss is a necessary and very difficult undertaking. Half of it is a matter of being ready for the task, and being determined enough to see it through. This is where the candle helps. It was designed to give you the willpower to achieve your goals.

CANDLE COLOR: Red, white, yellow.

CLEANSING: Rose water, mint oil, cinnamon powder.

DEITY: Venus, Lakshmi, Juno, Erzulie, the Three Graces, Muses of Venus.

OIL: Weight Loss, Success, High John the Conqueror, Venus, cinnamon, jasmine, lotus, mint, rose, carnation.

INCENSE: Success, High John, Venus, cinnamon, jasmine, frankincense, white sage, rose, narcissus.

FEEDING: Camphor, mint leaves, fresh or dry rose petals.

Weight Loss Spell

ITEMS NEEDED

A picture of the body you want with the face cut out and your own put in place of the other one (A photocopy is fine)	Mint leaves
	Rosemary
	Dry or fresh rose petals
	Lemon verbena (yerba louisa)
A bowl	Water
A letter of intention	Your personal perfume
	Camphor

CASTING THE SPELL: Light the incense and pass the photo of yourself through the incense smoke. Begin to visualize those pounds starting to melt away. Place the photo with the letter of intention. Add the mint leaves, rosemary, rose petals, and lemon verbena to the bowl. Add the water, with a spritz or a couple of drops of your perfume. Place your candle in the bowl, slip in the camphor, and let things settle.

Light your candle and say the incantation.

INCANTATION

Lately things are just not right, all I do is eat all in sight. No more midnight raids will I make for that extra piece of cake. Away, away, I banish thee, for it is a new me I want to see. Slim and shapely is what I desire, to walk, to walk I shall aspire. No more days of lethargy, you will see, a healthy, vibrant, and slim new me. So Mote It Be.

10.

Enchanted Mother Candles

*Y*ou *may have noticed* that there are other Mother Goddess candles that come before these last two in the book. I hold them all with the greatest reverence, and I love no one more than the other. Let me share some words of wisdom from my own mother: "I have five fingers on each hand, I do not love my pinky more than my thumb. If you asked me which finger I would choose to lose, the answer is unknowable. For I cannot say any one is less important to me than the other. I love each of them for different reasons, but I love them all just the same." Each aspect of the Goddess carries a similar dearness.

YEMAYA THE SEA QUEEN

Invocation to awaken the Ocean Mother.

PURPOSE: Let me tell an old story. (Well, at least going as far back as 1975.) A man named Clinton Stephen was working in the Magickal Childe, an occult shop in New York City. Lord Gwyddion was still an owner of the shop, and I visited there almost every other week, shopping, teaching Pagan Way classes, and just enjoying being treated as a celebrated guest by the people who worked there. Clinton was a Louisiana Swamp Witch. He was one of the most talented people I'd ever met, both in art and magick. He was personally

Yemaya

responsible for much of the creation of the *Magickal Formulary*, a book of oils that was written with Lord Gwyddion. I myself wrote one of the spells included in the book. He was a *Santero*, a Santerian priest. According to his tradition he was a child of Oshun and from a house of Yemaya. He also was studying to be a priest in the Voudon tradition of Haiti. Following is the tale he told me of the goddess Yemaya.

He said that she was a mermaid, and her son impregnated her. In her sorrow, she climbed atop a mountain. There she sobbed and sobbed until her tears filled the world below to become the oceans. Then her stomach burst and from her sprang the first Gods.

Lord Gwyddion went on to tell me that this story is similar to the legend of the Goddess Rhea—my very own namesake. The story he told me was that Rhea was married to Kronos, a very stern man. She was a very compassionate Goddess, the mother of all living things. A soothsayer had foretold that Kronos would be slain by one of his sons. So each time she bore him a child, he swallowed it whole so the prophecy would not come to pass. This continued for quite some time. Finally Rhea became weary and saddened by the sacrifice of her children. When she had her next child, she decided to give him up to be raised elsewhere. She swathed a stone with cloth and offered it to her husband instead of the baby. Being used to eating his newborn by now, Kronos paid no attention to what was being offered. The child was taken away by Gaia to be raised in the mountains. He came back as a full grown man, a mighty God named Zeus. He slew his father and from Kronos' head sprang the Greek pantheon, the mighty Gods of Mount Olympus.

Of course, I was now entranced with Yemaya and Rhea in every way imaginable. Both were mothers of sacrifice. They were willing to face adversity to see the greater picture. Would I have the strength to stand up for my beliefs and be a spokesperson for the Great Mother and her children?

I wanted to learn everything about Yemaya. I started asking a thousand questions and Clinton indulged me in all manner of ritual teachings in both Santeria and Voudon. I was back studying Santeria, my earliest exposure to magick and pagan religion. Then one night we were lounging on his rooftop. It was a clear night, and the evening sky was ablaze with stars. I looked up to the heavens and Clinton told me another story.

"Goddess Yemaya is like this, my Rhea," he said, as he put his hands on my shoulders. "The milky way is her hair, the moon her lovely face, the rest of space her body. The ocean waves are the bottom ruffles of her skirts, as she dances to the rhythm of life. Beneath the ocean waves she holds many mysteries and keeps all of her treasures underneath her skirts to give to her cherished children of earth."

I asked Clinton what treasures he was referring to. He answered me with a question of his own. He asked me how many times I had heard of people going to the beach and losing jewelry, money, and valuables? I thought for a second and replied, "Multitudes." Then he asked me how many ships have been sunk at sea? I answered, "Countless." He smiled. Now I was getting the idea. She holds physical wealth beneath her skirts. Not only that, but she is a time capsule slowly divulging secrets from her watery depths. Ancient civilizations are discovered under water, worlds that live in darkness and such depths of cold that we could not bear it. Ships that hold knowledge and historical facts are lying beneath her watery depths and only when she decides to allow these things to be discovered does it happen.

Yemaya gives multitudes of blessings to a home in abundance, peace, and protection. She is wonderful for bringing a clientele that is unique and elegant to your business. Call upon her for conception, happiness, money, house blessing, protection from harm, and all manner of things concerning the moon and ocean magick

CANDLE COLOR: Blue, white, silver.

CLEANSING: Lavender water, a few drops of gardenia oil, a few drops of cucumber oil.

DEITY: Yemaya, Melusine, Amphitrite, all Mermaids, Diana, Luna, Virgin Regla.

OIL: Yemaya, Sea Queen, Virgin Regla, cucumber, watermelon, gardenia, ambergris, wisteria, violet, lavender, ylang-ylang.

Apartment Hunting

INCENSE: Sea Queen, Moon, Virgin Regla, Seven African Powers, lavender, gardenia, violet, watermelon, wisteria.

FEEDING: Camphor, cane syrup, seven pennies.

Yemaya Spell

ITEMS NEEDED

A letter of intention
A bowl
Cane syrup
Yerba luisa herb
Lavender flowers
Sea salt
Water

Blue food coloring
Seven white flower heads to
   float in the bowl
A glass of Midori (a melon
   liquor) or white wine
Seven pink roses in a vase
   (optional)

CASTING THE SPELL: Light your incense. Write the letter of intention and pass it through the incense smoke. Place it in the bowl and put your candle on top of it. Pour in the cane syrup, followed by the yerba luisa, lavender flowers, and sea salt. Add the water and blue food coloring. Traditionally Yemaya likes dark blue water, although sometimes I like to make it a turquoise blue. The shade of blue is up to you—keep adding food coloring until it looks right. Add the white flower heads. Light some more incense, and place the glass of Midori or wine next to your spell. The following visualization is one of popular standing. The most common depiction you will find of Yemaya in popular art is one where she wears a long white dress and walks miraculously on the water. This is the image I chose for the purpose of this spell. It is one of the few pagan depictions of the old gods surviving in Santeria. Most all of the other representations are portrayed as saints.

Take a deep breath and visualize the Sea Queen in her long white dress, flowing black hair, and flower petals with silver coins flowing from her fingertips as she walks across the ocean to you. Light the candle and say the incantation.

INCANTATION

> *There she rises, above the mighty waves, under the glow of the*
>   *shining moon.*
> *She dances there upon the water in the moonlight.*
> *Her face shines like the North Star.*
> *Her complexion is the color of a moonbeam.*
> *Her lips, the color of the blooming rosebud.*
> *Her eyes are shaped like diamonds holding the truths to all the*
>   *world's secrets yet to unfold.*
> *Her hair is as fine as silk, and as thick as the honeysuckle thicket*
>   *may grow*
> *Her gown is woven of pure starlight, and of pearls and seashells*
>   *from the farthest depths of the ocean.*
> *She sings the song of life, death, and rebirth of new wonders.*
> *Then as the stars begin to fade*
> *The sun begins to rise and she descends back into the watery*
>   *depths, to places yet still unknown.*
> *There she sleeps until next nightfall.*

This incantation was written by my daughter, Tara Selivonchik, and it won first place in a poetry contest at her school. I have used it as an invocation to Yemaya ever since.

GREAT MOTHER

For invoking the Great Mother.

PURPOSE: The Great Mother seal was created on New Year's Day, 2000. It was just the way to start a new millenium. The Wiccan religion is coming into a new century, and so the enchanted candles needed something new to commemorate the turn of the century. What better than to celebrate the very deity that brings us all

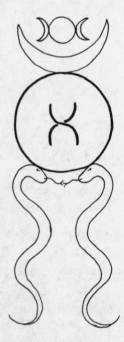

Great Mother

together? This seal was created under the auspices of the Great Minoan Mother.

As we came to use this seal we discovered what we already knew—that no matter what name is used, or what aspect is invoked, all Great Mothers are one and the same. No matter what tradition, all pagans come to the great mother for comfort, support, and love and to ask for her continued blessings. This candle is for adoring the Goddess in her many facets, asking for assistance with a problem, healing for the earth and her children, or for just showing gratitude for the Great Mother's presence in your life.

CANDLE COLOR: Green, brown, gold, white, yellow, red.

CLEANSING: Orange water, rose water, a few drops of mint oil.

DEITY: Rhea, Danu, Britomartis, Demeter, Eartha, Cerridwen, Rhiannon, Pellea, Isis, Astarte, Istar, Aradia, Gaia, Maia, Ariadne, Juno, Hecate, or any name you use to call out to the Great Mother can be used with this seal.

OIL: Any Goddess name oil available that you wish to work with, a blend of patchouli and musk, jasmine, honeysuckle, rose, apple blossom, gardenia, basil, sage, mint, veryain, or any fragrance that comes from Mother Earth. Apartment Hunting

INCENSE: Earth, patchouli, jasmine, pine, vetivert, benzoin, sandalwood, rose, frankincense and myrrh, cedar, sage, lavender, fruit fragrances.

FEEDING: Iron filings, dirt from the property where you live, honey, flower petals of any kind.

Great Mother Spell

ITEMS NEEDED

A bowl	Any kind of dry beans
A letter of intention	Vetivert or patchouli
Honey	Red wine
Wheat	Flower petals of your
Corn	choice

CASTING THE SPELL: Burn incense in the name of the Great Mother for the preparation of this spell. Before carving the candle, pass it through the incense smoke. Do the same with the bowl and letter of intention. Place the letter of intention in the bowl and put your candle on top of it. Add honey to the bowl, asking the goddess for sweet things in your life. Next, add the wheat, corn, and dry beans for prosperity and abundance. Add the vetivert or patchouli for protection from harm and continued prosperity and love. Offer a libation of red wine to the Goddess in her aspect of loving mother. Cast your choice of flower petals into the wine for a final loving tribute. Light your candle and say the incantation, acknowledging that it is the voice of the Goddess speaking to you from within:

INCANTATION

I am the beauty of the green earth and the white moon among the stars. I am all that encompasses the embodiment of the universe. So profound is my love unto all beings that in its boundless waves, eternity was born. My body of earth produces nourishment to sustain you. When you look up to me in the heavens I inspire you to dream. Children of every nation have cried out my name for eons of time. Each one a different name and to each call I answered. When you have a special need of me, all I ask of thee is to let there be compassion to all others, mirth and reverence within you, and knowledge that while you walk my spiral dance it never ends.

Now talk with Mother Earth, heart to heart. She will console you with her compassion, help you with her infinite wisdom, and set you back happily on your dance in the great spiral called life.

There is a song by the artist Sting along with Mary J. Blige called "Whenever I Say Your Name." It is technically a love song. For me it is one of the whispered prayers I sing to the Great Mother. Each and every word sung is how I live and feel the Great Mother. Whenever I call out her name she is there for me. The song so eloquently mirrors how I see her. The words fill my soul with her love. Always I trust my life in her, in the darkest times it is then that she cradled me. Her love has always seen me through. I know she is always there for me, and for us all: one Mother to infinite minions of children.

Appendixes

Appendix A:
Suggested Reading

There are so many wonderful tomes of information out there—this list only covers a tiny fraction of the books I would recommend for further research on the Craft. It is merely a starting point. No one book can say it all, not even this one. When I first started learning about the Craft, there weren't nearly as many books available on the subject—I was lucky if I could find a few. These days it is not a problem—all you need to do is walk into your local bookstore, and more often than not you'll find an entire bookshelf devoted to books on paganism and Wicca. So gather as much information as you can get your hands on! It's all right there, waiting for you. May you never thirst for knowledge!

Astral Projection

Melita Denning and Osborne Phillips, *The Practical Guide to Astral Projection*, Llewellyn, 2001.

Shakti Gawain, *Creative Visualization: Use the Power of Your Imagination to Create What You Want in Your Life.* New World Library, 2002.

Ophiel, *The Art and Practice of Creative Visualization (Revised Edition).* Red Wheel/Weiser, 2001.

Astrology

There are so many books on astrology, I listed two basics to get you started. Study this science and a new world will open up to you.

Bill Tierney, *All Around the Zodiac.* Llewellyn, 2001.

Kathleen Burt, *Archetypes of the Zodiac.* Llewellyn, 1988.

Colors

Raymond Buckland, *Practical Color Magick.* Llewellyn, 1993.

Joseph Murphy, Ph.D., *The Power of Your Subconscious Mind* (Revised Edition). Bantam Books, 2001.

Gemstones

I work with crystals on a daily basis. There are many books written about magickal stones and crystals. I listed these two because they pack a very thorough amount of information between their covers.

A. Melody and R.R. Jackson, *Love Is in the Earth: A Kaleidoscope of Crystals*. Earth Love Publishing House, 1995.

Scott Cunningham, *Cunningham's Encyclopedia of Gems, Crystal, and Metal Magic*. Llewellyn 2003.

Magick

There is so much more out there, but these books make excellent primers for you to begin exploring the world of ceremonial magick.

Raven Grimassi, *Witches' Familiar: Spiritual Partnerships for Successful Magic*. Llewellyn, 2003.

Konstantinos, *Gothic Grimoire*. Llewellyn, 2002.

———, *Summoning Spirits: The Art of Magical Evocation*. Llewellyn, 1999.

Donald Kraig, *Modern Magick: Eleven Lessons in the High Magickal Arts*. Llewellyn, 1988.

Michael Kraig and Mary K Greer, *Tarot and Magick*. Llewellyn, 2002.

Seals

I love seals and these books make them easy to work with.

Anna Riva, *Secrets of Magical Seals*. International Imports, 1975.

Sarah Morrison, *The Modern Witch's Book of Symbols*. Citadel, 1998.

Ray Buckland, *Signs, Symbols and Omens: An Illustrated Guide to Magical and Spiritual Symbolism*. Llewellyn, 2003.

Spell Books

These are some of the classics and well-loved spell books out there. I couldn't list them all or I would have ended up writing a catalog! New spells are always being devised and are loads of fun to work with. I thoroughly enjoyed these books and have had much success with them.

Ray Buckland, *Practical Candlburning Rituals* (third edition). Llewellyn, 1987.

Gerina Dunwich, *The Wicca Spellbook: A Witch's Collection of Wiccan Spells, Potions, and Recipes*. Citadel Press, 1994.

————, *Wicca Candle Magick*. Citadel Press, 1996.

Ed Fitch, *Magickal Rites from the Crystal Well* (third edition). Llewellyn, 1989.

Gavin and Yvonne Frost, *The Witch's Magical Handbook*. Reward Books, 2000

Migene Gonzalez-Wippler, *Rituals and Spells of Santeria*. Original Publications, 1986.

Bob Johnson, *Corporate Magick*. Citadel Press, 2002.

Ray T. Marlbrough, *Charms, Spells, and Formulas*. Llewellyn, 1986.

————, *The Magickal Power of the Saints: Evocation and Candle Rituals*. Llewellyn, 1998.

Edain McCoy, *Spellworking for Covens: Magic for Two or More*. Llewellyn, 2002.

Original Publications, *Helping Yourself with Selected Prayers*. Original Publications, 1995.

Anthony Paige, *Rocking the Goddess*. Citadel Press, 2002.

Jennifer Reif, *Morgan la Fey's Book of Wiccan Spells and Wiccan Rites*, Citadel Press, 2001.

Lexa Roséan, *The Supermarket Sorceress*. St. Martin's Press, 1996.

————, *The Supermarket Sorceress's Sexy Hexes*. Martin's Press, 1997.

————, *The Supermarket Sorceress's Enchanted Evenings*. St. Martin's Press, 1998.

————, *Zodiac Spells: Easy Enchantments and Simple Spells for Your Sun Sign*. Griffin Trade Paperback, 2002.

————, *Easy Enchantments: All the Spells You'll Ever Need for Any Occasion*. Griffin Trade Paperback, 1999.

————, *Power Spells: Get the Magical Edge in Business, Work Relationships, and Life*. St. Martin's Press, 2001.

Patricia Telesco, *A Floral Grimoire*. Citadel Press, 2001.

Valerie Worth, *The Crone's Book of Charms and Spells* (second edition). Llewellyn, 1998.

Witchcraft

These are among the classics of the Wicca books. They will give you a good working foundation.

Margot Adler, *Drawing Down the Moon: Witches, Druids, Goddess Worshippers, and other Pagans in America Today*. Penguin, 1997.

Ann L. Barstow, *Witchcraze: A New History of the European Witch Hunts*. HarperSanFrancisco, 1995.

Ray Buckland, *Buckland's Complete Book of Witchcraft* (second edition), Llewellyn, 1986.

———, *Wicca for Life: The Way of the Craft—from Birth to Summerland*. Citadel Press, 2003.

Scott Cunningham, *Wicca: A Guide for the Solitary Practioner*. Llewellyn, 1990.

Phyllis W. Curott, *A Book of Shadows: A Modern Woman's Journey into the Wisdom of Witchcraft and the Magic of the Goddess*. Broadway Books, 1999.

———, *Witch Crafting: A Spiritual Guide to Making Magic*. Broadway Books, 2001.

Gerina Dunwich, *Wicca Craft: The Modern Witch's Book of Herbs, Magick, and Dreams*. Citadel Press, 1991.

Stewart Ferrar, *What Witches Do* (revised edition). Phoenix Publishing, Inc., 1984.

Stewart and Janet Ferrar, *A Witches' Bible: the Complete Witches' Handbook*. Phoenix Publishing, Inc., 1996.

Raven Grimassi, *The Witches' Craft: The Roots of Witchcraft and Magical Transformation*. Llewellyn, 2002.

Judy Harrow, Alexei Kontratiev, and Maureen Reddington-Wilde, *Devoted to You: Honoring Deity in Wiccan Practice*. Citadel Press, 2003.

Lady Sheba, *The Book of Shadows*. Llewellyn, 2000.

M. Macha NightMare, *Witchcraft and the Web: Weaving Pagan Traditions Online*. ECW Press, 2001.

Christopher Penczak, *Gay Witchcraft: Empowering the Tribe*. Red Wheel/Weiser, 2003.

Maeve Rhea and Barbara E. Vordebrueggen, *Summoning Forth Wiccan Gods and Goddesses*. Citadel Press, 2000.

Herman Slater, *A Book of Pagan Rituals*. Red Wheel/Weiser,1978.

Starhawk, *The Spiral Dance*. HarperCollins, 1979.

Patricia Telesco and Sirona Knight, *The Wiccan Web: Surfing the Magic on the Internet*. Citadel Press, 2001.

Doreen Valiente, *An ABC of Witchcraft Past and Present*. Bookpeople, 1989.

———, *Natural Magic*. Phoenix Publishing, 1985.

Herbals

I love herbal magick; it was one of my first interests in the Craft. There were very few books about it back then—mostly what you learned about herbal lore and magick was by word of mouth.

Paul Beyerl, *The Master Book of Herbalism*. Phoenix Publishing, 1984.

Scott Cunningham, *Cunningham's Encyclopedia of Magickal Herbs* (second edition). Llewellyn, 1985.

Sarah Morrison, *The Modern Witch's Book of Herbs and Healing*. Citadel Press,1998.

Appendix B: Supplies

There was not enough paper for me to list all of the shops I wanted to include in this book. Each of these stores carry most of the products mentioned in this book, including oils, incense, herbs, magickal powders, and of course, candles.

Magickal Realms, "Home of the Enchanted Candle"
2937 Wilkinson Ave.
Bronx, NY 10461
(718) 892-5350
www.magickalrealms.com

Original Products Botanica
2486 Webster Ave.
Bronx, NY 10458
(718) 367-9589
www.originalprodcorp.com

Original Publications
22 East Mall
Plainview, New York 11803
www.originalprodcorp.com

Morgana's Chamber
242 W. 10th street
New York, NY 10014
(212) 243-3415
members.tripod.com/
    morganaschamber/home.htm

Sacred Space
1490 Montauk Highway
Mastic, NY 11950
(631) 281-5881
www.sharethesacred.com

Blue Moon Enchantments
560 Montauk Highway
East Moriches, NY 11940
(631) 878-5939

Realm of the Rainbow
46 Railroad Ave.
Sayville, NY 11782
(631) 563- 6318

The Awareness Shop
180 Main Street
New Paltz, NY 12561
(845) 255-5756
www.awarenessshop.com

Instant Karma
14 South Village Ave.
Rockville Center, NY 11570
(516) 763-0833
www.instantkarmastore.com

The Owl and the Serpent
15½ N. Front St.
New Paltz, NY 12561
www.owlandserpent.safeshopper.
    com
(845) 255-2882

Spellbound
5 Glen Toad
Rutherford, NJ 07070
(201) 896-8300
www.thestonecircle.com

Avalon
9 North Main Street
So. Norwalk, CT 06854
(203) 838-5928

Curious Goods Witchcraft Shop
45 Campbell Ave.
West Haven, CT 06516
(203) 932-1193

Mystical Horizons
313 Flanders Road
East Lyme, CT. 06333
(860) 572-9191
www.mysticalhorizons.com

Mystickal Tymes
127 South Main Street
New Hope, PA 18938
(215) 862-5629
www.mystickaltymes.com

Hocus Pocus
113 Meyran Ave.
Pittsburgh, PA 15213
(412) 622-0113

Moonbeams in a Jar
723 N. Market Street
Selinsgrove, PA 17870
(570) 372-0770

Isis Gifts and Books
5701 East Colfax Ave.
Denver, CO 80220
(303) 321-0867
www.isisbooks.com

Quantum Alchemy
913 Corona Street
Denver, CO 80218
(303) 863-0548
www.quantumalchemy.com

New Orleans Mistic
2267 St. Claude Ave.
New Orleans, LA 70117
(504) 894-0690
www.neworleansmistic.com

Lady Felicias
400 Vallette St.
New Orleans, LA 70114
(504) 263-2345
www.ladyfelicias.com

**Panpipes Magickal
    Marketplace**
1641 Cahuenga Blvd.
Hollywood, CA
(323) 462-7078
www.panpipes.com

Starcrafts
1909 Cable Street
San Diego CA 92107
(616) 224-4923
www.starcraftsob.com

Raven's Flight
5042-5050 Vineland Ave.
North Hollywood, CA 91601
(818) 985-2944
www.ravensflight.net

Ancient Ways
4075 Telegraph Ave.
Oakland, CA 64609
(510) 653-3244
www.ancientways.com

The Crystal Cauldron
360 S. Thomas St.
Pomona, CA 91766
(909) 620-9565
www.willowcrystalcauldron.com

The Witches Grove
711 Lancaster Blvd.
Lancaster, CA 93534
(661) 940-9902
www.witchesgrove.com

Whispered Prayers
120 San Juan Drive
Modesto, CA 95354
(209) 549-1727
www.whisperedprayers.com

Dolphin Dream
1437 N. Broadway
Walnut Creek, CA 94596
(925) 933-2342
www.dolphindream.com

The Gathering Tree
1558 N. Palm Canyon Drive
Palm Springs, CA 92262
(760) 323-4656

Gardenias
399 Dorchester Street
Boston, MA 02127
(617) 268-6600

The Broom Closet
35 Central Street
Salem, MA 01970
(508) 741-3669
www.broomcloset.com

The Cat, the Crow, and the
  Crown
63R Pickering Wharf
Salem, MA 01970
(978) 744-6274
www.lauriecabot.com

Practical Magic
190 Essex Street
Salem, MA 01970
(978) 745-8883
www.jodycabot.com

Nu Aeon
88 Wharf Street, Pickering Wharf
Salem, MA 01970
(978) 745-8668

Online Shops

www.easyenchantments.com: Author and teacher Lexa Roséan's Web site. She is one of my very own "children" in the craft. Her online shop is simply enchanting.

www.hecates-garden.com: Hecates Garden is a wonderful apothecary done by the illustrator of this book.

www.nixiemagick.com: Nixiemagick has some of the best handcrafted candles and excellent source of magickal items. Very Crafty.

www.companionplants.com: They carry the rare herbs as both live plants and seeds for every witch's garden.

www.angelfire.com/ego/magickalchilde/index.html: The Magickal Childe Formulary is back in print and available through this site.

Witchy Links

www.witchvox.com
www.avatarsearch.com

To get a listing of your local area shopping, events, meetings, and just for general networking, the above two Web sites have proven themselves invaluable to the community. I thank the people behind these sites for their tireless efforts. These sites have been a resource that has helped all pagan paths to grow.

There are so many wonderful sites out there—as many as there are stars in the sky. I salute each and every one of you.

Appendix C:
Gods and Goddesses Glossary

The Gods and Goddesses are the beings we petition to answer your magickal call. It's important to know to whom you're talking! All of the Gods listed in this book have heard me so often over the last thirty years that we have become personal friends. The deities I work with are my spiritual parents, both here on the earth and on the spiritual plane.

There is no spellcaster's union card given out just because you perform a spell. Practicing magick will not make you a witch or a pagan. Only your beliefs and initiation into a coven or serious self-initiation can make you either of these. Respect for what you are doing and respect for the deities that you are invoking are essential parts of this great work.

I was trained in an old school of magick where my High Priest, Lord Gwyddion, taught me the art of petitioning the Gods to help me with my life here on earth. As I progressed, he taught me the summoning of elemental spirits to help me with my tasks in life. The discovery of the enchanted candle was due to communication with these Gods. Without the many years of training and guidance by my teachers, this discovery may never have been mine. Here I give you a listing of many of the Gods and Goddesses that can be invoked by using these candle spells.

> *"The god will lay his hand where his signature lies."*
>
> —CORNELIUS AGRIPPA

Aine: Celtic moon Goddess of love. Grants pleasures, fertility, happiness. She seems to have both the qualities of Venus and the Crescent Moon Maiden, and can be invoked for any and all love spells.

Amaterasu: In most regions the sun is worshipped as a male deity. In Japan they recognize the feminine qualities of the sun. Her shining brilliance of lifegiving light and happiness is seen as a Goddess. We invoke her to shine her light and give us happiness, abundance, and wealth.

Amphitrite: Mother Goddess of the ocean, wife of Neptune. Her magick lies in the moon, secrets, women's mysteries, wealth, and people. She is invoked to bring customers to business and for psychic abilities. She also gives wealth and blessings for the home. I visualize her with the body of a mermaid. The dolphin is her sacred animal.

Anubis: The Egyptian God of the underworld, he is a guide through the realm of the dead. He gives knowledge of secrets, and will guide you safely when you are seeking answers that only the dead may know. We invoke him when we want to communicate with the dead or to help us discover secrets of magick in the underworld. He is often portrayed with the head of a dog and the body of a man.

Aphrodite: Greek Goddess of love, pleasure, and beauty. Her love of beauty is not so much for man-made objects, but a love of the beauty of young men and the pleasures that they can share. She enjoys bringing about love between two people. We invoke her to bless all love rituals, and to bring love, companionship, romance, and sex to our lives.

Apollo: Roman God of the sun, he is the archetype of man. He gives his radiant light to our souls, hearts, and minds so that we can become magnanimous, generous, and philosophical in our pursuits. We invoke Apollo to bring out in us the best qualities of ourselves so that we may be successful in life.

Arachne: I've included her because of her great skills in weaving. You can weave many forms of magick, but you must be ever mindful that what you weave in your magick must not include deceit or dark and arrogant thoughts. We invoke her for her ability to help us weave a web of magick that will be strong and crafty in its pursuit of catching what we want.

Aradia: Italian Goddess of magick, sorcery, and witchcraft. We turn to her for help in all of the magickal arts, including working with effigies, healing, potions, spells, and all works of magick, especially natural magick, the working of herbs, stones, water, fire, and earth.

Ares: The Greek God of war. He is both respected and feared by many practitioners of the magickal arts, and rightly so. He is a representation of the raw power of the Universe. Not to be treated lightly, the God of war can bring explosive changes into your life, for better or worse. We invoke the spirit of Ares to promote change in our lives.

Ariadne: Daughter of King Minos of Crete, consort of Bacchus, the God of wine. Because of her love of a man named Theseus, she defied her father and helped him to kill the Minotaur that was waiting to slay him. He left her because he claimed that the Goddess Minerva instructed him to do so. We invoke her for courage in making difficult decisions. We also see her as Mother of the Grape. We invoke her to bless the wine.

Arianrhod: Celtic Goddess of the Silver Wheel and sister of Gwyddion. She's a Goddess of the wheel of time, fertility, and female power. Her palace in the sky is said to be where souls go to await reincarnation. Invoke her assistance for seeking past-life knowledge, divination, fertility spells, and spirit contact.

Artemis: The Greek Goddess of the moon. Great Mother Goddess of nature, daughter of Zeus, associated with Diana. Protectress of her devotees as well as all animals. Goddess of the hunt. We invoke her for rituals concerning moon magick, and to remove veils when seeking mysteries of the unknown.

Aesclepius: The God of medicine, restorer of life. Due to his incredible healing powers Hades had him put to death, for fear that all who died would return to life. Apollo then had Aesclepius placed among the stars. We call upon his healing powers and oracles of the future and ask his assistance in finding the right treatment for a patient.

Astarte: Also known as Ostara or Ester. The Phonecian Goddess of love and spring. Rabbits are sacred to her, and so are red-dyed eggs, which represent fertility of the earth and the womb. We invoke her for love, the renewal of spring, the joy of new life, and fertility magick.

Asterion: Lord of light, a youthful aspect of the Sun God; the divine child from the Minoan Mycenian pantheon. We invoke him for compassion and light, and in reverence to all sons and their mothers.

Athena: Greek Goddess of wisdom, sciences, protectress of the city of Athens. We invoke her for guidance, wisdom, protection, and intelligence.

Aurelia: Roman Goddess of the dawn's golden rays. We invoke her benevolent rays to bring joy, happiness, and to replace the dark spots in our lives with light and opulence. She replaces sorrow with joy and sheds light on dark areas of your life.

Aurora: Roman Goddess of the dawn, she sheds her light to reveal new beginnings. She heralds a new day and new opportunities in life. Honor her by getting up early and watching a sunrise. Invoke her to bring joy, happiness, and a fresh start in life.

Bacchus: Roman God of wine, he blesses the vine and the grape. Son of Jupiter, he revels in gaiety, hedonism, lust, and abandonment to the senses. We invoke him for a good time at a party, esbat, or sabbat.

Balder: Scandinavian God of light, protection, wisdom, and the sun. Son of Odin and Freya. We invoke him for a good outlook on life, a positive attitude. Loki used mistletoe to trick him so that he can be slain. He can also be invoked to protect us from unseen pitfalls.

Bast: Egyptian Cat Goddess of love, joy, music, dance, art, and all acts of pleasure. We invoke the spirit of her for inspiration in creative endeavors, to give us a more carefree attitude, youthful energy, and a renewed lust for life.

Britomartis: Cretan Goddess of hunters and fishermen, moon Goddess, Great Mother, often associated with Artemis. Some legends have it that she is the lover of Artemis and she spurned the advances of King Minos and others who tried to seduce her. We invoke her for fertility, and abundance so that when we are fishing in the proverbial waters of life we have a good catch. She can also be invoked for lesbian love, and the courage to come out of the closet.

Cerridwen: Celtic Goddess of the cauldron of rebirth, great mother of fertility, granter of blessings, renewal of life. She rules over herbs, magick, astrology, and poetry. We invoke her as the dark mother of earth to bring back life and give wealth from her womb. We ask for her assistance in the learning and knowledge of all acts of magick.

Cernunnos: Celtic God of the hunt, Sun God, father of the woods, the green life, and all horned animals. He is the keeper of all herding animals (elk, reindeer, and so on). Said to be the God of the Witches, with Mother Earth as his consort. He is the God of fertility, the hunt, and our father provider. Invoke him for prosperity, guidance, and wisdom, and thank him for the food on our table.

Chango: Yoruban God of the Sun, a much-beloved God in Santeria who is honored by many pagans today. In Santeria he is associated with Saint Barbara. To my joy his pagan image is still alive and very popular today.

Invoke him for business matters, and protection. He also loves dancing, and is a real lover of beautiful women and having a good time.

Cupid: Roman God of love. He is the son of Venus and Mercury, which is probably where he gets his mischievous side. He is the winged messenger of love. The Victorians favored him greatly in their valentine art as a message of love and desire for courtship. Even cartoons have used Cupid as a character to indicate that two people are about to fall in love. We invoke Cupid to send messages of love, but beware, because he has been known to play tricks in affairs of the heart.

Daghda: Celtic Earth Father. He is the God of reincarnation. We invoke him to ressurect our lives out of the troubled times we are in. Like any good father, he helps us out.

Damara: British fertility Goddess, Goddess of Protection and Mercy. We invoke her to give us well-being and a sound and stable life. We ask her for mercy during hard times, and guidance to serve the earth.

Danu: Celtic Mother of All, great Earth Mother, and giver of all fruitfulness. Patroness of wizards, and queen of magickal wisdom. Invoke her for abundance, wealth, love, and protection.

Dawn: Roman Goddess of the morning's first light. She bears the birth of a new day. Invoke her for new beginnings, a fresh outlook on life, and healing of the soul.

Demeter: Greek Earth Mother, the daughter of Cronos and Rhea and the mother of Persephone. In Rome she was called Ceres. She controls the seasons, gives us wealth and abundance. We invoke her for guidance, wealth, and compassion.

Diana: Roman Goddess of the moon, the hunt, wolves, hounds, bears, lady of the crescent moon, archer, and twin sister to Apollo. I once read about a Roman festival dedicated to her in which chariots with beautiful maidens were pulled by bears. We invoke her presence for worship of the moon, stability, that for which we seek in life, as we hunt for those things we hold dear. Her lance strikes true and her hounds find all that try to elude them. We ask of her a direct line to that which we seek in all areas of life.

Dionysus: Greek God of wine, fertility, celebration. He has a dual nature: joy, happiness, hedonism, and frivolity on one side; brutal rage on the other. He was originally born a female, and when he reached adulthood he became male. He is a God who defies the bounds of sexuality, gender, love, and desire. We invoke him to be the life of the party, and to allow all inhibitions to melt away. To avoid the nasty side of Dionysus, put out plenty of bread to keep things even.

Durga: India's Goddess of protection and slayer of demons. We invoke her for protection from harm.

Eartha: One of the first Goddess names I learned when I first became aware that I was pagan. Another name for her is Mother Earth. We invoke her for her loving compassion, and pray to keep her well from all the harm that some of earth's children keep heaping upon her.

Elegua: The Yoruban God of all crossroads and the destiny of all. He holds the keys to all doors in life. Without his assistance none may pass through these doors. In Santeria he is worshipped at the beginning of every ritual, always fed first, and respected by all without question. We invoke him to open doors and to remove obstacles.

Epona: Celtic horse mother. We invoke her to help us carry our burdens until they can be relieved.

Erinyes: An aspect of the Greek triple will of the Goddess, also known as the Furies. The Furies punish crimes that are not satisfied by human justice. Invoke them only when you are certain that the crime is true and punishment by the law is not available.

Eros: The Greek God of love, passion and romance. He is often associated with Cupid, but I have found him to be less inclined to playing jokes. He has affairs in mythology that leave him quite injured and I believe that makes him more compassionate to a lover's call. Invoke him to bring out more of the romantic side in the person you love and desire.

Erzulie: A Haitian Love Goddess. She can be quite provocative, sensual, and flirtatious. She adorns herself with all manners of luxury, sweets, and adornments of jewels, flowers, and perfumes. She carries mirrors so she may look at how beautiful she is. We invoke the presence of Erzulie to answer the call of love, to seduce the one we desire, and to bring to us all manner of romance, love, coquettish behavior, and the finer things in life.

Fama: Roman Goddess of fame. Invoke her to gain recognition and fame in your life.

Fauna and Faunus: Roman God and Goddess of the forests, and animals of agriculture. We invoke them to keep our ideals of youth and a carefree attitude.

Femme Blanche: Haitian White Venus. We invoke her for assistance in clearing and cleansing problems with love.

Fortuna: Roman Goddess of luck and good fortune. We invoke her to smile upon us with all manner of luck and blessings in anything we undertake.

Freya: Norse Goddess. She is one of the fairest and most beautiful of all the Norse Gods. She is a Goddess of fertility, love, and beauty. Warriors cried out to her before battle to protect them and to keep the homeland safe while they were away. She is also the Goddess of the magician.

Gaia: Greek Earth Mother. Creator of the Universe, mother of the first race of the Gods and humankind. She assisted the Goddess Rhea in tricking Cronos by spiriting away Zeus to be raised by her in the mountains. We invoke her to assist in childrearing, birth, and for fertility in our lives.

Ganesha-Ganapati: India's elephant-headed God of intellect, communication, and remover of obstacles. Invoke him for all doors to open and all obstacles to be removed.

Graces: The three lovely daughters of the Greek Gods Zeus and Eurynome. Aglaia is splendor, Euphrosyne is mirth, and Thalia is good cheer. Invoke them to bring out the best qualities in yourself, and to bring hope and cheer to you when times are dark.

Gwyddion: Celtic God of civilization. Lord of light and a God of magick and transformation. Invoke his aid to help change those things that seem impossible and to help you live a civilized life when all is chaotic around you.

Hathor: Egyptian sky Goddess. Her domain is pleasure, joy, love, music, and she is a great protector of women. Invoke her for all of the good things life has to offer, and to protect you from harm when seeking these pleasures.

Hecate: Greek daughter of Perses and Asteria. Mother of the Underworld, Goddess of magick, ruler of the crossroads, and benefactor of all those whom she favors. She is the crone, the grandmother of grandmothers.

Hera: Greek Goddess of marriage. Beautiful and gracious, she is the queen of the Greek Gods, and the archetype of the perfect wife. Invoke the blessings of Hera on any marriage or handfasting, or for matters of the hearth and home. Her Roman name is Juno.

Hermes: Greek messenger of the Gods. Son of Zeus and Maia. He is hailed as the God of the merchants, and God of communication. He reigns over new inventions, for his lightning-quick mind is never at rest. He created the lyre and made it a gift to Apollo.

Hermes Trismegistus: The scribe of the Gods, who dwelt in old Egypt in the days when the present days of men were in their infancy. Instructor to Abraham. All esoteric teachings of every race may be traced back to Hermes. Even the most ancient teachings of India have their roots in the original Hermetic teachings. To master the simple principles that were taught by Hermes Trismegistus means to master the Universe. Invoke him for divine wisdom.

Horae Dike: A Goddess of justice. She and her sisters Eunomia (lawfulness), and Eirene (peace) are daughters of Zeus and Themis. Similar to the three graces, they each represent part of a law of three. Invoke her for justice—both physical and karmic.

Horus: Egypt's falcon-headed God. He is the son of Isis and Osiris, and is often depicted as a falcon—one that can survey from above, which means that he sees all. A Pharaoh often took his name to represent himself as the living God. In Egyptian mythology, Horus the Good conquers Set the Evil. Invoke him to overcome all adversity, and to aid in astral projection.

Hyacinthus: Greek God of rebirth. An everlasting youth, but always short-lived. The God's sorrow is expressed in the letters AI, the Greek word for woe, which are inscribed on the petals of the hyacinth. We invoke him for sorrowful love we lose in our youth, and so that the bloom of love may always return.

Inanna: Sumerian Goddess of the underworld. Invoke her for aid in overcoming obstacles, for dealing with family, for shamanic journeying, and for desperate aid in matters of love.

Iris: Greek Goddess of the rainbow. She is the daughter of an oceanid (ocean spirit) named Electra and a titan (giant god) named Thaumas. She is a special messenger to the Gods, and delivers messages between the heavens and earth. We invoke her to bring joy and promise of a fortunate change to our lives.

Ishtar: Babylonian Goddess. Mother of fertility, love, and war. Goddess of spring, light of the world, law-giver, opener of the womb, and lady of victory are some of her titles. Invoke her to bless the many areas of our life with all good things.

Isis: Egyptian Goddess, the wife of Osiris and mother to Horus. Associated with the Greek Demeter, fertility and motherhood are her primary domains. She is also a Goddess of intuition, psychic abilities, love, and compassion. She is the High Priestess of the Gods. Mother to all, she provides food for the dead as well as the living. Invoke her for love, fertility, magick, and your daily needs.

Jack of the Green: Celtic God also known as the Hidden One or Guardian of the Greenwood. Hidden in the green leaves of the forests, he is ever-watchful. He celebrates the coming of summer. Invoke him to help keep the green life we have and to promote more to come. He is especially important to invoke in urban areas where plants and trees are so few.

Janus: Roman God of the gates. A God of new beginnings, and spiritual doorways. Master of the gateways to the past and future, of protection, and of fortune for better or for worse. He has two faces, as doors and gates look both ways. He was so revered by the Romans that they named the first month in their calendar after him. We invoke him to help us start a new life, or to give us the courage to begin new endeavors. The second face keeps guard so that your past can never creep up on you.

Jove: *see* Jupiter.

Juno: Roman Goddess of marriage. *See* Hera.

Jupiter: Roman for Zeus. God of the sky, giver of all manner of luck, father of mercy, compassion, and wisdom. Jupiter's generosity knows no bounds. His feasts are massive, and his kindness is often shown as rewards for good deeds. Invoke Jupiter for wealth, beneficence, luck, mercy, and kindness.

Kali Ma: India's Goddess of death, destruction, and resurrection.

Kronos: Greek titan, husband to Rhea, son of Gaia and Ouranos. Kronos was father to the Olympians. Stern ruler of his land, he is associated with Saturn. When we need to be disciplined in our work we invoke Kronos or Saturn.

Kwan Yin: Chinese mother of boundless mercy, compassion, and healing. She will continue to help all who need her until all sorrow has ceased to exist. Invoke her aid for the general benefit of all, or for the healing of yourself or a particular person.

Lakshmi: India's Goddess of wealth, abundance, love, and protection. Invoke the presence of Lakshmi for gold, milk, cattle, horses, and for you and your loved ones to have rich, abundant lives. (To state that a Goddess gives horses and cattle means that she provides transportation and ease of lifestyle, and cattle for their milk which provides sustenance.)

Libertas: The Roman Goddess of liberty. She is the Goddess of freedom, and protectress of the right to pursue happiness. Invoke her for all manner of liberty, whether it be liberating thought or liberating oneself from a bad situation. She can also be invoked for aid in legal matters.

Lugh: Celtic Sun God. His festival is Lughnasadh (August 1). Among his many attributes are crafts, healing, prophecy, and hunting. He carries a staff that can give both life and death. His symbols are the raven and the white stag. Invoke him for strength, creativity, fertility, inspiration, protection, and guidance.

Luna: Roman Goddess of the moon. She is a Goddess of beauty, love, and grace, as well as psychic intuition and women's mysteries. In Greece she is called Selene. Invoke her for moon magick, love, and divination.

Lupa: The she-wolf mother of Rome. In the great city of Rome there is a large statue of Lupa standing over the infants Romulus and Remus while they suckle from her teats. Invoke Lupa for aid and support for adoptive mothers, stepparents, lunar magick, and for romantic love.

Maat: Egyptian Goddess of truth and justice. After death, one's soul is weighed in against the red feather of truth that sits in the crown upon Maat's head. If the soul and the feather weigh evenly, then you move on to your next life. If not, then judgment is passed and your sentence is determined.

Maia: One of Zeus's favorite lovers, and mother of Hermes. Maia is one of the few Goddesses that Hera is not jealous of. Invoke her favors for difficult relationships, and for problems with ex-lovers.

Math: Welsh god of enchantment and magick. We invoke his aid to assist us in the more difficult arts and spells of magick.

Mercury: The Greek messenger of the Gods. Invoke Mercury before any major undertaking in magick, to learn, for medicine, healing, and all forms of communication.

Morrigan: Celtic War Goddess. Great queen of magick and prophecy. Invoke her to watch your back in the proverbial battlefield of life.

Nemesis: Greek Goddess of avenging. She is feared for her retribution and punishments of evildoers. Her name has come to describe an adversary or foe. Invoke Nemesis for retribution.

Neptune: Roman for Posiedon, God of the sea. Earth Shaker is one of his titles. His symbol is the trident, and he rides upon a giant dolphin. Sailors placate him for safe travel; fishermen praise him for a good harvest. We invoke his mighty powers as one of the watchtowers of the west, and thank him for his multitude of blessings that come from the sea.

Nike: Greek Goddess of victory in battles and all games of competition. Invoke her to be victorious in your pursuits and to help you succeed in difficult endeavors.

Nuit: Egyptian Star Goddess. She protects the deceased and receives each spirit to become a star.

Nyx: Greek Goddess of chaos, and one of the first to emerge from that void. Mother of many self-created children. Invoke her for a cloaking device when you must do magick that requires hiding in the shadows.

Obatala: Yoruban God of peace. Father of purity and mankind. He is often called King of the White Cloth. He rules the head and bones. His wisdom is considered infinite and many people go to him with a problem that they cannot clear up. Invoke him for peace and to help resolve troubles.

Odin: Norse father of the Gods. He represents sacrifice for knowledge. He gave us the runes and divination. We invoke him for courage, wisdom and prophecy.

Oggun: Yoruban God of war. Also the tireless worker who builds cities and is the ruler over all railroads and automobiles. He is said to cause traffic accidents and for this reason his followers invoke him to prevent such tragedies. Invoke for safe travel and protection.

Oshun: Yoruban Goddess of love, marriage, fertility, gold, and flirtations. Her domain is the rivers and fresh water. She gives an abundance of wealth and blessings. She has a warrior side to her as well, and will protect her children fiercely. Invoke her for love, romance, protection, and wealth.

Uranus: Father of the sky. He rules electricity, lightning, and in some respects, the brain. He is the bringer of sudden inspiration and unexpected change in life. Invoke him for inspiration, but with the knowledge that he can bring sudden change and shake off all the dross that was holding you back.

Oya: Yoruban Goddess of storms. She is the wife of Chango and her job is to mix the magick that makes lightning in his special mortar. Legend has it that she swallowed some of the mix one day and belched fire. She rules the winds of change and cleanses all who encounter her. Invoke her for protection, cleansing, love, and change when you need it but can't bring yourself to face it.

Pacha Mama: Great Earth Mother of Peru. Goddess of planting, harvesting. She is honored by women as the "great serpent mother" or "huge dragon mother" who causes earthquakes. Invoke Pacha Mama for fertility of the earth and to offer thanks for the harvest. Ask her to protect your children, and to bless your life with insight.

Pan: Father of the woods and all its creatures. He is known to dance with wood nymphs and play enchanting music on his pipes. Lord of the Dance, virile fertility God, God of drums and music. Invoke him for fertility, passion, inspiration, celebration, and romantic love.

Parvarti: The benevolent aspect of Durga. She is the consort of Lord Shiva. We invoke her for honor and respect.

Pele: "She who shapes the sacred land" is one of the names of Pele. We invoke her with the greatest respect to help reshape our lives.

Persephone: Greek daughter of Zeus and Demeter, Queen of the underworld and wife to Hades. We invoke her for resurrection of our lives when we have been in the underworld too long.

Pomona: Roman Goddess of the orchards and gardens. Invoke her for abundance and long-awaited love.

Poseidon: Greek God of the sea. Son of Kronos and Rhea. Husband of Amphitrite. Earth shaker and storm-bringer. We invoke him to calm storms and honor him for blessings of the sea.

Ptah: Egyptian God of creation. Shaper of the worlds, patron of the arts and builders. Invoke him for knowledge, compassion, and inspiration in any artistic endeavor.

Ra: Egyptian God of the sun. He is a paramount force, a master of life. Invoke him for his healing solar power and to give us abundance in life.

Rhea: Greek Earth Mother. Wife to Kronos and mother of the Gods. We invoke her for help with children, life's problems, and compassion.

Rhiannon: Welsh Horse Goddess. Divine queen. Rhiannon had birds that sung more sweetly than any birds this side of the real world. She hails from the land of faery. She is a Goddess who speaks her mind and speaks the truth. We invoke her for courage when we need to confront a difficult task with eloquence and style.

Sappho: Greek poetess. Her vibrant love poetry was the first to appear from the women's point of view on women loving women. We hail her for her bravery and invoke her for the special charms that only two women can share.

Saraswati: Indian Goddess of speech, wisdom, and learning. She is dressed in white to represent her purity of thought. She rides on the back of a white swan to show her grace. We invoke her for assistance in all manner of writing, art, and music.

Saturn: Roman God of agriculture and crops. Saturnalia is a winter feast held in his honor to abolish the doldrums of winter. Invoke him to harvest the crops of the season and light the festival of winter.

Sekhmet: Egyptian Lion Goddess. Daughter of the sun God Ra. Healer and twin sister of Bast. Patroness of physicians and priests. Goddess of war and punishment. We invoke her for protection, healing, justice, and magick.

Selene: Beautiful Greek Goddess of the moon. We invoke her to bring us love and beauty.

Shiva: Indian God of victory over evil. Consort to Kali Ma. Invoke him to give life, wisdom, and to destroy those forces which prevent us from the good things in life.

Sophia: Greek Goddess of wisdom. We invoke her for a voice of reason when life gets too complicated.

Syrinx: One of the nymphs of Pan. He almost captures her, but she manages to allude him by turning into reeds. Pan then used those reeds to create his pipes which he uses to make love calls. Invoke her along with Pan for love spells.

Tara: Tibetan Goddess. White, Green, and Red Kurukula—there are twenty-one aspects to Tara in all, but these are the most commonly known.

> **White Tara:** Mother of peace, protection and insight. She has seven eyes that allow her to see in all directions. Invoke her for protection, a different perspective to a problem, and for peace.

> **Green Tara:** Lady of compassion. Invoke her to help you understand another and for financial blessings.

> **Red Tara Kurukula:** In this form, Tara is the Goddess of Enchantment, lust, and witchcraft to arouse desire in another.

Themis: Greek Goddess of justice and law. We invoke her to bring justice into our lives that the law of the land cannot provide.

Thor: Norse son of Odin, second in command to his father. Ruler of the sky and thunder. Rugged, powerful and lives by his own rules. We invoke him to take authority over those who wish to harm us. He is a protector to all his devotees.

Thoth: Egyptian scribe of the Gods. God of intellect, medicine, communication, and magick. His consort is the Goddess Maat. Invoke him for all aspects of communication and knowledge.

Venus: Roman Goddess of love and beauty. We invoke her in all matters concerning the heart.

Vishnu: Indian God of self-discipline. He is the consort of Lakshmi. Invoke him to help us get through a trying time in life that requires a lot of focus and self-discipline.

White Buffalo Calf Woman: Native American, Sioux Nation Mother Goddess who provides for her people. She not only taught them how to harvest and hunt, but also taught them how to pray and use the sacred bowl and tobacco. Her ethics taught them to honor and protect women. Invoke her to bring abundance to your table, to pray in gratitude, and for protection.

Yemaya: Yoruban sea queen. Great Mother of the oceans. Invoke her to bless your home and for abundance, wealth, and protection.

Zeus: Greek God of the sky, ruler of the Olympians. His symbol is the thunderbolt and the eagle. We invoke him for protection, justice, and insight.

Acknowledgments

There are so many people I wish to acknowledge, that I probably need to write another book just to do so. Let me start by thanking the Gods themselves, who have dictated this work through me. Through their inspiration and communication I am honored to have been their witness. Special thanks to my wife, Lady Zoradia (Sandra Rivera), who drew the designs in the last publication of this book. Throughout the preparation of this book she has advised and supported me when I couldn't see straight anymore. Thank you to my daughter, Tara, for her wonderful contributions as well as for the "Ballad of Yemaya" poem. To Lord Julian Aurelianus, for the countless phone calls I made with historical questions on deities and philosophies. To my coven for its support and input during this time. Many other people have helped in this work: Original Products Botanica, Original Publications, Carrie Ann Reda, Barry Johnson, Lord Tammuz, Joseph Balsamo, Magickal Realms and all its folk, friends, and customers. A special thank-you to Lady Venus for writing such a moving foreword, and to Lord Apollo for doing the illustrations. Thank you to John Reynolds "Vajaranatha" who taught me about the initiation practices to the Buddhist and Hindu deities mentioned in this book, and the art symbols that represent them. Blessed be to Raymond Buckland, whose writings and teachings on candle magic have inspired and guided me for many years. He is a true pioneer in the Craft, and I am grateful beyond words for his dedication to the Old Ways. Thanks to Eve LeFey for taking on this challenge with me, to our agent, Lisa Hagan, and our editor at Citadel, Bob Shuman, without whose support of my work this book would have remained an underground publication. Goddess and God bless all of you, for all of you have certainly blessed me.

In addition, Eve LeFey would like to thank the Coven of Eleuthia for their endless love and support, to her mom and dad for encouraging her to find her own spiritual path, and for respecting it when she did, and to the Gods for their inspiration and guidance in the writing of this book.

Index

About the Authors

LADY RHEA started working in an occult shop and studying the Craft in 1971. Since then she has become a High priestess in both the Welsh and Gardnerian traditions of Wicca. She co-owned an occult shop in New York City called Enchantments for several years, and founded the Minoan Sisterhood, a strain of Wicca based on ancient Greek deities and practices. While at Enchantments she self-published an early version of *The Enchanted Candle*, which gained popularity over the next seventeen years. She has also studied Santeria and has been initiated in the Tara rites of Buddhism. Rhea co-hosts the Official New York City Witches Ball, a fundraising event at Samhain every year. She currently owns a shop in the Bronx called Magickal Realms, "Home of the Enchanted Candle," with her life partner Lady Zoradia. She was born and raised in the Bronx, where she still resides with her daughter, Tara, and Lady Zoradia.

EVE LEFEY is a freelance writer, musician and composer. She's a second degree priestess with the Coven of Eleuthia, and lives in Brooklyn, New York, with her two cats, Anna and Lord Byron.